Music therapy: an art beyond words

Music therapy is a relatively new discipline; although the power of music to alleviate illness and distress has been recognised for centuries, it is only in the twentieth century that systematic research into the reasons for its efficacy has really begun. Leslie Bunt has written this book to explain the purposes and techniques of music therapy as it is practised today to a wide audience of mental health professionals, not just music therapists, and for all those interested in the use of creative arts in therapy.

After setting the development of music therapy in its historical context, and looking at its relationship with other forms of therapeutic intervention, he goes on to discuss, with practical examples, the particular contributions of the different elements of music (such as pitch, rhythm, timbre) to the therapeutic process. From this sound basis of understanding the reader is then easily led into the clinical chapters of the book describing detailed practice with both adults and children in schools, hospitals and the community. While not failing to acknowledge the creative and emotional power of the medium with which he works, Leslie Bunt makes it clear throughout the book that a strong research base is necessary if music therapy is to develop its full potential as a therapeutic intervention; that the way forward lies in the successful synthesis of artistic and scientific processes.

Leslie Bunt is a qualified music therapist, Director of The MusicSpace Trust and Research Fellow in Child and Mental Health, University of Bristol.

Music therapy

An art beyond words

Leslie Bunt

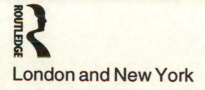

London and New York

For Sue, Laura and Jonathan

First published 1994
by Routledge
11 New Fetter Lane, London EC4P 4EE

Simultaneously published in the USA and Canada
by Routledge
29 West 35th Street, New York, NY 10001

Typeset in Times by LaserScript, Mitcham, Surrey
Printed and bound in Great Britain by
Mackays of Chatham PLC, Chatham, Kent

British Library Cataloguing in Publication Data
A catalogue record for this book is available from the British Library

Library of Congress Cataloging in Publication Data
Bunt, Leslie.
  Music therapy: an art beyond words/Leslie Bunt.
  p. cm.
  Includes bibliographical references and index.
  1. Music therapy. I. Title.
  ML3920.B85   1994
  615.8′5154 – dc20   93-24936

ISBN 0–415–08702–3 (hbk)
ISBN 0–415–08703–1 (pbk)

Contents

Acknowledgements

Above all I would like to thank the many children and adults who have inspired the writing of this book. The staff at the various schools, hospitals, units where I have worked as a music therapist since 1976. The Music Department, The City University, London, especially Professor Malcolm Troup for his support and encouragement. The students on the music therapy courses at the Guildhall School of Music and Drama, London since 1978 and more recently since 1992 at Bristol University. To colleagues, students and friends in Assisi and other Italian centres where I have worked regularly since 1982. To colleagues who have responded in discussions over the years to some of the themes in the book. Dr Hilton Davis, Department of Academic Psychiatry, The London Hospital, for acting as consultant to the research with children. To music therapy colleagues Sarah Hoskyns and Michele Scott for help in reading and commenting on parts of the manuscript. To staff and management of The MusicSpace Trust for their support in the final stages of the preparation of the manuscript. I would like to acknowledge the memory of a trustee of MusicSpace, Dr Allen Percival, strong supporter of music therapy and of late a dear friend. Various funding bodies: National Medical Research Fund, Music Therapy Charity, Barnwood House Trust, Gloucester and Emperor Fine Arts, London. To the anonymous reader for Routledge of the first drafts for constructive comments. To Dr Kate Cullen for compiling the index. To my wife, Sue Pontin, who has read all the chapters at least once and has made very helpful suggestions. I thank her for her constant support. To my children, Laura and Jonathan, for their understanding. To all other friends and colleagues whom I have failed to name but whose kind support during the preparation of this manuscript has been invaluable.

The author and publisher would like to thank the following for permission to reproduce copyright material:

1 Quotations from Myfanwy Piper's libretto by kind permission of Faber Music Limited (Chapter 8).
2 The Association of Professional Music Therapists: Table 1.1 Areas of work of members of the APMT.

3 The spiral of musical development: Fig. 4.1. From K. Swanwick and J. Tillman, 'The Sequence of Musical Development: A Study of Children's Composition', *British Journal of Music Education*, 1986, vol. 3, no. 3, p. 331.

Introduction

Music therapy is a relatively new discipline. It is being increasingly recognised at a time when there has never been such a variety of music available to so many people. We may go regularly to the concert hall, the opera house, to a jazz club or a pop concert. We may be members of a local choir, band or orchestra. Music of all styles is also available to us at the push of a button in the comfort of our own homes. We seldom meet people who report no liking for any kind of music whatsoever.

This thirst for music is demonstrated in many ways: singing or playing instruments together with family or friends; in most religious and secular festivals and rituals; and in the theatre. An outstanding actor of his generation, Antony Sher, writes: 'There is nothing more exciting than acting to live music, the make believe at its most indulgent and its most thrilling.'[1] It is difficult to imagine being unable to celebrate important life events without our favourite music. Favourite tunes have so many associations for us; we can even conjure them up at will and hear them inside our heads. Sometimes they creep in apparently uninvited. Our preferences for music are individualistic, relating to our personal and musical histories. There is a vast repertoire of both pre-composed music and traditional music from more oral traditions available to us. We would need more than our one lifetime to become familiar with a small fraction of all of this music.

What are the connections between us and music? The answers include: the pleasure gained from listening; the warmth and friendship from being part of a group making music; the stimulus and satisfaction from regular practice and rehearsal; the intellectual delight from exploring the intricacies of musical forms and structures; the physical energy released within us by both playing and listening to music, inspiring us often to move and dance. At the root of all these reasons lies the fact that music links with our innermost emotional, spiritual and most private selves. Music helps us to feel more human. It brings us into very close and immediate contact with the people around us and at the same time connects us both with images from the past and predictions of the immediate future. Without our involvement as either listener or player there would be no music. We are the necessary factor in giving rhythmic, melodic and harmonic meaning to the varying frequencies, durations, intensities and qualities that make up the physical world of sound.

A central theme of this book is that these needs, connections and uses of music can form an important contribution to present-day child and adult health care. A child may have a severe language problem or an adult may be very depressed. In a music therapy session we all have the potential to become an integrated part of the music, to move aside into a world beyond the verbal and physical. Everyday communication may be hampered by physical, intellectual, social or emotional problems. In music therapy we can understand more about such difficulties by observing how people respond to and make music. We can observe people becoming actively engaged in exploring a wide range of musical forms, improvisation being a key element of the work in this country. Music is very flexible and we can adapt it to make contact with people of all ages and abilities, to observe what they can do in a musical setting and to develop positive therapeutic interventions. What has music to offer a child or adult with a learning difficulty, or impairment of any kind? Can music help people overcome or cope with mental health problems? What is it about music that can be used as a healthy alternative to the pressures of life in the late twentieth century?

I hope that there will be something in this book for all interested in this emerging profession: music therapists and students, professionals in related fields and all who continue to be fascinated and affected by this enigma we call music.

Chapter 1

The growth of music therapy

INTRODUCTION

Music has been used extensively throughout history as a healing force to alleviate illness and distress, but only in recent times has the specific discipline of music therapy begun to evolve. This chapter will trace the emergence of music therapy, with particular reference to developments in the USA and the UK; define what music therapy is and consequently is not; survey areas of work; summarise some of the further historical reference points; and indicate the need for further research.

THE EMERGENCE OF MUSIC THERAPY IN THE USA AND THE UK

Into a richly diverse world such as music enters a mid- to late-twentieth-century phenomenon: the professional music therapist. There are turn-of-the-century historical antecedents for this emergence. William B. Davis has documented the activities of The Guild of St Cecilia, founded in 1891 by Canon Harford, himself an accomplished musician, to play sedative music to a large number of patients in London hospitals.[1] The Guild gained the support of leading reformers of the day, including Florence Nightingale, and received a great deal of media attention. Grand plans were made, including providing groups of musicians for other provincial cities, experimenting with both the uses of sedative and stimulative music and the rather more eccentric scheme of relaying live music via the telephone. In spite of the support of several physicians, a copious correspondence in the *Lancet* and the *British Medical Journal* and some early apparent success stories, the Guild folded under the pressure of criticism from the musical and medical press, lack of funds and Harford's own ill health. Davis adds that several similar associations were set up in the USA during the early years of the twentieth century. Like the Guild, they had a brief flowering resulting from the dedication of a single enthusiast.

In the early years of the twentieth century music was used in hospitals mainly to boost morale, as a general aid to convalescence and as an entertaining diversion.[2] Physicians invited musicians to play to large groups of patients on the vague assumption that it might activate metabolic functions and relieve mental stress.[3] Listening to music could provide an aesthetic experience of quality and was regarded by many as a very humane way of occupying patients' time. Anecdotal accounts of music's inherent worth abound in the early literature on music in medicine.[4] There seems to have been a general consensus that exposure to music could do nothing but good. Podolsky cites, for example, the case of a schizophrenic musician being administered daily doses of Chopin.[5]

The large influx into hospitals of Second World War veterans was significant for the development of music therapy. The medical authorities, in the USA in particular, were concerned to develop facilities for these returning veterans. Musicians, especially performers and music teachers, began to be employed regularly in hospital teams. But the medical and scientific communities were not so easily convinced by the early anecdotal stories of patients being reached by music when they responded to little else. Challenges were made to the musicians to verify and systematise their work, to assess the influence of music on behaviour and to examine the outcome of any musical intervention in specific treatment plans. Ainlay reports that until the 1940s and 1950s there appeared to be a general lack of understanding of music's value, apart from its general aesthetic and cultural aspects, from both the physicians and the musicians.[6] The musicians, quite understandably, lacked training in such assessment procedures and background medical and psychological knowledge.

The scene was set for the development of training courses for musicians wanting to develop their skills in this specific use of music. Some early key dates in the USA were:

- 1944 Michigan State University: first curriculum designed
- 1945 National Music Council formed a music therapy committee
- 1946 Kansas University, Texas: first full academic course taught
- 1950 National Association of Music Therapy (NAMT) formed
- 1971 American Association of Music Therapy (AAMT) formed.

The NAMT and AAMT currently support undergraduate and postgraduate degree courses and award full registration for entry into the profession after a period of internship.[7]

One pioneer who developed an international reputation as a concert cellist, teacher and music therapist was Juliette Alvin. She was a pioneer in the UK, where some key dates were:

- 1958 Society for Music Therapy and Remedial Music formed; soon renamed the British Society for Music Therapy (BSMT)[8]
- 1968 Guildhall School of Music and Drama, London: first course taught by Alvin[9]
- 1974 Goldie Leigh Hospital, south London: first course taught by Paul Nordoff and Clive Robbins[10]
- 1976 Association of Professional Music Therapists (APMT) formed[11]
- 1981 Southlands College, London: new course set up by Elaine Streeter[12]
- 1991 Bristol University: first part-time course.

In April 1980 the issue of appropriate pay and conditions of service was addressed in the House of Commons. This was the result of response to growing pressure from the APMT and support from colleagues on the need for a separate identity for the profession. A discussion paper had been in circulation that assumed that music therapy, alongside the other creative therapies, could be subsumed under the umbrella profession of occupational therapy. While wishing to link up with other professions, music therapists felt strongly that their discipline needed its own independent structure. The discussion in parliament makes interesting reading:

Art and Music Therapists (Pay)
6. Mr Mikardo asked the Secretary of State for Social Services what steps he plans to take concerning the 1979 salary increases for art and music therapists, following the Clegg commission's refusal to recommend appropriate salary levels for them.

Dr Vaughan: These salary levels are at present determined by the Department by relating them to the salaries negotiated for occupational therapists by the professional and technical A Whitley Council. Now that the council has agreed on a settlement of the Clegg award to occupational therapists, new salary levels for art and music therapists will be fixed, with effect from 1 April and they will be announced as soon as possible.

Mr Mikardo: I thank the Minister for that reply. However, is he aware that this relatively small group of professional workers, who make an important contribution to therapeutic treatment, are the only public service employees who have no real negotiating machinery? Their wages are fixed unilaterally by their employers. Is it not time that this nineteenth-century Dickensian anomaly was got rid of, and that we moved into the twentieth century?

Dr Vaughan: I am sympathetic to the remarks of the hon. gentleman on this matter. Discussions are taking place with this sort of goal in mind. I should like art and music therapists to be formally allocated to a Whitley Council, so that their pay and conditions can be properly negotiated between NHS management and the staff organisations concerned.[13]

This 'Dickensian anomaly' was eventually discarded in 1982 by the award of a career and grading structure for music and art therapists by the then Department of Health and Social Security.[14] This placed music therapists alongside speech therapists, physiotherapists and occupational therapists, for example, as recognised members of a para-medical profession. The profession was no longer to be regarded as an *ad hoc* group or falling under the structure for occupational therapists. The profession is currently negotiating for full state registration as part of the Council for Professions Supplementary to Medicine (CPSM).

WHAT IS MUSIC THERAPY?

This is a question that seems to fascinate people, but it is notoriously difficult to find a definition that will suit all people in all contexts. I must have struggled to answer this question hundreds of times when talking to clients (from now on this term will replace 'patients' wherever possible), children, parents, carers, students, fellow musicians, music therapy colleagues, other team members and friends. To many people the linking of the words 'music' and 'therapy' is very obvious, especially if they have discovered other self-help uses of music besides entertainment.

We can begin by describing how music therapy provides an opportunity for anybody to make a relationship with a trained music therapist where aspects of problems or difficulties can be addressed. The music is not an end in itself but is used as a means to an end. As Michel points out, any definition of music therapy is not self-evident; it is not as if music therapists are helping people's music as speech therapists may be helping speech and language development.[15] In music therapy we are trying to make contact with another human being through music. We can observe how clients use the music and how any problems may get in the way of interactive communication.

Musicians may be interested to hear more of how the music is adapted to suit the needs of different people. Here the discussion might focus on compositional and improvisational techniques. Hospital managers, debating whether to set up a music therapy post, may need convincing of the efficacy of music therapy. Here the discussion would be directed towards indicating some of the therapeutic outcomes of the work and that music therapists are often working towards non-musical aims. Definitions have changed in emphasis over the years as the profession has adapted to different needs and contexts. For many years a standard definition in the UK was Alvin's: 'Music therapy is the controlled use of music in the treatment, rehabilitation, education and training of children and adults suffering from physical, mental or emotional disorder.'[16] The word 'controlled' implies that the music is used in a clear and focused manner, and the definition as a whole makes for rather a therapist-centred approach, as if the therapy is done to the children and adults. Terms go in and out of fashion, and the words used to describe the various problems and difficulties are linked to philosophical, ethical and moral issues of the day. There would be hot debate among contemporary music therapists over both the word 'control' and the use of the terms 'treatment, rehabilitation . . . and training'. Alvin's use of 'suffering' is also rather outmoded. Today we stress a positive outlook towards health, whilst still being fully aware of the pain and horrors involved in illness.

A softer version, which bears some resemblance to Alvin's definition, comes from the Australian Association for Music Therapy: 'Music therapy is the planned use of music to achieve therapeutic aims with children and adults who have special needs because of social, emotional, physical or intellectual problems.'[17] The term 'therapeutic aims' is also at the centre of a definition published by the NAMT: 'Music therapy is the use of music in the accomplishment of therapeutic aims: the restoration, maintenance and improvement of mental and physical health.'[18]

To some extent any factor that helps in the prevention or alleviation of illness or problems can be regarded as therapeutic. The word 'therapeutic' is somewhat over-used today and I want to side-step becoming involved in a discussion of the differences between therapeutic music-making and music therapy. Therapy itself implies the concept of change and many definitions refer to changes in behaviour: for example, 'The therapist uses music, in a therapeutic environment, to influence changes in the patient's feelings and behaviour.'[19] The music therapist is using music to alleviate or change behaviours within the creative context of a developing relationship. This factor permeates the relationship-based approach of Paul Nordoff and Clive Robbins.[20] Alvin also writes: 'The success or failure of music therapy depends on human as well as musical factors of the relationship.'[21]

Schneider and colleagues felt that there were three stages in the early evolution of the discipline in the USA: an emphasis on the music without recognising the importance of the therapist; the disregarding of the music by the therapist in favour of a developing relationship; and, third, a position somewhere between the two extremes.[22] We can see these different emphases continuing to dominate discussions at both national and international levels. In the UK the music and the musician as music therapist have always been central considerations. In other countries music therapy is practised by musical psychologists, physicians and educationalists, the music being used here more as an adjunct to another therapeutic modality such as psychotherapy, or as part of an overall, rather than a primary, mode of intervention. Bruscia, in his comprehensive text *Improvisational Models of Music Therapy*, considers this adjunctive approach as 'music in therapy', differentiating it from music used specifically 'as therapy'.[23] Benenzon feels that a music therapist must be specifically trained as such and need not, of necessity, be a trained musician.[24] There are different international standards regarding training with first degree, diploma or postgraduate opportunities. Some courses only train postgraduate professional musicians of a certain maturity and with some working experience with a variety of client groups; other courses train students straight from school on first degree programmes. With an internationally expanding profession it is even more important to discover areas of common ground and to support the natural evolution of any international standards and codes of practice. Different countries will develop different definitions of music therapy relating to their own musical and cultural histories and particular patterns of care. Various philosophical and political positions cannot be underestimated.

To return to definitions, Pamela Steele reminds us of our major responsibility to listen as music therapists: 'Perhaps the most primary service which we offer our patients within the space and time of the therapeutic environment is our willingness and ability to listen.'[25] She also draws our attention to the notion of 'attendance'. This is echoed by Kenny: 'Attendance implies a mutual interchange, an alert, resourceful, caring, vigilant patience and guidance.'[26] And in another NAMT definition:

Music therapy is the specialized use of music in the service of persons with needs in mental health, physical health, habilitation, rehabilitation or special education . . . the purpose is to help individuals attain and maintain their maximum levels of functioning.[27]

The complexities of definitions have preoccupied music therapists throughout the history of the profession, and the need for a thorough overview led Kenneth Bruscia to write an entire book on the subject. After examining the nature of music therapy and defining both music and therapy, he proposes a working definition which is then systematically broken down into smaller aspects. This working definition is presented here as the first of three definitions to summarise this section:

Music therapy is a systematic process of intervention wherein the therapist helps the client to achieve health, using musical experiences and the relationships that develop through them as dynamic forces of change.[28]

The second definition is from a recent leaflet published by the APMT:

Music therapy provides a framework in which a mutual relationship is set up between client and therapist. The growing relationship enables changes to occur, both in the conditions of the client and in the form that the therapy takes . . . By using music creatively in a clinical setting, the therapist seeks to establish an interaction, a shared musical experience leading to the pursuit of therapeutic goals.[29]

The third is a simple definition proposed as a final summary of some of the most important aspects in the definitions quoted so far:

Music therapy is the use of organised sounds and music within an evolving relationship between client and therapist to support and encourage physical, mental, social and emotional well-being.

AREAS OF WORK

If we look back over the development of music therapy in the UK, we see that two main areas have been work with adults with learning difficulties (previously categorised as mentally handicapped) and with adults with mental health problems (adult psychiatry). Again there are historical reasons for this fact, given that some of the first fully trained music therapists began to find employment in the large institutions responsible for the care of these two client groups. Music therapy was found to be a point of contact for many residents living in these institutions, especially those with long-term problems, such as profound physical and mental disabilities or chronic schizophrenia. Many of these people had lived in the hospitals for many years. As in the pioneering years in the USA, these individuals and groups of adults were referred to music therapy on the assumption that exposure to music and work with a caring therapist could do nothing but good. Gradually more systematic reasons for referral were itemised. Music therapists began to evolve assessment and evaluation procedures. In the area of learning difficulties it became increasingly clear that music therapy could help maintain and develop such areas as physical skills, cognitive potential, motivation, speech and language skills, non-verbal expression, social skills, choice-making and independence, for example. In adult psychiatry some of the noted areas were: changes in mood, releasing of tension, expression of feelings, social interaction in a group, and development of self-esteem. Music could be a medium where feelings could be articulated and shared, thus providing a different point of access for future verbal elaboration. Music therapy was seen to be contributing more than the general enrichment of a person's quality of life. What is emerging here is the beginnings of specific contributions to therapeutic models of care. I shall continue to explore later how music therapy is not about teaching people to play an instrument or sing, about having a recreational time (although this does often happen and cannot be overlooked). It is not solely a means of occupying people for a short time with music as a diversionary and entertaining activity.

Other areas of work soon evolved, and in the UK these included: the child with all manner of learning problems, including speech and language, other cognitive and emotional difficulties; the child and adult with visual and hearing impairments; the older person, including people with both neurological and psychiatric problems; the adult offender. Music therapy is currently developing interventions into the area of hospice work, both in cancer care and in the specialised area of people living with the AIDS and HIV virus, and into the area of sexual abuse.

British music therapists currently work in hospitals and units for adults and children with learning difficulties, physical disabilities, mental health problems; in pre-school assessment centres and day nurseries; in special schools; in day centres, hospitals and residential homes for older people; in centres for people with visual and/or hearing impairments; in the prison and probation service; in hospices and in private practice (see Table 1.1 for a breakdown of areas of work). As music therapy becomes more recognised and understood, a wider range of client groups is emerging: music therapists continue to work in the important areas where there are chronic difficulties in communication but are also able to take on work in areas not regarded as a high priority a few years ago. Could we have imagined the growth of music therapy for the professional musician that is a distinct strand of the profession in the USA today?

I shall be elaborating on many of the traditional and more recent areas of intervention in later chapters. I shall also be discussing how music therapists have responded to changes in the policies relating to models of care for adults and children with any kind of special need.

SOME HISTORICAL REFERENCE POINTS TO MUSIC THERAPY

At the start of any new profession it is expected that searches will be made among related disciplines for common reference points and patterns that can serve as

Table 1.1 Areas of work of members of the APMT

Area of work	No.
National Health Service – adult psychiatry	36
National Health Service – adult learning problems	43
National Health Service – general	2
Local Authority Social Services – psychiatry	1
Local Authority Social Services – learning problems	13
Local Authority Social Services – physical disability	1
Education – Special Schools	41
Freelance	25
Charities	41
Other non-specified areas	11

Note: In addition to the above areas there were:
  – 17 associate members either not working as music therapists or working in other countries
  – 28 student members
  – 5 retired members

Source: Association of Professional Music Therapists Survey of members, 23 October 1990.

guidelines and theoretical frameworks for the work. The case has been no different in the evolution of music therapy.

Many of the early pioneers cited, as supportive evidence, sources from mythology, biblical stories and the uses of music in tribal medicine and other cultures. There is a large literature on this historical use of music.[30] Passing reference is made here, with a brief return to this perspective in the final chapter. It is often pointed out that music is the oldest art form associated with helping the ill. Benenzon adds that the use of music to influence the human body was first mentioned in writing in Egyptian medical papyri dating back to 1500 BC.[31] The Greeks developed both the rational concepts of order and harmony and the unrestrained and purging aspects in relation to the use of music to alleviate disorder. It is not surprising that the Greeks are often regarded as the forerunners of music therapy:

> Even if Greek medicine was still empirical and subjective . . . the Greek physicians knew how to observe carefully the symptoms of disease . . . . The Greeks applied music systematically as a curative or preventive means that could and should be controlled, since its effects on man's physical and mental state were predictable.[32]

Other commentators have discussed how most humane treatments in the history of psychiatry have included music. Goodman traced this history from early Arabic–Hebraic traditions.[33] A further historical reference point is the story of tarantism from the Middle Ages up to quite recent times in parts of southern Italy. Here music and dance were used, often for a period of days and involving teams of musicians, to combat the sudden frenzy followed by complete inertia induced by a real or imaginary sting from the tarantula spider. Hence the origin of the dance named the tarantella.[34]

Music took on a developing secular role during the Renaissance. The discoveries of the anatomists were greatly to develop a scientific and physiological basis to medicine. However, the older beliefs that evil was inherent in illness, especially mental illness, could not be completely suppressed by these new developments. Of relevance to the emergence of music therapy was the increased use of music as an individual and fundamentally human act of expression, interchangeable in the early beginnings of opera with speech itself. The physiological effects of music began to be recorded as the beginnings of a less indiscriminate approach to the use of music in medicine evolved. There was much interest in the effects of music on health in Parisian medical life in the mid-nineteenth century, a treatise by Dr Chomet, 'The Influence of Music on Health and Life', discussing the preventive uses of music.[35]

The lack of sustained and rigorous experimentation can be observed in many of the early uses of music in medicine. It was still apparent during the middle years of this century and led to a warning by the physician Licht that is still relevant today:

> Musicians must be cautioned to consider that their sincere efforts may result only in discrediting music as a therapeutic agent. As a result its acceptance on the basis of such merits as it may possess may be undeservedly delayed because of the antagonism aroused by extravagant claims made in its behalf.[36]

A physiological basis to music therapy played a large part in the emergence of music therapy in the USA, with a body of physiologically based research measuring the effects of music on specific client groups. We are currently witnessing a re-appraisal of this early work in the research concentrating on the measurable and predictable effects of music, sound and vibrations on our physiology (see Chapters 2 and 3).

Such physiological research led to the possibilities of a medical model providing a reference point for the emerging profession. The advent of psychoanalysis and the work of Freud and Jung and their successors provided another major reference point.

By contrast to the growing interest in a psychoanalytical approach to music therapy, other therapists turned to behaviour therapy and the direct observation and documentation of more external behaviours. Carefully planned research recorded positive effects of music on a wide range of behaviours and skills. As we shall discover, this reference point contributed a great deal to the growing acceptance of music therapy during the 1950s to the 1970s, particularly in the USA, where music therapy developed its place as a science of behaviour.

During recent decades the third force of humanistic psychology began to wedge its way between the two pillars of psychoanalysis and behaviour therapy. Many expressive-arts therapists, including music therapists, would agree that their work embraces such humanistic goals as 'helping individuals to realize their potentials'.[37] The influential humanistic psychologist Carl Rogers lists the three core factors of empathy, acceptance and genuineness that are the basis of any therapeutic relationship.[38] Further reference points come from the more cognitively based therapists and from the vast amount of research on adult–child interaction that took place particularly in the 1960s and 1970s. The work on mother–infant interaction in particular will become the framework for the discussion of the uses and effects of music therapy with children (see Chapter 4).

There are both advantages and disadvantages in forming close relationships with existing frames of reference, as we shall see later. A major personal motivation for writing this book is to demonstrate that music therapy has reached the stage in its evolution where it can begin to form its own methodology while still keeping close contact with related fields. I am optimistic about this but still agree with Even Ruud: 'While the ultimate goal of Music Therapy is to establish itself as a unique discipline, up to now it has been necessary to build Music Therapy's underlying processes upon prevailing theories in psychology and other treatment philosophy.'[39]

RESEARCH AND MUSIC THERAPY

A common criticism levelled at music therapy is that there is an insufficient body of research to account for the effectiveness of any intervention. We can argue that the profession has almost a moral responsibility to indicate the effectiveness of the work. What are the links between therapeutic objectives, the music therapy process and eventual outcomes? Parents will often ask how music therapy can specifically help their child. If I go to a therapist and embark on a period of intensive personal therapy, I want to have some indication of what may be expected to happen during the process and to have some understanding of the therapist's theoretical orientation. At a very basic level I also want to know what I am getting for my money. The various budget-holders are reluctant to part with funding unless there is a clear indication that employing a music therapist will contribute in a specific way to the clients for whom they are administering public funds. These factors are even more acute in the present times of economic restraint, accountability and emphasis on providing services that are looked on as being cost-effective.

Research is one way of indicating change and of monitoring both the outcome of a piece of work and the processes by which any outcome is reached. As will be seen in future chapters, there has been an extensive history of research in the USA and to some extent in other countries. In the UK there has recently begun a tradition of setting up specific research projects, although we are only beginning to open up an area that needs extensive exploration.

The need for more systematic research was highlighted in 1982 by a survey of the first thirteen volumes (1968–82) of the BSMT's publication, the *British Journal of Music Therapy* (*BJMT*). This followed the same process as was adopted by Jellison in her review of the first twenty years of publications in the USA by the NAMT, the *Music Therapy Annual Books of Proceedings* (1952–63) and the *Journal of Music Therapy* (*JMT*) (1964–72). She used the categories:

(a) philosophical – analysis, criticism, speculation
(b) historical – reviews, surveys of past information
(c) descriptive – current music therapy status: case studies of individuals and groups; descriptions of work settings and training programmes; indicators of the growth of the profession
(d) experimental – results of structured research, presentation of research plans.[40]

The survey of the British journal revealed much descriptive material during this period, and the order of categorisation followed the expected pattern: descriptive, philosophical, experimental and historical (see Table 1.2). The dearth of research work during the first stages of the profession was as predicted. It is interesting to compare the patterns of Jellison's American survey and this study. Jellison's survey followed an identical pattern of categorisation to the British one, and there was a very comparable closeness in the percentage scores relating to the mode of inquiry (see Table 1.2).

Table 1.2 Categorisation of *BJMT*, *JMT* and *JBMT* and percentage scores

Journal	Descr.	Phil.	Exp.	Hist.
BJMT ('68–'82) n=115	62	25	8	5
BJMT ('82–'87) n=19	63	27	5	5
JBMT ('87–'91) n=41	41	27	27	5
JMT ('52–'72) n=485	57	31	11	1
JMT ('73–'78) n=115	42	18	39	1

n=number of articles

Surveys: *BJMT* (1968–82); *JMT* (1952–72); *JMT* (1973–8) – see notes 40–2.

Gilbert's later American survey can be studied to track the development of published research.[41] We can assume that as more clinical work becomes available for careful description and analysis more systematic research and potential theory-building can develop. As in any new profession, competent practice commonly precedes the development of research. There is a body of extant clinical work about which questions can be asked. Gilbert's study demonstrated the predicted growth of experimental work. In 1984 I asked the question: 'As more clinical material becomes available and the profession grows, can we predict a growth in research papers in GB, as noted in the later trend in the United States?'[42]

During the mid-1980s plans were made for a British journal that would focus more on reporting current clinical work and research. In 1987 the *BJMT* developed into a joint publication between the professional association (APMT) and the British Society (BSMT) and was re-named the *Journal of British Music Therapy* (*JBMT*). Before the first issue of the new journal further articles had been published in the remaining five volumes of the old one (1982–7) and, as can be seen in a second *BJMT* survey (see Table 1.2), the order of categories and percentage scores in this last stage of the *BJMT* is similar to the findings of the earlier survey. There continued to be an emphasis on descriptive and philosophical articles, with a marked absence of experimental material. I predicted with the start of the new journal, now with the added impetus from the professional association, that work of a more experimental nature would be published. As can be seen from the most recent survey of articles published during the first four years of the new *JBMT*, this has become a reality (see Table 1.2). The experimental and research-based writings now occupy the second rank, alongside the philosophical writings. We can also see that there is a marked increase in the total number of published articles during this initial phase of the new journal. This 1991 survey compares favourably with Gilbert's 1979 study. The percentage of descriptive material is almost identical and there is this marked increase in research-based material. We can conclude that the changes from 1952 to 1978 in the USA have a similar pattern to the changes from 1968 to 1991 in the UK, a pattern that relates to a comparable stage in the development of the profession and one that confirms my 1984 prediction.

Articles of a more historical nature are ranked in the lowest position in all of the American and British surveys. Most emphasis is on describing current work, methods of training and places of work, and expressing different viewpoints about work in progress. This work will in time become the historical past of the profession. 'The music therapy profession is young but as it matures and creates its own "past," accurate historical documentation may increase to analyze the past in order to interpret the future.'[43] As a final observation, it is interesting that there is still a prevalence of philosophical writing in the survey of the new *JBMT*, which may say something about a British and European predilection for philosophy and debate.

SUMMARY

At the NAMT's 1988 conference Carolyn Kenny used a life-span approach to describe the evolution of music therapy. During its infancy and childhood the profession was learning basic rules for survival, acquiring all the necessary tools of the trade and working hard to set up jobs for the newly trained therapists. In adolescence there was much research and exploration, experimenting with various styles of work and research designs, as if in an attempt to see if the various clothes and styles would fit. Kenny pointed out that music therapy in the USA is now into mature adulthood, when a deepening understanding results in attempting to stand on one's own. There may even be a sign of mid-life crisis brewing, with re-evaluations of the past and searches for new meanings and directions.[44]

In the UK, the BSMT can be proud of its first thirty years of life and the APMT can boast of entering its late teenage years. The days of breaking up into little factions holding and proclaiming the sole version of the truth seem to be disappearing. We are beginning to respect and encourage many differing styles of work, approaches and opinions. We can present our practical work and ask research-type questions in a climate that is more open to mutual respect and debate. We need no longer worry that asking an outcome-based research question, for example, will trouble some of our fellow music therapists. Like our American colleagues we are at a stage when we are beginning to gain sufficient confidence to evolve our own styles and research methods, to become our own discipline, without constantly looking over our shoulders for guidance or referring to other traditions.

There seems to have been an upsurge of interest in all kinds of therapies in recent times, and we can draw parallels between the emergence of music therapy and other therapies that complement the traditional medical model of health care. As the discipline develops on its life's journey, we can observe further areas of debate and questions that have occupied and continue to concern clinicians in such related disciplines as clinical psychology, speech therapy, physiotherapy, art therapy and psychotherapy. The questions are perennial and will be elaborated in later chapters:

- How can we observe, record and describe the outcome of the work?
- How can we disseminate information more efficiently?
- How can we create more opportunities for work?
- Is a new music therapy service cost-effective?
- Where is the locus for change: the music, the therapeutic relationship, or an interaction between them?
- What are the links between the musical processes and the therapeutic outcomes?
- What language shall we use to describe all these changes?
- How can we observe any outward manifestations of responses to music that are so often deeply private and personal?

No two people respond to music in an identical way. No music is ever performed in the same way at the next hearing. In notating a piece of improvised music musicians have great difficulties in agreeing the length of the sounds, the relative loudness of the sounds and the way in which each pitch is notated. These are some pointers to the unique potential of music as a highly expressive art form but they also indicate profound difficulties in the understanding of its nature and the application in music therapy.

Music therapy offers the opportunity for interaction on equal terms. A major challenge when working with people of all ages and with all kinds of problems is to adapt the music and style of interaction to suit each unique situation. When working with a chid with a short concentration span, for example, we can observe the responses during short bursts of musical interaction and note the way in which these responses may alter over the period of the work. It would be inappropriate to bombard such a child with richly complex music that might heighten any confusion. It may be sufficient, as a point of initial contact, to work with one or two beautifully produced sounds. We can work hard to be equal partners within the music, while obviously recognising that an adult music therapist brings to the interaction additional years of life and musical experience. On the other hand, an older person with a long musical history may need more complex music and may quickly indicate a preferred musical style.

Music has long been used as a means of expressing both group and personal identity. We have tended to lose touch recently with these traditions in the West. Are we in danger of overlooking these more human aspects in our striving for musical excellence and perfection? A further change is the way in which society is coping with people with serious disabilities and problems, people previously residing in the large institutions. With the closing-down of these hospitals many people are being thrown back on the resources of family, friends and the local community. Can music be used again in the time-honoured sense of being a means of social integration? What part can music therapy play in helping people to gain or re-gain contact with each other through music? Has it the potential to integrate people of all ages, both disabled and able-bodied alike? The emergence of the professional music therapist could not have happened at a more crucial time in relation to changes in society and in music itself.

Chapter 2

The relationships between music therapy and other forms of therapeutic intervention

INTRODUCTION

How is music therapy practised? What actually happens in a session? This chapter starts with a description of a child's individual session. The session will be looked at from a variety of perspectives, indicating the areas that are common to other forms of therapeutic intervention and those more related to music therapy. A description of a session with a group of adults follows. We shall explore some of the features linking a music therapy group to all kinds of group work and begin to identify some contributions specific to music therapy.

Connections will then be elaborated, from the descriptions of both the individual and the group sessions, with such established therapeutic models as: a medical model, psychoanalysis, behaviour therapy and humanistic psychology. My own therapeutic orientation will become clarified. By the end of this chapter I hope that it will be apparent that music therapy can contribute to both child and adult health in a very positive way and that 'music therapy is a rational discipline which adds to music a new dimension, binding together art, science and compassion'.[1]

AN INDIVIDUAL SESSION

This is a description of John's second music therapy session. He was attending a child development centre with his parents for a two-week assessment period. During the two weeks John and his parents were seen by a team of specialists: doctor, speech therapist, psychologist, physiotherapist, occupational therapist, psychotherapist, music therapist and social worker. At the end of the assessment period all the therapists met with the parents and discussed their findings at a case conference chaired by the consultant paediatrician.

John is 3½. His parents are concerned that he is not talking; at home he is exposed to both English and an African language. They are also worried because he appears to be quite withdrawn at times, finding it difficult to make contact with the other children and adults around him. He does not seem interested in exploring the games and toys presented to him during some of the assessment sessions. The occupational therapist observes John tapping a table top and suggests that music therapy may be an appropriate medium for observing a wide range of his behaviours.

John has his first two music therapy assessment sessions on the same day, one in the morning and the other after lunch. He attends with his mother. The second session is filmed for future observation. This is a description of John's use of the second session, drawn from frequent viewings of the video film and discussions with students and colleagues. I also report some of my thoughts and feelings during and after the session to act as a supporting commentary to John's music-making. This contributes to the rather intuitive and fundamentally subjective nature of this description.

The setting is a small room. I am seated at the piano. A drum and free-standing cymbal stand to the side of the piano. I have selected this arrangement of drum and cymbal close to the piano on the basis of the experiences of the first session, when John played for the most part on these two instruments.

John comes in, moves quickly to the drum and cymbal, takes up the drum-sticks that I offer him and starts to play. The contact with the instruments is immediate. He plays in short, sharp, loud bursts of sound. I explore on the piano a variety of musical ideas to try and match some of the excitement and energy that he is generating. I am trying to find some point of contact and to meet these short bursts of expressive energy. His mother, who is sitting just behind him, laughs and smiles and encourages her son verbally. Music based on the alternating intervals of fourths and fifths in the bass with clear, short melodies that I play or sing seems to attract his attention and to support and sustain his drumming. It is as if these short ideas are musical calls or reflective echoes of his own playing. I continue to call his name in short vocal phrases and draw attention to the situation: for example 'Hello, John. John is playing his drum.' We play loud music together. The phrases become longer and the music more sustained. He vocalises freely with repeating streams of 'da, da, da . . .'. The vocal sounds contain some basic rhythmic patterns and are closely connected to his loud drum-playing. He points to another stick, using the vocal call of 'da'. We begin to establish more sustained contact and the beginnings of an interaction through the music. During this early part of the session John returns from time to time to his mother, who is positioned very close behind him. He also on one occasion waves his drumstick towards her and vocalises to her. This looks to me like a kind of greeting gesture.

John drops the sticks on the floor and takes a long time picking them up, bending from the waist rather than getting down on hands and knees. He returns to the drum and cymbal and starts up the excited 'da' playing and vocalising again. He plays the cymbal by itself and this builds for about twenty seconds as a sustained outburst. Up to this point he has made rather indiscriminate use of both cymbal and drum. I match this loud resonant cymbal sound with high-cluster piano chords. It can clearly be observed from the video that at this point his whole body is in constant motion, synchronising with the sounds he is making by moving from head to foot. He slows the music down, using larger arm movements on the cymbal. I sing longer phrases and introduce long, sustained vowel sounds. John leaves his playing area of the drum and cymbal and comes across to my playing area of the piano. He looks straight into my face and sings long 'ees' and 'ahs', gradually adjusting these vowel-based vocal sounds to the tonality of the music I am improvising. At this point I recall being very moved. His face becomes very animated, with much smiling; the music appears to have stimulated him to a high level of arousal. I have the strong feeling that John is trying hard to communicate with me and that he finds a spontaneous sense of release in his worlds of sound and music. I have the intuitive feeling that he is trying to say, in his own way, something like, 'At last I am beginning to get through to someone in this building and to communicate what I want. No more strange words and tasks to confuse me.'

He jabs out with one stick to make one single sound on the drum. This suddenly interrupts our close vocal contact and takes us off into a new direction. I try to reflect the feeling behind this gesture and respond with a short and loud piano chord; he repeats it. I play two connected sounds; he plays three, then one again. We play an interactive turn-taking game, almost like a conversation in sound. There is much laughter and sense of explorative play. We are beginning to have a shared musical experience, becoming more of a partnership in the music we are making up together. I feel that we have now moved from the tentative, fragmented start of the session to a point where there is more mutual understanding and shared meaning. It seems that we both are able to start up musical ideas and immediately to persuade the other to join or imitate the gesture and mood. All this happens without many words being said.

The session continues for a further ten minutes, to complete a total time of around twenty-five minutes. The second half continues with an alternation of the fast, rhythmic 'da' activity and the slower, vowel-like vocalising and playing. These two areas seem to be two distinct musical moods. He moves in ever-increasing circles away from the area of the drum and cymbal and from where his mother is sitting. He uses the limited space to move and dance. During one of these movements he points to and vocalises his need for a third stick, which he uses with the others as part of his dance. At this point I wish I understood more about African dance. He explores more of the room and gestures and vocalises to me, pointing to the camera in the corner of the room. I assume that he is trying to tell me something about the camera. The music continues to engage his body totally; even when away from the two main areas of musical activity, he has been moving and dancing in relation to the music he is making or hears. At one point he adapts immediately in response to my change from a fast four-beat to a slower, rocking three-beat tempo. After the session his mother comments on his love of dancing and of television programmes such as *Top of the Pops*, when he will imitate the dancers. During the second part of the session I observe that his playing becomes increasingly organised and that there is more awareness of the music I am making. At one point, for example, he imitates my soft sound on the cymbal. His music is more sustained, with fewer fleeting changes of mood. He is able to move at a slower pace and at one point becomes much stiller and claps gently in time to a slow tempo. I am left at the end of the session with the feeling that we have travelled a little farther on the musical journey we started that morning. We were able to find contact in the music and to sustain this for increasing lengths of time as the session unfolded. The vocalising we made together felt to be both very exciting (the consonant-based 'da') and very intimate (the vowel-based sounds). I felt that John had expressed a lot of his feelings in his music and had communicated them to me. I felt that I had supported some of these feelings and that we had reached points in the session when we were communicating with each other. I was not just providing a mirror which could reflect back John's every gesture and mood: I was able to find some music that would pick up, help to articulate and elaborate his ideas. He in turn was picking up some of my ideas and was becoming increasingly able to incorporate them into his own playing. Although we had only had these two sessions on that day I felt that I was beginning to get to know John and some of his needs through the music.

REFLECTIONS ON THE INDIVIDUAL SESSION

It is clear that this one session can provide us with more than just information about John's musical play. It can help us observe the way he interacts with another person and to discover some of his specific needs. Music is an all-embracing form, providing a rich source of information that can be viewed from a range of different standpoints. We observed John physically moving and dancing about the room, organising himself in space and time and manipulating the instruments. We heard him making a variety of vocal sounds in response to a range of musical stimuli. We made observations about his level of attention which led to assumptions about his concentration during the session. We noted his social skills and the way he related to a rather unfamiliar adult. We made intuitive judgements about the quality of his interactions and the range of feelings he was expressing and trying to communicate. We noted his level of motivation to participate and the way in which he picked up another person's ideas. Music can therefore help us understand a great deal about the physical, intellectual, emotional and social needs of a child. We are given a very comprehensive picture by observing a child in this way in an individual music therapy session.

The video film made of this particular session was viewed together with other members of the team as part of the assessment procedure. If we eavesdrop at this meeting, we can note how the session can be viewed from within some of the broad standpoints of these different professions.

The speech therapist notates phonetically the various sounds John makes during the session, observing the range of vowel and consonant sounds, the pitch and intonation of the sounds. She (all the other staff in the discussion are female) notes that the short 'da' sound occurs when John is very actively involved both playing and dancing; the more melodious and sustained vowel sounds occur when he is less active and in closer contact with me. She tracks the way we pick up the sounds from each other and use them in a non-verbal interaction. She is interested in when and how the sounds occur, in the variety and complexity of the sounds. She notes how John appears to understand what is expected of him in this setting and that the space is a place for making all kinds of sounds and music. John appears to understand simple and short commands. His responses in the music therapy session provide her with further information for an assessment of his speech and language development. Like the family, she is concerned about the apparent delay in his speech. However, the session has given her more evidence of the sounds he can make and indicators of his general level of verbal understanding.

The psychologist notes the way John responds immediately to the various musical and gestural cues. How planned and organised are these responses? Are his responses at an instinctive and reflexive level, or is there some intention behind them? She is able to observe the changes in attention and how these relate to his level of interest and engagement. His attention seems to be more sustained as the session progresses. What are the most significant events that tend to keep him focused on the activity? How does his response relate to my behaviour?

The physiotherapist observes a whole range of both gross and fine motor skills. She sees John handling both one or two beaters while drumming and three when dancing. She is quick to comment that his whole body seems to come alive with the sounds, resonating throughout in response to the physically stimulating music he hears and makes. His movements appear to be the mainspring of all his music. At times his movements are fast and active, even somewhat chaotic, but he is also able to be more focused and still. She notes, with some concern, that he finds it difficult to pick up the sticks from the floor. He tends also to have some problems in hand and eye coordination, especially when playing very fast music. Often, when highly aroused and excited, he misses the edge of the cymbal and drum, continuing to beat the sticks in the air. It is clear that in the softer and slower playing John is more accurate with his coordination, appearing to take more care in the placing of the drumsticks.

The occupational therapist observes how John plays with the instruments. How does he use this opportunity to invent a variety of expressive musical play? How does he use the instruments? How motivated is he to interact?

The psychotherapist comments on the quality of the interactions between John and myself. How do we know that the music he is making is an authentic reflection of what he is feeling? How do the instruments and his singing provide a vehicle for John to express himself? What is he expressing in the music? What am I picking up about his emotional needs from the quality of his playing and singing? What am I reflecting back? Is the music I am making an empathic response to John's mood? We discuss my feelings during the session: the levels of excitement and range of energy, mixed with moments when I was very moved by the vocalising and close contact, the sense of the evolving trust which John was beginning to show in me and the setting. When he was vocalising with long vowel sounds, within the tonality of the music, smiling and looking straight into my face, there were tears in his eyes. We discuss the need to maintain some sense of detachment even at such very close moments in the music. I need to find the balance between trying to sustain a close and warm contact with John and yet being a strong and consistent support for him.

The social worker makes observations about the interactions between mother and child and offers insights into how the behaviour of one influenced the other during the session. She talks of how music therapy could provide the opportunity for the parents to observe John building up a relationship with another adult. She also suggests that music-making could become a regular family activity, with John having an important place within the family dynamic, given his obvious curiosity and interest in the sounds.

In summary, I, the music therapist, report that music therapy seems a very appropriate means of intervention for John. Some of the reasons to support such a claim are:

- Music therapy can provide an opportunity for John to explore a wide range of feelings, such feelings being supported in a safe and consistent environment.
- We can build on what seems to be a strong motivation to participate in sound and music-making.
- Music therapy provides opportunities for developing very focused listening skills, a prerequisite to any speech and language work.
- The rhythmic and melodic aspects of music can be a stimulus for evoking, extending and organising his vocal sounds.
- We can help John to develop more control over his gross motor movements when playing the larger instruments.
- More control over gross movements could then lead to work on fine motor skills and increased hand and eye coordination when playing smaller instruments, or instruments needing specifically focused movements.
- Music therapy would provide an opportunity for developing his attention and concentration skills.
- The sound and music-making will take place in interaction with an adult, involving both synchronous and antiphonal play.
- John will be able to learn that he can influence immediately the behaviour of an adult.
- John will be able to develop more control over his range of feelings.
- He will be able to communicate these feelings and have immediate feedback in an improvised and symbolic medium that bypasses words.

A GROUP SESSION

This group session took place on an acute admissions ward in a general hospital's psychiatric unit. It is a short-stay ward for people in acute phases of illnesses such as manic–depressive psychosis, anxiety and schizophrenia. This is a general and once again very intuitive description, transcribed from notes, of one particular group session.

Setting, aims and boundaries

The setting is an airy day-room on the ward. It is eleven in the morning. A space is cleared at the end of the room and, before the session can start, I ask if the television can be turned off. The setting is not ideal, but the most comfortable and contained space on the ward. The nursing staff announce the start of the music-therapy group and invite people to move into the room. Some have attended for previous sessions but, being a short-stay acute unit, some new members can be expected.

In this kind of setting each group needs to be considered in its own right as a once-off experience. An overall aim is to try and find a musical means of meeting as many needs of the people in the group as possible at that particular moment in time. I have a loose overall framework in my mind of an opening, a middle and a closing section. Some musical structures will be set up, in the hope of providing a sense of security. But within such structures there is freedom to improvise and explore. We must always be prepared to change direction to accommodate the needs of the group. The particular direction which each group takes depends very much on the nature of the group, the problems presented and many other external factors.

Boundaries are established at the start of the group. The group is scheduled to run for an hour and a quarter and people are free to come and go as they wish. I have asked other staff not to interrupt the session if at all possible. These boundaries of time and space are set to facilitate a sense of safety for expressing feelings. These feelings may develop in any direction, one of the features of improvised music being 'that it is not pre-determined and unfolds moment by moment in accordance with what each person actually does'.[2] I stress that there is no question of a right or wrong way to play an instrument. Strong feelings may be expressed on the instruments. There is a further boundary which excludes physically violent behaviour.

The story of this group

A psychology-student assistant and I have brought with us a variety of tuned and untuned percussion instruments. The selection is from all over the world and includes: Chinese gongs and cymbals, Indian bells, African talking drums and West Indian bongo drums, as well as a large xylophone and other more familiar Western-style percussion instruments. There are also some rather unusual blowing instruments, some often creating a humorous effect. Some of the instruments produce a beautiful sound by the slightest means; others are more challenging and require finer control and dexterity.

The arrival of the instruments attracts some tentative interest and curiosity.

We place the instruments on the carpet and small tables at the centre of a circle of a dozen chairs. By this stage a group of eight people has assembled: five women and three men. The initial feelings that I pick up from many in the group are those of apathy, tiredness and tension. I sense a heaviness and lack of motivation and, from some people, the feeling that they have come to the group to give it a try, as if it was the best activity on offer at that moment. I quietly invite the members of the group to explore the instruments and to use an acceptable instrument as a way of introducing themselves to the group. I try to communicate that not playing is also acceptable, everyone needing differing lengths of time to become acquainted with the instruments. Some people choose to play, others introduce themselves verbally. A few spontaneous comments occur about the quality of each sound, whether the sound is acceptable or too jarring. Some people find the sounds of the shaking instruments too intrusive and harsh.

After the introductions on our instruments, I set up a basic heartbeat pulse on a drum, checking with the members of the group that this pulse is neither too fast nor too slow. Several members find it too fast and I adapt the speed. I invite people to join me if they wish and some members add their own unique pattern in turn and continue to play. Some people join after a while; some do not play. The piece gradually builds up to a loud climax. Some members of the group comment about the effects of the different instruments, their likes and dislikes and the physically arousing nature of getting louder. I invite the members of the group to change instruments if they wish. We repeat the structure with the additional complexities of playing faster or slower. Spontaneous comments are made relating to the excitement of playing fast and the difficulty of controlling slower speeds. As usual the music becomes spontaneously louder as we go faster and softer when slower. One of the women says she feels rather embarrassed and would be happier playing with eyes closed. We experience the structure again, this time with our eyes closed, concentrating on internal listening. This opening structure, with an emphasis on rhythm, energises some of the members and they become more active. I feel that this kind of opening section to the group provides a sense of personal freedom within some organised structure. Members of the group can make up their own pattern, yet this relates to a central pulse which provides a sense of clarity and solidity.

I sense that people would feel comfortable playing some music for each other, a kind of musical dialogue. I begin by observing one of the group, intuitively absorbing an impression of this person, and play a short pattern of sounds on some bongo drums as my personal message. She replies on her instrument to me, adding patterns of her own. She then plays for another member of the group. This structure offers the opportunity for some interactive musical activity. It provides an opportunity for individual members to express a variety of feelings. Each dialogue is completely different. Up to this point I have the sense that most people in the group feel rather low, many people also appearing to be very anxious. There is not a great deal of talk, and what talk there is tends to relate to the individual sounds and the music we are making.

By this stage most members of the group have explored some of the instruments. We have another change of instruments, if wanted. I propose that we put all our instruments together to make up an improvised piece. Such a piece could start without any planning or we could choose a theme. Our first piece is a short free improvisation which sounds rather scattered. For a second piece the theme of 'climbing a mountain' is introduced by a member of the group as an image on which the group can focus. One member feels that the theme is too difficult and comments that she would not be able to get above her depression. Another member takes up the Swanee whistle and says that he wants to fly high like a large bird at the top of the mountain. The music starts out of comparative silence with slow, long and heavy sounds, taking a long time to reach any level of speed or excitement. The music moves gradually towards a momentary climax and ends with a loud outburst of activity. After the improvisation, all the members relate in turn where the music has taken them: individual musical journeys and inner fantasies. Some members of the group comment how they feel still not far from the bottom of the mountain; the man who chose the Swanee whistle is very much at the top, soaring away with the birds. One woman says that she is stuck in a swirling river and cannot get out. One of the men suggests that we come back down to the base camp at the bottom of the mountain as the theme for a second improvisation. Other instruments are chosen for this return journey. The group improvises again, starting from where they each left off. The music becomes slower and ends in a calmer mood. We talk about the return to base camp, and the session ends with this moment of quiet reflection as the group disperses for lunch.

My function during the group

My function has been that of a facilitator. I used an instrument to introduce myself, as did the other members of the group. I introduced the structure of playing some music for another person. The move to a less directive approach occurred as the group members began to become more familiar with the instruments and to suggest musical structures themselves. I was able to observe the musical flow of the group, introduce musical techniques and suggest small variations. I was able to observe how various members of the group coped with the different instruments, supporting people with their choice of instrument and, when necessary, helping in the choice of another instrument if a particular sound was not wanted. I tried to give my full attention to listening to the sounds people made, observing how the instruments were used, as well as the behaviour of the various members of the group and the interactions between people. I observed the process of this group's particular journey. I listened to the individual feedback from each person and helped to relate the personal comments to the kind of music that person made and how the instruments were used. In this kind of group I am making connections between the music the adults make, their behaviour in the group and their comments. During this session, for example, I was able to draw attention to the loud, screeching and swooping music made by the man who played the Swanee whistle as his expression of flying high with the birds over the top of the mountain.

FURTHER REFLECTIONS ON THE GROUP SESSION

This was an open group, and for some people a first exposure to music therapy. We can consider the experience as complete in itself. A prime factor in acute work is a changing population on the ward week by week. Can we imagine that some of the group decide to move from this open setting and make a commitment to attend for a more extended period of music therapy away from the ward? This opportunity was introduced into this particular unit, with some members of the morning group returning for a longer period of work, even after being discharged from the ward, at the same time and place for an agreed number of weeks. How could music therapy help such a group? We can begin by exploring features that are complementary to factors in any group therapy process. On the basis of his extensive experiences of facilitating all kinds of groups, Irvin Yalom has described several core 'curative factors' specific to group work, regardless of the particular therapeutic methods and the therapist's personal style. He places these factors into the following main categories.[3] How do they relate to both short- and long-term music therapy?

1   Instillation of hope

At the start of any group process instilling a sense of hope is a prerequisite for both the group members and the therapist. We all hope that the experience of making music together will be beneficial. On a practical level the understanding that there is no right or wrong way to play may eventually decrease any initial fears and anxieties about touching the instruments. It increases a sense of playful curiosity and interest. Being given permission to explore and experiment, within a secure and safe setting, often provides the necessary springboard for the group to start working.

2   Universality

We observed how even in this one-off session the group began as a collection of isolated and quiet people, rather preoccupied with their particular problems. There was an opportunity for sharing some of these fears and preoccupations, for unifying what had previously divided. Playing new instruments also unites people in the task of exploring how to play, as they master any difficulties together.

3   Imparting of information

There may be the need to impart information about a particular instrument, way of playing or musical structure. Any information about the dynamics of the group and observations about each member's place and behaviour in the group will tend to be implicitly understood, each client learning about the processes as the group evolves.

4   Altruism

During this group session a sense of caring for other members of the group was beginning to emerge. The suggested theme for the final improvisation took account of some of the feelings expressed by certain members of the group. We had not all made it up to the top of the mountain and some people needed to re-assess their position. Group work provides many opportunities for supporting each other; in this example we noted the beginnings of such sensitivity in the musical dialogues developed between people in the group. People often talk of how both the music and the group-work can take the focus away from their immediate problems, helping them to see the situation from a different per-spective and in the light of other people's experiences and difficulties. Helpful insights about each other's behaviour can occur, often being more easily accepted from other group members than from the therapist. Such learning will hopefully be carried over outside the session.

5   The corrective recapitulation of the primary family group

In the example the group members were beginning to show signs of accepting and encouraging one another. Over a period of time, in more extended work, some of the patterns and habits from earlier in life that may have contributed towards particular problems can be explored in the trusting setting of the group. In music it is possible to try out different ways of playing. Taking risks may be easier for some people in a musical rather than a verbal medium. A timid person may risk getting very angry on the drums, without setting in motion reactions that might occur using words.

6   Development of socialising techniques;   7   Imitative behaviour and 8   Interpersonal learning

Clearly the interactional and fundamentally non-verbal nature of music-making provides many opportunities for the development of these factors. Music is very much a social act: people can listen, imitate and learn from each other, even trying out and discarding different styles of interacting. Alternative ways of behaving can be explored in the safety of the musical setting. We shall see later that groups may be set up to develop specific social tasks: for example, a pre-discharge group of adults with learning difficulties to prepare for a move into the community. Each member can begin to find an individual place and role in the group and to explore ways of feeling increasingly comfortable in relating to others. Each member can learn that they can make a unique contribution to the whole.

9   Group cohesiveness

Many observers, even of one session, comment on the fact that music can quite quickly bring people together and provide a sense of group cohesion, a sense of immediate belonging. People appear to be attracted to music and will stay with it for quite some time before becoming overwhelmed or satiated. We may not need to draw attention to this verbally, as in the cohesive silences that often bind people together at the end of a shared musical experience. Whether we listen to music or make music together, the very structure of organised sounds themselves provides a unique opportunity for such integration. People can use the music to work through problems with the support both of the therapist and of each other.

10   Catharsis

Cathartic moments are a clear feature of making music and are very likely to occur in moments of free improvisation. The purging of the emotions has played an important part in music's functions since time immemorial. A whole range of both negative and positive feelings can be freely articulated in music. Group members can learn how to channel and express such feelings in constructive ways, supported by the therapist and the group in a safe and consistent place. Music-making is very much a physical and releasing activity.

11   Existential factors

Yalom's final category refers to all those outside factors that affect any group at any time or place. In this category he placed such major issues as recognising our own mortality and the fact that, however close to people we may get, we have to take responsibility ultimately for our own lives.

In summary, we can list some more specific features of a music therapy group. These include the following.

– A range of instruments is offered and the choice of what to play from within this range is not imposed; there is a freedom of active choice-making within the limits of availability.
– The emphasis is on interactions through sounds: therapist/individual client, client/client, client or therapist/group.
– Music-making can be highly motivating, aesthetically satisfying and a deeply sensuous experience.
– A musical gesture can immediately influence the behaviour of another person and have a direct effect on the nature and direction of any improvised music.
– Improvised music-making has the potential to bring people together on equal terms in how and what is expressed.
– Music can be an expressive enactment of a person's emotional, social, intellectual, physical and spiritual life, enabling personal insights to be gained into areas of difficulty and concern.

- Music can be regarded in many ways as a metaphor or symbol; we invest musical events with significant meaning, inner images becoming manifest in articulated outer forms.
- When people make all kinds of music together the combined result can still be meaningful, unlike the confusion of meaning if we all talked at once.
- The music therapist is in a privileged position as an attendant listener, facilitator and catalyst enabling this creative process to begin, take shape and grow (such growth even occurring during one session).
- The music therapist can find ways of adapting the music to the individual or group, and not vice-versa.
- The journey of discovery is a shared one, involving trust, learning processes, joint negotiations, shared meanings and the dynamic processes that are at the root of any relationship.
- This journey can be at one and the same time both a private and a public event.

MUSIC THERAPY AND A MEDICAL MODEL

Both the individual and the group session described above took place in hospital settings where the music therapist was part of a team. Observations from John's music therapy sessions were presented at a case conference chaired by the consultant paediatrician. The conference started with the well-established medical practice of summarising the child's history, charting significant features from birth up to the present day. Each therapist then presented his or her own assessment using, for the most part, language comprehensible to all. The music therapy report did not itemise detailed musical features of the session but drew from the music observations that would help the conference understand more about John, his particular problems and his needs. During some conferences the various observations might have included the listing of physiological symptoms, leading to a possible diagnosis. If, for example, symptoms indicated a diagnosis of epilepsy, a well-documented treatment strategy could be introduced. In John's case no clear pattern of symptoms emerged. The results of various tests indicated that no biochemical causes could account for the apparent developmental delay. The problems were related to an unknown aetiology. Nevertheless in preparing a treatment strategy all members of the team were invited to propose various courses of action that could lead to a possible amelioration of the problems. The family was soon to return to Africa, and recommendations were made regarding various approaches. The importance of developing his motivation for music became a key part of the discussion. This did not mean that the family should rush and find John a music teacher on their return home, but that they should encourage all possible kinds of spontaneous music-making, perhaps with the support of a local musician.

In the psychiatric unit the music therapist was a visiting member of the therapeutic team. Observations about how the patients (the term was used in this context) used the session were presented to the nurses on duty and to other team members. At this unit it was common for team members – nurses, psychologists, the art therapist and the occupational therapist in particular – to sit in on the music therapy sessions to observe the patients in a different setting. Through discussion with these team members information about any of the patients could be fed back to the appropriate medical team. The importance of the medical model in this particular unit was paramount and was often demonstrated by the way in which interviews with the doctors would take precedence over attendance at a group.

We can describe a fundamental feature of a medical model in its simplest terms as the search for a biological basis to illness. Are there any links between biochemical changes in the body and the presenting illness? There is a well-established historical pattern throughout medical practice: the taking of an accurate history; diagnosis of symptoms; treatment leading to, wherever possible, a potential cure. Treatment strategies are based on a proven use of a particular combination of drugs, surgical intervention or pattern of care with a particular collection of symptoms. There is a vast array of highly detailed scientific evidence indicating the effectiveness and outcomes of these various treatment strategies. A large amount of human and financial resources is made available to medically based research, in the area both of physically and of mentally based disorders.

The main question here is whether music therapy bears any resemblance to such a model, even if described in this basic form. Can we view an applied use of music as a form of medical intervention and treatment? Are there any observable causal links between the range of symptoms, the application of specific music-therapy strategies and the resultant outcomes? One immediate difficulty of linking with this model seems to be that, while appreciating music therapy's contributions to the healing process in general, a music therapist working in the West today would find it difficult to make outright claims for a cure through music. In spite of this caveat, music has been observed to effect changes on a physiological and very basic level of functioning. In her short overview of music therapy in the latest *Grove Dictionary of Music and Musicians*, Natasha Spender refers to comatose patients regaining consciousness after prolonged exposure to music as an example of music influencing function at a very basic level of response.[4] Today there is a growing interest in researching the use of music therapy with people in various states of coma following road-traffic accidents: for example, the work of the music therapists at the Royal Hospital in Putney, London. Conversely, there is also documented evidence of the very rare condition of musicogenic epilepsy when a particular piece of music, a melody, a harmonic passage or even the sound of bells can induce fits and temporary loss of consciousness.[5]

In the early development of music therapy much emphasis was placed on physiological research and the formulation of biologically based reference points in attempting to explain the influence of music. Many physicians were among the early advocates of music therapy, and it is understandable, given the fact that music therapy wanted to gain access to a medically dominated culture, that early researchers began to explore any potential physiological connections. Arrington summarises some of this early work, noting measurable changes when listening to music in areas such as: metabolism, breathing, pulse rate, levels of fatigue, attention, rate of activity, muscle reflexes and electrical conductivity of the body.[6] Clearly both John and members of the group displayed such changes during the music sessions. John certainly became more aroused and his attention became more focused as the session progressed. If we had linked him up to the appropriate recording apparatus, there would doubtless have been noticeable physiological changes over many parameters during the session. The group also showed visual signs of becoming less fatigued during the session. We are well aware of some of these changes when we listen to music. Some people even find it difficult to work unless music is being played in the background. Particular pieces of music do appear to have profound physiological effects on people. Recently I have found that sitting still and listening to a piece of music such as Arvo Pärt's *Tabula Rasa* after a busy day can take away any headache and feelings of tension. The music seems to help me reach a deep level of meditative relaxation. Or does it? Does the music not merely act as a trigger to help me to be in a more relaxed frame of mind, to become more relaxed? As Ruud indicates, any physiological responses may create the kind of environment that is necessary for the emotional arousal.[7] The right conditions can give more opportunity for an emotional response to occur. It would be dangerous to predict that this piece would have the same influence on anybody else. In fact when I played it to groups of students in Italy some found it extremely relaxing and stress-reducing while others had the completely opposite responses, those of intense irritation and boredom. If the same piece of music can have such positive and such negative influences on people, music therapists need to be aware and respectful of such a powerful medium. Two earlier researchers have warned about predicting responses to listening to music. Ellis and Brighouse found that recorded music could produce significant changes in respiration but not heart-rate, warning that, since individual responses to music are so complex, predicting general reactions to music is very hazardous. [8] Weidenfeller and Zimny carried out a series of experiments with children and with depressed and schizophrenic adults, hypothesizing changes in the electrical resistance of the skin relating to calming or exciting music. The results enabled them to discuss how different music could be used to modify general emotional levels, lowering or increasing levels of activity.[9] Rieber noted that fast music in particular had a marked effect on the activity level of children at play.[10] This is no startling revelation to parents and people who work regularly with children and it is clear that fast music activated John in his session. The adult group also became increasingly energised through-out the session with a marked increase in the speed of the improvised music. Such early studies made an impression on the development of a music therapy presence within medically dominated settings in the USA, providing reference points for almost a physiological and biological basis for the development of music therapy. Many of the studies on the hypothesised links between music and muscle-tone, pupillary reflex, digestion, postural response and the like demon-strated measurable and in some ways predictable physiological changes while listening to music.[11]

This early research can be criticised for focusing on instantaneous results from one-off experiments and on short-lived effects. Much practical music therapy takes place over extended periods of time. Very often we also see that only a small range of classical music is presented for listening and many of the once-only reactions may relate simply to the amount of pleasure or displeasure aroused by the piece. The music is for the most part pre-recorded, which does not take account of the use of live interactive music-making at the centre of much current music therapy practice. If experiments were to include a therapist and client making music together, this would of course increase substantially the number of uncontrolled variables and, as we shall see in later chapters, be a very difficult medium in which to develop research projects. As I have noted, it is also notoriously difficult to separate the physiological from the emotional in terms of a sensory response to music. Spender wonders whether changes in respiration caused by changes in the tempo of the music, for example, could on the one hand be interpreted as increased emotional arousal or on another as a kind of musical synchrony as observed in marching to a steady beat.[12] Is marching a basic physiological adaptation to the outside musical stimulus, a kind of nervous arousal, or a more complicated and individual psychological response? Marching to a steady beat does, however, demonstrate a very basic function of music. It is very difficult not to synchronise with the beat; the music appears to relieve the strain of marching, as every army has observed throughout history. John's attention was very much held by the rhythmic activity. He appeared to stay with the music when other activities did not capture his interest. What is difficult, in a case such as John's, is to state categorically that his outpouring of active musical behaviour, the enormous range of physiological changes he underwent during those twenty-five minutes, is directly related to the stimulus of the music he was hearing and making. We could also look at the way John began to build up expectations within the music and became more accustomed to the complexities of the music as the session evolved. We shall return to this notion of expectations in music. At the moment it is enough to say that we would have to do a very sophisticated piece of comparative work in collaboration with other disciplines, including bio-electrical engineers using the latest in computer technology, in order to begin to sort out all the interacting complexities. But something at a very basic level of functioning is clearly taking place.

We are beginning to see a re-evaluation of this physiological research in the current growing interest in vibro-acoustic therapy (see Chapter 3). Passing refer-ence must also be made to the work on music and bio-feedback. There is some work concerning EEG monitoring while listening to music, and several studies have shown increases in alpha rhythms (brain waves associated with an increase in relaxation), particularly when trained musicians are tested while listening to music.[13] As with my listening to the Arvo Pärt piece, any increased alpha could be connected with the music-listening, or there could be many other influences. What about the familiarity of the music? It is hard to know what these changes mean. Nevertheless the work on bio-feedback and music has practical implications for helping people use a method to influence their own state of relaxation and, potentially, to reduce levels of anxiety by listening to preferred music. There are practical implications in working with people with learning difficulties and perceptual problems.

An early music therapy pioneer, Ira Altshuler, was interested in these physiological and almost primitive responses to music, evolving a principle of working that has very practical links with this discussion on music therapy and a medical model. This was the 'iso principle', a principle which is not outmoded today and can be regarded as at the heart of much current music therapy practice. 'Iso', based on the Greek,

> simply means 'equal'; that is, that the mood or the tempo of the music in the beginning must be in 'iso' relation with the mood or tempo of the mental patient. The 'iso' principle is extended also to volume and rhythm.[14]

In the individual session I searched for a way to be in 'iso relation' with John, exploring various moods, speeds and rhythms to match his playing and find a point of contact. Once we reached this point, then we began to interact musically. The group members took some time to find a way to make music together. As the therapist I needed to observe carefully the speed and mood of the opening musical gestures made by the members. I searched for musical ideas that might sum up these various moods and shapes, to find a musical common denominator that would help to bring the group together, to find some sense of group cohesion via the music. This seems to be what Benenzon means when he talks about a 'group iso', although further elaboration is surely needed to understand what he means by such concepts as 'universal iso'.[15]

One of the most recent uses of music therapy within a medical or physiological model is in the management of chronic pain. Mark Rider is one of a group of American therapists who are investigating the relationships of music to the body's immune system.[16] Such research also has implications for work within the fields of palliative care, for people living with cancer or with the HIV and AIDS virus.

This discussion of the use of music largely within a medical, physiological or biological framework implies that music can have a measurable and predictable effect on human behaviour.[17] There appears to be a body of evidence to support such a physiological base to music therapy. Much of the early work needs now to be replicated using more sophisticated measuring equipment and experimental designs that are robust enough to account for the many individual differences and variables involved. There needs to be more research into the long-term effects and the use of active techniques. To work within this model, Ruud adds, music therapists need to accept that music has the potential of influencing underlying physiological behaviours. As we have seen, it is very difficult to be categorical about the use of music and to isolate the physical from the psychological and the emotional.

MUSIC THERAPY AND PSYCHOANALYTICAL THEORY

Near the end of the nineteenth century the mind was beginning to be subjected to the same scrutiny as the body. An evolving science of consciousness created a split among the early pioneers. On the one hand, the leading psychologist Watson regarded consciousness as almost a remnant of medieval thought, advising study only of overt behaviour that was measurable and observable. We shall see in the next section how this kind of thinking evolved into behaviour therapy. On the other hand, the medically trained Freud began exploring the uncharted areas of the unconscious. The emerging discipline of psychoanalysis was to provide the twentieth century with a radically new theory of mind and personality, a theory with implications in all areas of art and science.

What can psychoanalysis teach us about the forms of music and the way in which people make use of music? The psychoanalytical literature contains a wide range of viewpoints on the meaning of music with a main focus on: the personality of musicians, the pleasure derived from music and musical forms, and the relationship of art and the creative process to key psychoanalytical concepts.[18] Freud himself was not able to derive much pleasure from music, being unable to rationalise how it affected him.[19] We can look to Freud for insights into the creative and artistic processes in music therapy. To begin with, we must understand that the creation of a finished artistic product is not a major factor in music therapy. The process itself matters more than the final result, although often the result can be musically very satisfying and beautiful. We must differentiate between using our creative imaginations improvising music and striving for musical perfection in the finished created or re-created piece of music. A Freudian interpretation of the artistic and creative process primarily seems to emphasise sublimation, which can be understood as the transfer of usually sexual and instinctive impulses from direct and outward expression into more civilised and acceptable forms. We can infer therefore that a musical composition such as an improvisation is an acceptable form in which we can expose some of our wilder and more out-of-control feelings. Is this what was happening when the group was exploring a range of rhythms together – rhythmic work often producing such cathartic moments? After a particularly vivid improvisation people often comment with such statements as: 'That was primitive'; 'I didn't know I had that in me.' Such experiences certainly seem to relieve tension.

Freud also suggested that the artist creates in order to compensate for inadequacies of personality, the process itself being very close to a kind of neurosis or obsession. History contains many examples of musicians with major personal difficulties in their private and domestic lives who may possibly have turned to their music to compensate for problems in coping. This way of escaping reality may be similar to fantasising, and Freud makes links with day-dreaming and the exploratory play of children as further reference points with regard to the nature of creativity. There is much discussion on regression, as if a root of artistic inspiration stems from an unconscious return to a very egocentric and primitive stage in our psycho-sexual development. Are the members of the music therapy group returning unconsciously to a pseudo-weaning stage, one where the boundaries between self and reality are blurred? Do we all want to float in this narcissistic 'oceanic' state? Perhaps we are in danger of becoming music-addicts, using music to escape from growing up and facing reality? On another level, are we using music as a substitute for sexual experience? If such blissful moments as the intimate togetherness after sexual intercourse are denied us, can music fill the gap? Are these the areas of inspiration – the narcissistic, the primitive, the sexual – that we use to create a form of art such as music?

Rollo May, in an essay on the nature of creativity, criticises this Freudian overemphasis on sublimation and regression as a source of creativity. He argues that: 'if we create out of some transfer of affect or drive, as implied in sublimation, or as a by-product of an endeavour to accomplish something else, as in compensation, does not our very creative act then have only a pseudo value?'[20] Anthony Storr also challenges such classic Freudian interpretation, questioning why a work of art or creative process is of necessity a substitute for something else.[21] Why cannot the work of art or creative process stand up by itself? The improvisations made by the hospital group were unique creations, music made in a particular time and space by a group of people who would never create the identical music again. Even if we were to record the improvisations, transcribe them and re-create them there would always be subtle differences in performance. I like to think that these moments of creative impulse are born for the moment and do not stand in for any other energy or source of conflict. Every act of creative or re-creative music-making is a new and totally unique experience.

We can infer from our observations of individuals and groups in music therapy that making music together to some extent provides an opportunity to escape from the immediate concerns of the moment. But need it be called escape? We could also think of it as a positive side-stepping from present preoccupations. A further feature of a music therapy session is access to an inner world of inspiration that does not need verbal interpretation and can bear little resemblance to everyday life. Side-stepping present preoccupations and exploring inner inspiration could lead to criticisms of music therapy as providing a mere temporary diversion or additional luxury, particularly in the present economic climate. I hope it will become clear that, as in any school curriculum, the opposite could be the case, with music occupying not a peripheral but a central position.

A Freudian interpretation might regard improvised music-making as a form of musical day-dreaming or fantasy. But this invitation to explore sounds and music provides more than a primitive excursion into uncharted waters of creative inspiration, a quick dip into all-embracing oceanic feelings. Music therapy is more than a temporary diversion: it presents people with a challenging opportunity to look at aspects of themselves in a different light. As in any therapy, such a process can be painful. The musical end-result may be pleasurable at all levels, including intellectually; but it may also be disturbing, helping people to confront difficult and conflicting issues. Music is a transformation process that can take people to many depths and heights, all richly imbued with private fantasies, dreams and symbols. Yet the articulated forms of music are the link that can bring these areas from the internal to the external world. Music therapists do not want to increase sliding into neurotic, obsessional or introverted behaviour through the very form of the creative intervention on offer. Time and time again we observe in music therapy sessions rather the opposite, an opening-out of a personality. This clearly happened to John during the one individual session and is apparent to all who have viewed that particular video film. We see adults visibly grow in confidence as they discover they can make beautiful sounds which not only give themselves pleasure but can also be appreciated by other members of the group. Such creativity seems to link more centrally with a high degree of emotional health and maturity.

Jung discussed creativity more in terms of a process of change and growth, 'a living thing implanted in the human psyche'.[22] He linked creativity closely to the play instinct: 'The creation of something new is not accomplished by the intellect but by the play instinct acting from inner necessity. The creative mind plays with the object it loves.'[23] In many ways Jung regarded creativity as a far more active and dynamic process than Freud did, placing less emphasis on regression and sublimation. This concept of growth is echoed by May, who defines creativity as 'the process of bringing something new into birth'.[24] Jung would often encourage patients to paint out their dream recollections and fantasies and his writings are important reference points within the discipline of art therapy.

The American music therapist Dorinda Hawk Hitchcock has recently summarised Jung's contact with music therapy.[25] She describes how in 1956 Jung met the concert pianist Margaret Tilly and was given a session of passive music therapy. Tilly played music to Jung. Members of Jung's family were musicians, and Jung, unlike Freud, had extensive knowledge of the repertoire. Before she played to Jung, Margaret Tilly asked him about his relationship to music. During his early career he had heard many great musicians perform but had stopped listening to music as it apparently exhausted and irritated him. His resistance was very unlike Freud's reluctance to listen to music: 'because music is dealing with such deep archetypal material and those who play don't realise this', he is reported to have said.[26] Tilly then understood that Jung cared too much about music, and not too little as she had been led to believe by previous reports. Margaret Tilly played to Jung as she would have done to any of her clients, beginning by playing music to match the kind of mood and personality of the person with whom she was working (the 'iso' principle). Many key Jungian concepts such as the parameters of extrovert/introvert, masculine/feminine, thinking/feeling influenced her choice of musical material in her work, which ranged from pre-composed music to improvisation based on folksongs. Jung proposed various hypothetical cases and asked Tilly to demonstrate how she might play and help the person in each case. He also asked her to relate some case studies. According to Jensen, Jung is reported to have said to Tilly:

> This opens up whole new areas of research I'd never dreamed of. Because of what you have shown me this afternoon – not just what you have said but what I have actually felt and experienced, I feel that from now on music should be an essential part of every analysis. This reaches the deep archetypal material that we can only sometimes reach in our analytical work with patients. This is remarkable.[27]

Such a reaction was very different from Jung's earlier opinion of music therapy. He was familiar with the subject of music therapy and had read a great deal but was apparently not interested because he found the work sentimental and superficial. Hitchcock proposes that there is a need for more research within Jungian frameworks. Are there such features as musical universals or musical archetypes? What are the links between music, symbol, metaphor and myth? How can music be part of every analysis? Are the reported comments from Jung a challenge to music therapists to work alongside analysts in formulating a clearer psychoanalytical theory of music?

Perhaps the contributions of both Freud and Jung relate rather too specifically to the creation or effects of the final artistic product and we should be looking at developing more of what Erich Fromm calls a 'creative attitude'.[28] In music therapy we are providing opportunities for developing active listening, awareness and response. We are concerned with such highly creative factors as encounter, engagement and focused absorption.[29] There are opportunities to interact with the music, with the instruments available, with the music therapist and with other people in the group. Fromm cites the example of a 2-year-old child rolling a ball on the floor again and again and never seeming to be bored. He points out that the child delights in seeing the ball rolling, and for the child it is not registered as a simple mental fact. A music therapy group can provide a space for people of all ages to listen and see, almost with the kind of rapt and concentrated attention of this 2-year-old. This quality of attention also, according to Fromm, 'requires the capacity to be puzzled'.[30] As adults we feel that to admit puzzlement may make us lose face; to admit we do not know may let us down. We also become more creative as we experience and work through conflicts, reconciling apparent opposites (see Chapter 8). Can we allow ourselves to be open enough to rediscover this sense of puzzlement and wonder when listening to or playing music?

The Freudian concept of sublimation became less rigid during the 1930s. There was less emphasis on an inner conflict as the root of any creative process. We need to practise our skills to appreciate and play music which the ego finds highly satisfying. The ego is acting here more as a regulator of the admittance of primary process material – all that is irrational, unrelated and illogical – into everyday secondary process thinking – all that is regulated, rational, highly focused and logical. Noy gives much attention to the concept of mastering and, in art in general, to the ability to detach oneself from the centre of this inner conflict – a concept very much developed by Melanie Klein and her followers.[31] Within these terms music and music-making could be regarded as a defence mechanism, protecting the self against being overwhelmed.[32] We can organise all these internal impulses through the active processes of variation and repetition into pleasure-giving musical structures. The ego is able to make sense of, and be in control of, all the stimuli. This is a far more active response to music than the earlier emphasis on regression. Ostwald points out the paradox of the interpretation when the regressive nature of music is organised by the ego almost as a defence against regression: 'This combination of and interaction between deepest regression and highly developed organisation makes music a unique experience.'[33] Ruud feels that this active sense of mastering musical stimuli, a developing sense of being in control, was very much used as a base for many of the early assumptions about music therapy.[34]

To summarise this section on music therapy within a psychoanalytical framework, it is apparent that to work within the model necessitates a sympathy with one of the various analytical schools of thought. We have briefly touched on pointers from the deterministic, reductive and medically based Freudian model, the more all-embracing Jungian approach, and the later notions of mastering. Some form of personal analysis is now almost regarded as essential for a therapist working within such approaches. Regular supervision is recommended. Music therapy does seem to share certain concepts and attitudes of the psychoanalysts, and joint interventions could be highly stimulating, to take Jung's suggestion a stage further. The highly complex and subtle communicative systems at the heart of much music therapy practice could develop into analytical studies in their own right, excluding the additions of insightful interpretations from a different discipline. Both client and therapist are more often than not actively involved as participants in the interactive music therapy process. This immediately separates the actively involved music therapist from the more traditional passive role of the analyst in most schools of psychoanalysis.

MUSIC THERAPY AS A 'SCIENCE OF BEHAVIOUR'

'Music therapy is a method of behavioural manipulation and therefore can automatically be considered as falling within the purview of the behaviour modification movement.'[35] Although this statement was written over twenty years ago, it sums up a period of work in the 1960s and 1970s when many leading music therapists, particularly in the USA, advocated such an objective and scientific approach. The vast range of music appears to give as many possibilities of application as there are individual needs and problems, and it is not surprising that one of the directions the emergent profession followed was to consider music therapy as part of the behaviour modification movement. It is possible to regard music as not only a stimulus but also a reward for eliciting and maintaining certain behaviours. If we think again about John's individual session, we can observe that his very act of playing the drum can, from a behaviour-therapy perspective, have an in-built reward system. At a simple level of description, John plays the drum, and the sound comes back to him as his sound. He has made the sound, the sound gives him pleasure and he repeats the experience. The effect of one pleasurable musical gesture has an in-built reinforcing effect, so this one gesture stimulates and elicits the next. There is also the additional reinforcing effect and reward of the adult supporting, encouraging and responding to these gestures. The therapist can also choose to support and encourage certain behaviours and not others. In John's session I was keen to encourage him to sustain contact on one instrument for as long as possible. I gave him a great deal of positive reinforcement by joining him in the sounds he made, feeding back to him immediately and elaborating on his musical ideas. We could apply the behaviour therapist's terminology of rewards, tokens, contingencies, goals, positive and negative reinforcers to this process. John had a reward both from the instrument itself and from my response. We could think of a pleasurable musical experience as a kind of token, contingent on behaviour within the session that relates to the ground rules, boundaries, aims and objectives. In John's session such objectives included exploring a wide range of musical stimuli to find the kind of music that would engage him for the longest period.

The act of music-making itself is a very positive reinforcement for most people. People of all ages are able, in most cases, to stay with music for long periods without becoming over-stimulated and satiated. There are obvious exceptions due to particular problems. Great care is needed when working with some autistic children, for example, not to over-stimulate an often already highly aroused child. Learning procedures are clearly involved in both short- and long-term music therapy. Even in the individual and group sessions described in this chapter we can surmise that John and the adults learned more about how to use the instruments as the session progressed. People are engaged in constant processes of discovery while making music, since music offers such endless opportunities for creating new and exciting ideas. It is also possible to link both short- and long-term aims for intervention with specific activities and individual needs.

To work within a traditional behaviour therapy framework a music therapist would need to address such systematic questions as:

- What is the observable behaviour that needs changing?
- Does this behaviour need increasing or decreasing?
- If the behaviour is causing problems, what situations are currently reinforcing such behaviour and thus preventing changes from occurring?
- What system of reinforcement (for the most part we can assume positive) can be introduced and applied to alter the behaviour?

There are many examples in the music therapy literature of very successful interventions clearly based within a behaviour therapy framework, considerably helping to promote music therapy's external validity. Rigorously controlled studies, with much reliance on statistical and comparative evidence, examined the effects of music on small aspects of carefully defined behaviour. According to such evidence, music appears, to list a few examples, to be effective in developing reading, numeracy and imitation skills.[36] Music can also reduce aggression, stereotyped behaviours, hyperactivity and maladaptive behaviour.[37] Token economy systems and time-out procedures have also been used.[38] So has rock music, as an incentive for groups of children with learning disabilities when recordings of the music are withdrawn upon responses defined as disruptive or inappropriate.[39] The Orff-Schulwerk music education methods have been applied effectively in a behaviour therapy context.[40]

Louise Steele set up a community music therapy project, the Cleveland Music School Settlement, following a clear structure of behavioural analysis. 'Music is used in therapy as a reinforcer, as an extra-auditory cue, as a music learning experience, and to set the occasion for modifying non-musical behaviour.'[41] Steele and her team carefully planned any new intervention. First of all there would be a period when the specific behaviour or behaviours to be modified would be observed and charted without any music therapy intervention. This could take the form of three observation points at equally spaced moments in the three months preceding intervention. This observation period is known as the baseline period (A). The targeted behaviour(s) is then monitored at equally spaced points during a three-month period of music therapy intervention (B). A return to the baseline period (A) enables more observations of the behaviour to be made in a setting outside the music therapy. If our hypothesis is that music therapy intervention can have a marked influence on sustaining attention, for example, then we must first chart the child's or adult's attention in a context such as a classroom or any other non-musical setting (baseline observation). We then have observations made of the child or adult in the context of music therapy. If we find that any increase in attention observed during the music therapy is sustained in the return to the baseline period after the intervention, then we have some evidence that can be statistically tested to indicate that the music therapy may have had an effect. This is a simple example and there are many more complexities and variables involved. If the ABA design is used on a series of interventions, then more evidence can be collated. A further period of intervention often follows the return to baseline (ABAB), or many baseline measures may be charted, usually the observations being started at different times – a multiple baseline design.

A major strength of this behavioural approach is that no claims are made other than those relating to the clearly stated objectives. The work cannot be criticised for being too anecdotal, subjective or over-sentimental. On the other hand, the work can be seen as rather mechanistic and rigid to the extent that two researchers proposed the creation of 'a technology of music therapy which would provide the clinician with a ready source of information relating behavioural and treatment variables and encourage the operational description of behaviour'.[42] Can music therapy fit so rigidly into such a box, enabling us to look up a particular problem (A) in our book of tricks to see how to apply musical technique (B) to reach the chosen treatment objective (C)? In order to provide a control for the many variables involved, there is also the primary use of recorded music within this model of working. McGinty, as late as 1980, reported that over 68 per cent of her surveyed music therapists in the USA used record-listening as a main activity.[43] A behavioural approach, by definition, is reductive and predictive, with causal relationships being set up between behaviour, intervention and therapeutic outcome. If we relate this to music therapy, we observe that specific responses are linked to specific musical events and eventual outcomes as in the proposed 'technology of music therapy'. This approach has been criticised for the focus on small bits of behaviour in undue isolation (the symptom rather than cause argument) and the apparent neglect to focus on purpose, choice and consciousness.[44] In the traditional behaviour therapy approaches there has been an emphasis on measuring those behaviours that are clearly observable. Many music therapists consider that such an emphasis excludes the more private and inner states often regarded by them as central to the work.

Recently behaviour therapy has begun to look at more internal patterns, and more flexibility is developing. Blackman has summarised some of the basic approaches of a more radical behaviourism as advocated by Skinner in his later work.[45] A stimulus-and-response model of behaviour has developed into an approach relating the behaviour both to the setting-conditions in which it occurs and the consequence of the behaviour in those conditions. We can describe such a model as A:B:C, with A the setting, B the behaviour and C the consequences.[46] There is a two-way movement represented by the colon, with influences passing in either direction. If we think of John's session in terms of this A:B:C model, then it is clear that any isolated moment of behaviour, be it playing the drum, vocalising or moving around the room, can be directly related to the setting-conditions, be it the previous music, the choice of instruments available, the particular mood of the music or his level of attention and tiredness. Such behaviour will then have direct and immediate knock-on effects on any following behaviour. We noted, for example, that a move to slower and quieter music elicited longer vocalisations using vowel sounds. In turn such behaviour became the setting for a new behaviour, as in the moment when he changed directions and began short, rhythmic patterns on the drum to break up the longer vowel sounds. According to the radical behaviourist, mental and social life can be included in a behavioural perspective, mental life being regarded as a form of behaviour which is subject to similar environmental influences to overt behaviour. Blackman points out that we cannot understand a person and their actions without a close observation of the contact and interactions with others. There is a reciprocal process in wanting to reinforce those who reinforce us, and social reinforcement is a situation where one person's actions are reinforced by another's pleasure or displeasure. John soon learned that his pleasure could be increased by joining me in my music. I was in turn pleased with the music we made together, and the session could be described as spirals of pleasurable joint activity with John clearly perceiving that I was enjoying his sounds and music as much as he was.

In summary, a behavioural music therapist must be consistent and rigorous in the approach. Understanding and acceptance of definitions are crucial, for example in using terms such as 'appropriate' or 'inappropriate' behaviour. Behaviour therapy has been remarkably successful, for example, in reducing some of the anti-social behaviours of both children and adults with severe learning disabilities, making it possible for many to live outside large institutions in more community-based group homes and hostels. Clear operational definitions and a systematic approach to intervention, constantly called for by the behaviourists, are very necessary for efficient practice. The more recent exploration of social and interactional processes by the radical behaviourists indicates less rigidity. However, behaviour therapy is not the only model that can stand up to the rigours of scientific investigation.

MUSIC THERAPY AND HUMANISTIC PSYCHOLOGY

During the last few decades there has evolved what is known as a 'third force' psychology finding a path between psychoanalysis and behaviour therapy. Many new therapies all cluster under the umbrella term 'humanistic' – some are offshoots of psychoanalysis and existentialism, others are less orthodox. Worthwhile goals include helping people realize their full potential and an emphasis on the notion of growth rather than treatment. The therapist as an expert to be consulted by the potentially dependent patient is replaced by a more collaborative process of joint negotiation, the term client being used in preference to patient. These humanistic therapies claim to be concerned with areas that have not been so explicitly highlighted by the psychoanalysts and behaviour therapists, such as:

- respect for individuals and their unique differences
- the notion of 'wholeness'
- development of purpose and personal intentions
- freedom of choice
- self-growth, or self-actualization, particularly in relation to others
- creativity
- love
- peak experiences
- self-esteem.

Several of the terms listed here are rather cliché-ridden and associated with a particular philosophical and ideological viewpoint. The terms have a high moral content. Within humanistic psychology a main emphasis seems to be on experiencing present feelings and issues in what is referred to as the 'here and now'.[47] In humanistic psychology the therapist is more often regarded as a catalyst or facilitator. Two major pioneers in this field are Fritz Perls, with the growth of Gestalt therapy, and Carl Rogers, with his client-centred style of therapy and counselling. There is an increasing acceptance of more complementary kinds of intervention, particularly Eastern systems, homeopathy and the more holistically based therapies.

The work of many music therapists seems to fall within a humanistic framework. A music therapist is aiming to maximise growth and potential, often as part of an evolving group process. We are very much concerned with encouraging creativity and our clients' expressive behaviour. Alvin used to describe her course in London as based in humanistic psychology. The Bristol University course has an introduction to counselling skills as an integral part of the training. Ruud describes the work of Nordoff and Robbins as a relationship-based model of therapy rooted in humanistic psychology.[48] William Sears considers that 'experience in self-organisation' and 'experience in relating to others' are major factors in music therapy processes.[49]

A criticism of humanistic psychology is that there is a dearth of carefully planned research. But the objectives of this approach can still be included in research projects. A music therapy researcher could devise a research strategy that would not lose any sense of respect for the integrity of each individual. Devising research does not mean that any therapeutic approach would be less warm or client-centred. Research based within a humanistic perspective could help music therapy to develop alternative strategies to a rigid behaviourist application of recorded music and also help to dispel some of the profession's early cosiness and general assumptions of inherent worth. Working within such an approach, we could begin to evaluate the use of live music in a fundamentally interactive and ever-changing setting. My colleague Sarah Hoskyns and I have drawn up a simple list of proposals that begins to address some of these issues. Research in music therapy could be enhanced by:

- a careful and systematic period of observation, both visual and aural
- the formulation of simple and clear questions
- the definition of terms and construction of observational frameworks which need to be agreed upon to an acceptable level of reliability
- a detailed plan for the analysis and evaluation which leads on to the drawing of interpretations and inferences.[50]

In order to reach an 'acceptable level of reliability' two or more people need to agree on the meaning of a particular observational definition. This often means only accepting a term if practice indicates agreement over 80 per cent of the time. These proposals stress that inferences are made after extensive questioning, observation and analysis over a period of time. We need to make many observations before we can infer, for example, that someone's quiet drumming is indicative of feeling depressed. Conversely, although loud drumming may indicate anger, it may also be a moment of excited celebration. Music is rich in ambivalent forms and derives some of its most potency from its very wordless and rather enigmatic quality.

SUMMARY

Music therapy appears to have many relationships with these traditional models in health care. As in the growth of any new profession, music therapy has looked backwards and sideways for sources of reference and to gain further understanding. Doubtless we shall continue to do so, as in our discussion of work with children (see Chapter 4). The recent developments in cognitive therapy may provide further parallels. For example, in helping a client move from the fixed rigidity of an obsessional beat to a more planned and fluid way of interacting we may be mirroring a process in cognitive therapy, namely the substituting of more positive thinking for the automatic cognitive distortions that may overwhelm a person under stress.[51] Much interesting work could develop in charting any parallel processes between music therapy and counselling. But we return to the contention that music therapy will eventually be able to step outside existing frameworks and orientations, 'to establish itself as a unique discipline'.[52] We could begin to develop a perspective from within the evolving discipline of music therapy itself.

Finally, to return to our opening individual and group examples, I hope it is clear that the underlying assumptions behind these examples are rather eclectic. I have a leaning towards humanistic philosophy with an open-ended approach and a stress on active interaction. Some subjective and intuitive observations and inferences were included in the examples but they tended to emerge from the musical content itself. Such inferences are not related to any one particular analytical tradition or therapeutic model. We now need to turn our attention to the content of the music itself. Perhaps by a deeper understanding of music and musical processes we shall begin to become aware once again of the central position of music within music therapy.

Chapter 3

Sound, music and music therapy

INTRODUCTION

A music therapist is sitting with a group of pre-school children and their parents.
The therapist, who is a violinist, slowly and quietly takes the instrument out of its
case, checks the tuning, tightens the bow and plays a single low sound, one
beautiful tone. The sound emerges imperceptibly out of the relative silence, is
held constant, rises to a peak of loudness and dies away back into the silence. The
children look to the source of the sound, attend to it as if drawn along and sharing
in this brief sound journey. The image of a railway track springs to mind, the
children on one track, the music therapist and the violin on the other, with the
sleepers linking them through the ebb and flow of the sound. No words are
spoken, yet the atmosphere in the room changes completely and some form of
non-verbal communication has seemingly taken place. This is a simple example
of an opening gesture in sound but it contains some of the essential 'sound
elements' that are the music therapist's basic tools of the trade. We are assuming
that the reactions of the children and the changes in atmosphere have been
brought about by the interactions of the fundamental elements inherent in the
sound: the unique quality of the sound produced by the violin; the duration of the
sound; the growing and fading of the level of loudness and the pitch of the sound.
What can science, in particular the psychology of music, teach us about these
basic elements? Each is present in any one sound but for simplification we shall
start this chapter with a brief survey of the relationship of each sound element to
music therapy. Alvin based much of her teaching on a commonsense study of
these basic elements of sound, observing that in any collection of sounds there
was usually one element in a dominant position.[1]

These basic elements can inform us how we perceive sounds, particularly
physically, but cannot help us in our understanding of the relationship between
tones. This brings us closer to the world of music. Our violinist begins to explore
other sounds and to organise them into rhythmic patterns and sequences of tones.
More than one sound is played at the same time. We add into our melting-pot the
more complex ingredients of rhythm, melody and harmony, the 'musical
elements'. We shall explore the vital importance of these elements in music

therapy, again supporting this by evidence from clinical practice. As with the descriptions of our four basic elements of sound – timbre, duration, loudness and pitch – the arbitrary and rather reductionist breaking-up of these ingredients is mainly a matter of convenience. Most music is made up of a complex web of expressively organised sounds. We also cannot overlook the fact that each element, even if we can regard it as a self-sufficient idea, is bound additionally by context, learning, behavioural state and cultural conditioning. The individual personality and unique musicianship of our violinist are also major factors in the communication process. It is possible to play one note on the violin, or any other less complex instrument such as a chime bar, in all manner of ways from the musically expressive and beautiful to the blatantly ugly and careless.

We have a lot to discover about our fundamental emotional responses to music. We will need to face such philosophical questions as 'What is music?' and can look at this daunting question in relation to understanding more about how people use music in music therapy. It is reassuring to observe today how many more musicians are taking an active role in researching some of the psychological and motivational aspects of music. In this way we can place the experimental examination of bits of sound (analysis of computer-generated pitches and rhythmical patterns, for example) in the context of observations relating to larger sections and forms of music (emotional reactions to loudness levels, melodic and harmonic structures, for example). Howard Gardner, for one, feels that the future lies in such a 'middle ground' approach with an emphasis on the neurological and cognitive underpinning.[2] Some of this more recent cognitively based approach will be included in the discussions of the musical elements, the origins of music and our emotional responses to the shapes and forms of organised sound. We shall begin to explore how our minds invest with musical meaning what on the simplest level is a series of interconnecting and differing durations, pitches, and changes in timbre and loudness levels.

I recall the feelings of panic when asked by my first placement supervisor during my music therapy training to move from the piano and to use one chime bar, sitting on the floor with a group of children with severe learning difficulties. I felt that I was supporting the children's music-making at the appropriate level with my expressive piano-playing. I felt very secure at the keyboard. What could I do with one chime bar? I felt that it would be impossible to interact with one sound or help sustain a musical experience. I began to learn that being simple, listening, waiting and not 'doing' are some of the hardest lessons to learn in music therapy. I began to learn that it was possible to support and express a wide range of emotions with the use of my voice and a simple instrumental accompaniment. As a practising music therapist I continue to observe people of all ages responding to the stimulus of a sound – and sometimes these are very simple sound shapes – with the sound making an apparent change on or in the person, or the person doing something with or to the sound. On a more complex level I observe how the shapes and forms of music influence people, noting both positive and negative aspects of how 'people do things to music and music can do things to people'.[3] If we observe how the different ingredients of sound and music are used by our clients, we can begin to assess our clients' reactions, relate such reactions to any problems, and explore the evolving therapeutic relationships. We begin to develop what Alvin neatly calls 'constructive therapeutic work'.[4]

When we play an instrument or sing a sound we also introduce the concept of resonance. Our bodies or the instrument itself vibrate in sympathy, acting as sounding-boards and adding changes to the quality, loudness, pitch and duration of the sound. Material substances resonate at a specific frequency: we can find the natural resonating frequency of rooms, wood, metal and glass, and even, according to some ancient healing traditions, our own unique resonating tone. Alvin used to define being musical as being resonant to sound. Gary Ansdell also uses the metaphor of the sounding-board in relation to the music therapy process:

> In a musical situation perhaps the visual metaphor of 'reflection' could be replaced by the aural metaphor of the 'sounding-board.' The musical-therapeutic process acts as a sounding-board to amplify and reflect back aurally what is given. It enables you to listen to yourself and others in a different way.[5]

TIMBRE (OR TONE COLOUR)

'Laboratory tests have demonstrated that differences in tone colour are the first differences apparent to the untrained ear.'[6] A young baby quickly learns to discriminate between the sound of a human voice and other significant sounds, marking out timbre as an early area of differentiation of sound. Differences in timbre enable us to distinguish between a flute and a clarinet playing the same pitch at the same level of loudness, or even two of the same instrument. After any musical performance we often hear comments that relate to personal taste and thereby to differences in timbre – 'I liked the sound of the flute more than the clarinet'; 'I didn't like the tenor's voice'. Such comments support the idea, again proposed by Copland, that 'we respond to music from a primal and almost brutish level – dumbly, as it were, for on that level we are firmly grounded'.[7] So what is timbre? If we listen to one deep bass note on the piano we can hear other sounds vibrating simultaneously with this one note. We are hearing the sound of the whole string vibrating (the fundamental tone) and the other vibrating parts of the string (the overtones). Any particular timbre results from the combination of the individual patterns of overtones and their relationship to the fundamental tone. On a more everyday level, an understanding of timbre enables us to give meaning to sounds and to attach labels to significant events around us. We hear a door slam and recognise the sound, without even needing to see the particular door.

Timbre is not just about the relationship of overtones to the fundamental tone; other factors include:

– the mental preparation for the sound, the inner hearing of the sound

- the beginning attack and ending fading of sounds
- slight changes in pitch due to vibrato
- the overlap of sounds
- the technical ability and personal touch and style of the player
- the resonating capacity of the instrument itself and of the entire space where the music is being made
- the link with loudness: an increase in loudness opens up more overtones and changes the timbre
- the harmonic context.

Timbre has long been associated with making an immediate and sensuous impression on the listener, adding meaning to sounds. In Western classical music this has resulted in the use of timbre for creating atmosphere and mood and for emphasising musical ideas and lines. As listeners we can all list our favourite examples where timbre is a dominant element, when we feel that a composer has used the timbre of a particular instrument to great effect. As players we will all have favourite composers who write well for our instrument, with good understanding of the range of colours available. There is a growing curiosity in exploring other musics and instruments from other cultures: Indian bells, Chinese gongs, African drums and South American pan-pipes are becoming increasingly popular. One very distinct timbre is the sound of the Balinese 'gamelan' and several complete 'gamelan orchestras' have been brought back from Bali and re-assembled in this country. There is also the rapidly expanding world of electronic and synthesised sound. Timbres can now be created and composed.

Timbre can be used to excite interest, curiosity and attention. Pleasure can be gained from discovering the origin of the sound and the substance from which any instrument is made. Adults seem to share with children this fascination with the shape, colour and size of instruments, even if it takes rather longer for adult inhibitions to be put aside and for instruments to be explored with the spontaneity of a 4-year-old. How is the sound made? What is the instrument made of? Can I play it? Where does it come from? Where can I buy it? These are the kinds of question that I often meet when introducing a new group of adults to a wide range of tuned and untuned percussion instruments. The group may then need support and time to give themselves permission to explore and play with the instruments, to contact the carefree child part of themselves. These extra factors are stimuli in their own right, in addition to the sound-producing timbre of the instruments. The experienced educator David Ward often refers to the integrated nature of stimulation through music, how an instrument can offer a child with learning difficulties, for example, all manner of additional visual and tactile stimulation.[8] Differentiation of timbres can form a major contribution to a developing sense of sound discrimination so vital for language development. Carers and workers with children with learning or language difficulties will be familiar with the use of different instruments and sounds as a means of helping the development of aural discrimination.

If provided with a comprehensive range of instruments to explore, people of all ages will often develop a certain personal preference for a particular timbre or group of timbres, continuing to return to these instruments. Such a discovery is often a point of entry for the music therapist and the beginnings of contact and some shared activity. It may take weeks or months to discover or it may happen in the first session.

Colin was attending a music therapy group in a psychiatric day hospital. On being offered a choice of instruments he chose to play the chocolo, a shaking-type instrument used in West Indian reggae bands. This quickly became his sound, his voice in the group. We observed how attached he became to this one instrument even during the first session. He needed to leave the room but carefully hid his instrument under his chair before leaving. On returning he became very angry on finding another member of the group with his instrument. He would not accept another choice of instrument and did not settle until his instrument was returned to him. It was only then that he felt comfortable about playing his sound and taking an active part in the musical improvisations again.

Alvin records the striking response of a 9-year-old autistic boy to a small instrument imitating the sound of a nightingale. Brian tended to remain immobile and inactive, not reacting to environmental sounds or to any musical sound. Alvin played the nightingale sound after many weeks of 'sterile attempts' at trying to interest Brian in sounds and music:

> The effect on the boy was immediate and surprising. He suddenly came to life, his eyes brightened, his face lit up. Even his posture changed. He straightened up his neck and emitted rapid bird-like shrill sounds in response to the nightingale, then stopped waiting for a reply. At the same time he made bird-like movements of his neck and head. He also made ritualistic movements of his finger-tips, tapping rapidly on the table. The same response happened several times before he left the hospital. He held real dialogues with the bird.[9]

A specific timbre which is unique and special to each and every one of us is our voice. We do not choose our voice-print, it is something that we are born with. What we can do is to try and be aware of our real voice and use it confidently as a means of self-expression. Singing is a very exposing and risky business. Memories of school music-making, not being allowed to join the school choir, tend to plague a lot of adult groups in this country. 'I can't sing' is a common complaint, not heard so often in other cultures where there still exists a lively folk and singing tradition. There also seems to be a relationship between the sophistication of the equipment for listening to music and our lack of confidence in singing. I have heard many anecdotal reports from parents and colleagues that today's high technical standard of recorded music inhibits singing to children at home or at school. It is difficult persuading colleagues and parents that live singing with a significant adult is far more enriching for any child than being placed by an expressionless tape-recorder or loudspeaker. By the age of 2 most children can sing. Something to do with what other people do to our vocal confidence, particularly significant adults, seems to change this natural ability into something very different as we grow up.

We can alter our voices, we are aware of how our voices change in different emotional contexts. I am aware of a change in timbre, a lowering of pitch and loudness level if I am feeling nervous. Conversely, my voice will change timbre, become higher in pitch and louder if I am more confident (or acting as if I am so). Alvin used to talk of helping people to find the identity of their voices, their personal sounds. Sometimes the voice may be hampered by a particular physiological problem which in turn may produce an emotional disturbance. But most people can sing, and before we begin to sing we can cry, laugh, hum and vocalise. We may need help to explore or re-explore these processes before we can feel free enough to use our voices in singing or chanting.

Of all the elements timbre seems to have a very direct associative potential. We do not know why people are drawn to various sound sources. It may be a question of curiosity. There may be biological links – does the sound link with the sound of our mothers' voice? There may be connections with the natural world or specific life events. What this element does teach us is that in therapy people of all ages are disturbed by an imposed choice. People have a right to explore a range of musical sounds and experiences for themselves. As music therapists we are in a privileged position to observe people's choices and to begin to explore a channel of musical communication (our railway track metaphor again). Offering people a range of choices so that preferences can be observed does take time, often a great deal of time, and patience.

LOUDNESS

Loudness is also a basic perceptual attribute of sound. Physically it is related directly to the energy of the source of the sound, which in turn affects the power, the intensity of the sound and finally our subjective impression of the loudness. The term 'loudness' is used here to cover the continuum from very soft to very loud. There is a direct correlation between the amount of energy at the source and our subjective perception of the loudness of the sound. Scientists have devised the unit of the decibel to measure the different levels of loudness. At the extremes of the scale are two thresholds: the threshold of hearing (0 decibels) and the threshold of pain (around 130 decibels). In the West today, with our highly mechanised life-style, we are only too aware of the threshold of pain, exposing ourselves to high levels of loudness in busy cities, airports, on roads and in discos, with the risk of premature hearing problems. If invaded for extended periods by high levels of loud sounds, our ears need time to recover, for example from the ringing in the ears and dulled sense of hearing after an evening at a loud disco. If we surround ourselves with high levels of loudness too soon, perhaps by a return visit to the disco on the following night, then we may not be allowing our ears sufficient recovery time. At the other end of the scale we need to pay attention to how loud a sound needs to be before it reaches a sufficient level to be heard. This is particularly important when making music with people who have hearing impairments and with the elderly. As with preference for timbre, people appear to have a preferred level of loudness. For one person some music may be too loud, whereas for another the opposite is true. This is particularly noticeable in group work where care is needed in observing the individual members' reactions to loud sounds. Some people may even demonstrate a form of loud-sound phobia.

Musicians make use of a rather vague and imprecise range of terms from *pianissimo* to *fortissimo* in describing loudness. It is all relative and depends greatly on the nature of the music being made, the size of the group, the shape and size of the room and how the room is carpeted and furnished. There are other associations:

– the threshold of masking, i.e. the level of sound necessary to cover another and gain significance (this is very obvious in group work)
– the overlap with pitch, particularly at the extremes: for example, when pitch seems to increase with loudness in high passages
– the resonance and physical properties of instruments and, when we sing, our voices and whole physiology
– the strength of the movement needed to make an instrument sound, including the physical preparation for the movement
– the motor control needed to control the level of loudness and the shifts in level, with much control being needed in very soft playing
– contextual aspects such as location and distance – where is the sound coming from, how near, how far?

As in all the sound and musical elements, learning and cultural processes are very significant. It is very much common knowledge that most of our responses to music are learned, although there appear to be certain basic features to which we all respond. We all seem to react to a sudden loud sound in a similar way (a reaction exploited to great effect in horror films), and a simple soft sound tends to create a general calming atmosphere. The soft and delicate sound of a pair of Indian bells often serves to focus the attention of a group of children or adults at the start of a session. Changes in the level of loudness can also be used as a means of gaining attention, the changes initiating new perceptual activity.

Silence is crucial for giving space and significance to a sound and can almost be regarded as an element in its own right. Breaking a silence has both a physical and a psychological impact. Silence acts on the memory and can build up pleasurable feelings of expectancy – when is the next sound going to come? The imagination can be let loose – what will the next sound be like? Sometimes silence can cause suspense and in some cases anxiety. When I used to live in the country several visitors, accustomed to a louder city environment, commented how they missed the usual high level of sound, finding the relative silence rather unsettling.

Is there a human need for loudness? At birth the young infant certainly has no inhibitions about making loud sounds, making an immediate impact on the surrounding environment. Could we replace the Victorian maxim with 'children should be seen and heard'? If we as adults are worried about the expression of loud sounds in children, are we not building up frustrations and contributing to the likelihood of future fear and anxiety of being loud in adult life? I often need to explain to parents that it is acceptable for their child to make loud sounds in the music room. If the child has a language or speech problem, it seems very appropriate that loud sounds are encouraged as a way of communicating possible feelings of frustration or confusion. If an adult is depressed, the music therapist can be supportive in encouraging some of the anger, possibly turned inwards and feeding the depression, to be turned outwards in loud, expressive playing on the instruments.

In music therapy practice we observe people making use of the full range of loudness. But I hesitate to make too many assumptions about people's feeling states from their loud or soft playing. There are too many subtle variations. An autistic child, for example, may be using loud drumming as a way of withdrawing from contact with the therapist, the loud sounds being used as a barrier to more direct communication. Loud playing could indicate a release of physical tension or a desire to communicate aggressive and frustrated feelings. It could also indicate confidence, focused attention and internal strength. Some people do find it difficult to project themselves in loud sounds, even to the extent of stopping a movement so as not to make a loud sound. A group of adults who are used to being very sensitive towards each other may need to be given permission to make loud sounds, even if another person's sounds cannot be heard in the process. Even professional orchestras find it difficult to sustain a real *fortissimo*, appearing to be satisfied when the music returns to a comfortable *mezza forte* – the middle-ground position which is safe and involves little risk-taking. Conversely, real sustained *pianissimi* are seldom heard in our concert halls. Soft sounds can create a safe, intimate and enveloping atmosphere. They can often be used to calm when sounds are felt to be too loud. On one level soft sounds may indicate timidity and shyness, on another a conscious plan to focus the attention of others. One of my most effective school teachers was a master who hardly ever raised his voice, the softness of both voice and manner gaining immediate attention. At the other end of the spectrum a master who shouted found it very difficult to calm our rowdy class.

Mike was 10 years old when he started music therapy. He had mild learning difficulties overshadowed by behaviour problems. The particular problems concerning the teachers, and the main reasons for the referral, were outbursts of destructive and aggressive behaviour. There was a history of a difficult birth, including some asphyxia. At the start of the work his music was very loud with an interest in rhythmic patterns and imitative interplay which was accurate. I had the impression that he was surprised when I supported these loud outbursts by playing even louder on the piano. I tried to contain these loud sounds in the improvised music, which contributed to a growing trust. As his trust in me and the situation grew – I was not going to stop this loud playing – he began to be interested in sounds at the opposite end of the spectrum. He would come to the piano and ask for quiet sounds, what he called his 'sleep music'. He would often pretend to sleep as the soft sounds seemed to envelop him. We could begin to interpret this behaviour from all kinds of theoretical standpoints, even making connections with his difficult birth. For the present I was interested in his active and creative use of loud and soft sounds. Once he had explored the extremes of very loud and very soft sounds he became increasingly interested in the middle range of loudness. We could assume that being provided the freedom to explore within this wide range of loudness gave Mike opportunities to make inner connections with troublesome areas of his life and to begin to explore ways of integrating and balancing such aspects of his personality.

PITCH

Pitch is the subjective aspect of a sound where such descriptions as 'high' and 'low' are used. We use the notion of pitch to help us determine the relative position of a sound in some form of scale, be it the Western chromatic range of twelve notes (semi-tones) or the more complex Indian system, where quarter-tones are found. Pitch is a fundamental 'sound element' and there are direct associations with the 'musical elements' of melody and harmony. We often use visual cues to help in developing pitch discrimination: for example, in shaping a sound with up-and-down movements in various teaching techniques such as the Kodaly method, or when conducting a group of singers. When we look at the shape of various instruments such terms as up and down or high and low can cause some confusion. To take two examples: we need to move in a horizontal plane from left to right to play higher sounds on the piano and on the 'cello we go down on the top string to play the highest sounds. But there is a clear link between the frequency – the number of cycles the sound wave vibrates per second – and our subjective impression of the sound. The faster the vibrations, the higher is our subjective perception of the pitch and vice versa.

We can normally hear from around 20 to 15,000 cycles per second (alternatively labelled as Hertz – Hz.): that is, from the lowest sounds of a tuba or an organ to the highest overtones of an orchestral piccolo. There are cultural conventions with changes in a pitch standard over the centuries. Today orchestral musicians in this country will tune to an A of 440 cycles per second; this would have been different in previous centuries, and there are differences today in other countries. Tuning systems also change, the concert grand of today sounding very different from a keyboard before the time of Bach. Sensitivity to the upper and lower end of pitch discrimination does relate to the person's age and there are many individual variables, not least among people with hearing difficulties. The thresholds are not the same for animals, as in the classic example of the dog whistle which we cannot hear but dogs can.

Pitch involves a basic association between tension and relaxation: the law of gravity implying an effort in going up and relaxation in coming down (McLaughlin refers to out-going tensions when we go up in pitch and in-coming tensions when we go down; Cooke adds the notion of out-going or in-coming feelings of pleasure).[10] Singers and string, wind and brass players are only too aware of the physical relationships between levels of tension, relaxation and pitch.

A simple practical exercise can demonstrate this link of pitch with our bodies. Try to be as relaxed and comfortable as possible. Now close your eyes and relax your breathing with slow deep breaths. Try to clear your head of thoughts and hum a sound that is comfortable for you. Play around with this sound, explore the vowel sounds and experiment with different consonants. Try making the sounds go up and down in pitch. By now you should be aware that different parts of your body are resonating with the various pitches you are sounding. What happens if you make the sounds go up or go down? Are you aware of where any tension is occurring? Is your throat becoming tighter as the sounds become higher in pitch? There are many variations on this little exercise. You may like to explore groups of sounds; you could explore these elemental sounds with other people. There is nothing startlingly novel about these exercises: such exploration with sound has been practised for centuries in the East, where there is much written on the connections between pitch, different parts of the body and physiological states.[11] A detailed study of the placing of the vowels and different parts of the voice is also at the basis of good *bel canto* singing.

Pitch is further influenced by temperature (we speak of players 'warming up'), timbre, loudness, the harmonic context and the effects of vibrato. There also appear to be biological influences, with certain sounds, such as high screams or low thuds, causing distress, and there being an apparent preference for safe middle pitches, which we may be associating with the pitch area of our mother's voice. We have already observed a preference for the middle range of loudness and it appears that we prefer the middle sound of three pitches, whether the sounds themselves are in high or low registers.[12]

Strong physical responses to pitch, particularly to the extremes, can be observed in music therapy. Some children and adults seem to be stimulated by particular areas of pitch. High cluster sounds, for example, often stimulate and excite. A client may come into the music room and demonstrate an immediate preference for high-sounding instruments, returning again and again to the high-pitched instruments. Conversely, a sudden low sound may cause distress and physical discomfort. Individual responses may occur in all parts of the body.

A child with profound physical and mental disabilities was referred to Juliette Alvin for an assessment, almost like a last resort. Could sound and music make an impression when no other medium appeared to influence the child? There was a great deal of scepticism as to whether any sound would have any effect. Alvin played some sounds on her 'cello and, with her typical emphasis on detailed observations, watched for even the slightest physical movement or possible reaction to the sounds and the specific pitches that she played. At the end of the session the doctor accompanying the child reported that his initial scepticism had been confirmed and there had been no observable reaction to the sounds. In a characteristic short retort Alvin apparently replied 'Look at the child's foot', as she had been working with responses in the child's feet, in particular the connections between low sounds on the 'cello and movements of the foot.[13]

I often refer to this example to remind us of the unpredictability of responses to sounds and how vigilant music therapists need to be in observing the minutest of responses. We are fortunate that pitch is a basic element of both the sound and verbal memory systems and that specific pitch work has potential in helping sort out prosody, intonation and general comprehension of language and speech. But we are now moving towards the more complex musical worlds of melody and harmony.

A recent development in the specific use of low frequency sound is 'vibro-acoustic therapy'. The first attempts, using a kind of 'low frequency sound massage', were devised by Olav Skille in Norway in 1980. Tests continued in Norway and other countries during the 1980s. The equipment is basically 'a bed/bench or chair with four to six built-in loud speakers. This is connected to a signal unit with six channels containing a cassette player which can run various tapes.'[14] The client lies on the bed or sits in the chair and sound is directly transferred through the mattress or cushions. Special tapes have been made with a mixture of music which tends to be gentle and rhythmically rather amorphous. The important extra ingredient is the pulsed low frequency tone. The researchers create this tone by placing two tones in close proximity, for example 40 and 40.5 cycles per second:

> As far as the use of specific tones is concerned, subjective tests have indicated that the most significant frequencies range between 40 and 80 Hz. The lower frequencies, 40 to 55 Hz. will predominantly set up a resonant response in the lower lumbar region, pelvis, thighs and legs. As one moves through the frequency range so the sound is resonated in the more dense tissues of the body in the upper chest, neck and head.[15]

The first stages of the research are demonstrating quite striking effects of this vibroacoustic therapy on clients with wide-ranging problems: profound physical disabilities, rheumatoid conditions and pulmonary disorders. The therapy appears to have positive results in the relief of pain. A lot of the research has been carried out with people of all ages with severe mental and physical disabilities, often those very groups of clients who have severe difficulties in engaging in more active music therapy approaches. In England Tony Wigram has been pioneering this work at Harperbury Hospital, a hospital for adults with severe learning disabilities, where he has recorded positive evidence on the reduction of muscle-tone and spasm. One client showed marked reduction in muscle spasm in the back, arm, legs and trunk, also initiating movements. Tony Wigram and his physiotherapist colleague Lyn Weekes report that after only three treatments there was an improvement in this client's respiration. A second client began to vocalise in the sessions, with more relaxation in her shoulders and more chest movements. This client, who has severe spasticity, demonstrated much reduction in muscle-tone and spasm, being able to lie on the flat surface, rest her head and extend and flex her legs, which were previously locked in spasm.

People often fall asleep while being massaged by the sounds, and work on the treatment of insomnia and stress is also being developed. Wigram and Weekes have found that other staff have wanted to explore the positive effects of the vibroacoustic unit. They report positive influence on back problems, neck strain and headaches. The team at Harperbury is currently undertaking a series of more rigorously controlled studies on the specific effects of this very physical and sound-based therapy. The team investigated the influence of low frequency sound on the hypothesised reduction of muscle-tone in cerebral-palsied clients. Two conditions were used, one with music plus the low frequency tone and the other with only the music. External assessors made, before and after treatment, measurements of the range of movements in a variety of joints. There was a more significant decrease in muscle-tone in the additional low frequency condition than in the condition when only the music was used. From the early evidence of this project it seems clear that specific and carefully controlled use of pitch can be of positive therapeutic benefit.

DURATION AND TIME

The element of duration is concerned on a physical and measurable level with the length of time a sound lasts. Sounds of long duration will obviously create a slower tempo than sounds of quick duration. On a far deeper philosophical and musical level we can link duration to the movement of time in music: 'The statement of music is made moment by moment, what it expresses comes to life as it moves in time.'[16] This dependence on time contributes to making a sound musical. We shall explore duration here as a link between the sound elements of timbre, loudness and pitch and the musical elements of rhythm, melody and harmony.

There are so many different subjective perceptions of time: the time of the scientist is not that of the poet; the time of the Zen meditator is not that of the head of a big business corporation; we talk of 'having a good time' and even of daring to 'kill time'. In the West we tend to be rather over-burdened by reliance on clock time, mapping out our days with appointments. In his illuminating book *Space, Time and Medicine*, Larry Dossey narrates the incident when he decided not to have his broken watch repaired. At first he thought that this would cripple his activities as a busy hospital doctor. He would not even be able to take a pulse. In fact he found the reverse was true, not wearing a watch became a liberating experience for him, enabling him to free himself from the contemporary addiction to clock time.[17]

How do we perceive time and the different durations of sound? Do we have inner biological clocks? We are intimately connected with a whole range of biological tempi – heartbeats, walking, thyroid activity, metabolic rate, neural activity and the longer cycles such as menstrual and kidney cycles.[18] A baby is quickly exposed to a variety of time and durational experiences: *in utero* and at the breast; the early beating of the feet, movement of limbs and rocking movements. McLaughlin feels that tensions in time occur as there are disturbances in these normal inner tempi.[19] This leads to the question as to whether there is a natural tempo (the ancient notion of *tempo giusto*) from which point all other tempi are judged as faster or slower. If we are used to playing music either alone or with other people, we will be aware of the difficulties of sustaining both a very slow tempo, when we may have to subdivide the main pulse, and keeping a fast tempo up to speed. We do seem to overestimate short sounds and underestimate long sounds. More accuracy occurs in the area of our heartbeat tempo, that is 75–100 beats per minute.

It is rather striking that the durations of our heartbeats and of our spontaneous and preferred tempi do seem to fall within a similar range.[20] Is this sufficient evidence for the notion of an internal regulator or biological clock? We meet this spontaneous and economic tempo in music therapy when a new group, improvising together for the first time, will often settle into this comfortable heartbeat and body-based tempo. This usually follows on after a period of random exploration of the available sounds. Perhaps the natural durations of our physiological functioning may go somewhere to explain certain primary relationships between us and music, a basic physical response to sound. This reliance on durations and time is also cross-cultural and could be described as a universal characteristic of all sound and music. There is a great deal of dance and folk music from various cultures that accentuates these fundamental body-based connections. Much rock music has a heartbeat inner pulse that provides an enlivening and immediate appeal. Within Western classical music I find certain elements which seem to be very much in touch with these physical relationships: for example, the work of many Baroque composers, the physicality of Stravinsky, the balance of durations in Verdi and other composers from southern Europe. Conversely, I find it difficult to relate in any physical way to the music of a composer such as Hindemith where I find myself thinking about the durations rather than instinctively feeling the relationships. We can be excited physically by changes in tempo, enjoying the classic Rossini *accelerando*. We can also be calmed by longer durations and slower tempi with extensive use of *ritardandi*. These changes can occur irrespective of the detailed rhythmic structure.

In his well-known book *Awakenings*, Oliver Sacks gives examples of the effects of different durations on adults with post-encephalitic Parkinsonism. He provides ample evidence that these inner biological pacemakers and regulators are very impaired in Parkinsonism. He claims that music's reliance on time is a strong factor in helping to free the Parkinsonian while the music lasts. Dr Sacks narrates the example of Edith T., who was a former music teacher:

> She said that she had become 'graceless' with the onset of Parkinsonism, that her movements had become 'wooden, mechanical – like a robot or doll', that

she had lost her former 'naturalness' and 'musicalness' of movement, that – in a word – she had been 'unmusicked'. Fortunately, she added, the disease was 'accompanied by its own cure'. I raised an eyebrow: 'Music', she said, 'as I am unmusicked, I must be remusicked.'[21]

The implications of helping people to become 'remusicked' go far beyond the confines of Parkinsonism. There appears to be a strong connection between a person's perception of time and of illness, disease and health in general.

Some commentators do not support the notion of a biological clock regulating durations. Ornstein, for one, prefers a cognitive definition and sees time as a mental construction, making close links between the length of the durations and the available cortical space we set aside. He questions whether our experience of duration is proportional to the amount of space the brain makes available for the analysis and storage of incoming sound events and the number of such events. In one experiment he played subjects three tape-recordings of equal clock-time length. The recordings were made up of short tones sounded at irregular intervals. The subjects perceived the tape with more sound events as being of longer duration. On the basis of Ornstein's experiment we could deduce that we estimate the passing of time to be longer when more material needs processing, and that our estimation decreases with less information.[22] Any developed unit of time is therefore only an arbitrary invention.

There are other physiological influences on our perception of time. We are aware of the feeling that time seems to pass faster in relation to clock time when we are suffering from a high temperature. We have only to spend a brief period of time with young children to be part of a more cyclical world where there is little of the break-up of linear time that seems to plague our adult life. My 5-year-old son is now beginning to map out in his mind what next week means; previously it could have been tomorrow or the next hour, and yesterday could easily have been last year. When we become deeply involved in a task, time seems to pass quicker than when we are bored by more mundane activities. We can all remember those special moments, almost outside time, when time appears to stand still. Musicians are fortunate to be working in a form that seems to provide opportunities for peak experiences of such a kind to occur. Ancient systems of meditation also focus the attention away from a linear towards a more cyclical notion of time. We may have similar experiences when in the company of someone we love, or during moments of deep spiritual or religious contemplation.

In spite of the complexity and variety of the theories of duration in music therapy, we can make assumptions about correlations between physiological functioning and durations. We can talk about a harmony or disharmony with time, being in phase or out of phase with time. The timing of responses is very often a major problem with clients of all ages. I feel that attempting to understand the particular and unique time framework of each of our clients is a major responsibility and challenge for music therapists. A young child may only be able to cope with a small amount of sound information at any one time. There may be the question of over-arousing an already excitable person. The duration of the sounds may be the reason why somebody has stopped attending to the sound. The sounds may be too fast or too slow. The session itself may be too long. We need to set aside both time and space to make contact with each person's unique temporal framework – to go alongside and 'meet the clients where they are', to make use of an often-quoted therapeutic maxim. The outside world of durations can begin to be matched with what is within us.

Understanding and matching the speed of a child's movements is the crux of the following example, which also links with the following discussion of rhythm.

Natalie, a bright 7-year-old, was about to move up into the junior section of her school, which meant moving upstairs. She had a mild cerebral palsy, a diplegia, and with this physical problem an associated lack of self-esteem. She walked with an irregular pattern and for quite some time the physiotherapists had been trying to work towards a more organised walking pace and pattern. Could music therapy help? We found that her preferred and spontaneous tempi were slower than the tempo of the physiotherapists' clapping being applied to help organise the walking. From making music with Natalie we were able to discover the point at which her pulse became steady. We hypothesised that from discovering her own comfortable tempo we could work from within to outside, not imposing an external pulse on Natalie. This steady pulse became the basis of a song that she practised with the other members of her family, as she walked down the street, at school and at times when she felt anxious about any movements, such as facing the gym apparatus. She came back to her next appointment and walked slowly and carefully down the corridor at a slower and more organised pace. She was using the internalised tempo of the song by inwardly singing the song to herself, helping her own self-organisation. This developing self-organisation was transferred to other areas of her life such as control of movements on a horizontal plane. As the short period of sessions progressed so did her confidence, with a more upright girl leaving the room at the end of each session (we measured her at the start and end of each session). The physiotherapist at the school reported, even a few years later, that this musical interlude had provided her with a secure basis for when she found herself losing control or feeling afraid. We had discovered her comfortable tempo together, but Natalie herself was making an intelligent use of the musical material as a self-help tool.

Working specifically with long and short sounds can help with the initial focusing of attention. Children and adults can be encouraged really to attend to a long sound on a cymbal, for example, listening to every nuance of the sound as it dies back into relative silence. Try and imagine one long sound (for example, on a stringed instrument) of a steady pitch, loudness and timbre. We need to give sufficient mental preparation to the start of such a sound, however simple it might be. When this sound stops we realise that it was there, that something has taken place. Both the starts and ends of sounds are important, with sounds being given space to travel to their natural conclusion.

A very sensitive 10-year-old girl, who had severe language and speech problems, once gave me a salutary lesson about respect for durations. We were taking turns vocalising with the support of a few chime bars. I played a short sequence of sounds and she replied. I was about to set up a new sequence when she stopped me and pointed rather angrily to her chime bar, which was still resounding. Her sounds had not yet finished and I had the impoliteness to interrupt what she was expressing. For the sounds to have their full meaning for her they needed to travel to their natural end.

The philosopher Susanne Langer is quick to point out that while we can hear that there are fast and slow sounds, that sounds start and stop, what is taking place is only a semblance of musical motion.[23] Nothing actually moves in the sense that we can physically displace more concrete objects from one place to the next. When we consider larger tonal and rhythmic forms we enter into the more complex worlds of perceived motion where we can even contemplate such a notion as 'sustained rest'.[24] The music may come to a point of rest but there are implications within that moment for what is to come, a musical sense of an implied movement forward. This leads us from the world of the simple 'sound elements' – timbre, loudness, pitch and to some extent duration – to the forms and patterns in the more 'musical elements' of rhythm, melody and harmony.

RHYTHM

Rhythm occupies a crucial place in music therapy and follows on naturally from a discussion of duration and time, with which it is inextricably linked. Even within one long sound there are the inner rhythmic fluctuations of the wave form.

> Of the elements of music . . . it is rhythm that is acknowledged to be the vital therapeutic factor by virtue of its power to focus energy and to bring structure into the perception of temporal order.[25]

> Without rhythm there would be no music . . . the unique potential of rhythm to energise and bring order will be seen as the most influential factor of music.[26]

Both these quotations stress the energising and organising aspects of rhythm, central ingredients of both music and music therapy.

There are many definitions of rhythm, and a study of the many factors involved is complex. Paul Fraisse refers to Plato's fundamental definition in *The Laws* that rhythm is 'the order in the movement'. Fraisse adds: 'Rhythm is the ordered characteristic of succession.'[27] We can form a mental conception of large cyclic rhythmic movements such as the succession of the seasons, day and night; we also have inner perceptions of the close links to our bodies of the rhythms of dance, poetry and music, forms of activity generated and organised by human effort. Rhythm is the basis of all neural activity. It has a central part in many creation myths. In many respects rhythm remains a mystery. 'Rhythm, which is the cradle of Being, is itself the supreme paradox. It is the never-resting point at the non-existing centre of existence.'[28]

Howard Gardner is not alone in suggesting that understanding rhythm does not rely solely on the auditory pathways and mechanisms.[29] People with hearing impairments often report that rhythm is the ingredient that provides the easiest access to comprehending music. There are many examples of musicians with hearing problems with highly sophisticated rhythmic understanding – we think immediately of Beethoven's later years. Today the percussionist Evelyn Glennie is performing music of intricate rhythmic complexity.

The physicist Fritjof Capra has described how rhythmic patterns manifest themselves at all levels from the sub-atomic to the large cyclical changes of ecosystems and whole civilisations. Rhythmic patterns are therefore both universal and at the same time individual expressions. Post-Einsteinian physics is re-shaping our whole attitude to time and rhythm, with implications for how we understand illness. There are pointers for furthering our understanding of both music and music therapy in the work of contemporary physics, an area currently being explored by the American music therapist Charles Eagle. As Capra has stated:

> The notion of illness as originating in a lack of integration seems to be especially relevant to approaches that try to understand living organisms in terms of rhythmic patterns. From this perspective synchrony becomes an important measure of health. Individual organisms interact and communicate with one another by synchronising their rhythms and thus integrating themselves into the larger rhythms of their environment. To be healthy, then, means to be in synchrony with oneself – physically and mentally – and also with the surrounding world. When a person is out of synchrony, illness is likely to occur. Many esoteric traditions associate health with the synchrony of rhythms and healing with a certain resonance between healer and patient.[30]

At its simplest level rhythm can be a repetition of the same stimulus at a constant frequency of occurrence, as in clockwork or the repeated pulsing of a metronome. We can observe this in a basic pattern such as walking, when one event predicts the next. We can regard such activities as spontaneous, and, as we noted in our discussion on duration, they occur within a given tempo range with slight environmental and individual differences. We are aware of such differences when walking down the street with another person. As we get to know the person better we are able to synchronise the walking so much more easily, lovers demonstrating beautiful synchrony. Such factors gave rise to the notion that rhythm is closely based on motor function, with the nervous system playing a determining role in the organisation and control of rhythmic patterning.[31] Gaston considered that this concept contributed greatly to the early acceptance of music therapy, the discipline being grounded in very basic patterns of human behaviour.[32]

The development of expectations and anticipation is crucial in our understanding of the rhythmic process. This development introduces further expressive functions such as the pause between two events in time and the concept of accent. An accent can be created by changes in loudness or duration, not underestimating any tonal implications. A regular pulse, for example, can be elaborated with such rhythmic details as different accents, thereby adding to the definition and location of a beat. When working with children and adults with profound learning difficulties we are often met with a lack of understanding of pulse and that one sound event can generate the next, a kind of pre-pulse behaviour. We observe musical playing that consists of a random series of events with a large gap between the sounding of each event – approximately two seconds is regarded as the time-limit between the perception of two events belonging to the same present.[33] There are also temporal restraints imposed by the memory. An emphasis on rhythmic play can help, in such instances, to predict and anticipate events and to associate two or more events within the same present. Serial connections can then be built up in the memory, forming musical messages. Order is not only given to the present but to what Natasha Spender describes as the 'temporal map of the immediate future'.[34]

Anne is 2½ years old and has profound and multiple disabilities (a diagnosis of Rett's Syndrome). When presented with a skin-top tambour she reaches out and makes an occasional stroking movement. I reply in a similar fashion. There is a long delay before her next 'sound gesture', which again I reflect back to her. Over the weeks of short individual sessions her 'sound gestures' come in quicker succession and after twelve sessions she is beginning to play in short bursts of sounds, playing at times two separate sounds. She starts to vocalise and I observe a connection between a vocal sound and the short rhythmic patterns. For the most part I regard her behaviour as essentially pre-pulse activity but with signs of the beginnings of connections between two events within the same present. It may be that she is learning about connections from our interactional dialogue, where each group of sounds (child and adult) takes place within a short space of time, very much within a two-second interval.

In addition to periodic activity such as walking, there is also the notion of each person's individual tempo witnessed in such characteristics as rhythmic tapping and finger-strumming. Rocking and hand-flapping also can be included here, behaviours that are frequently observed when communication with the environment is greatly reduced through impairment or disability. The rhythmic behaviour could be viewed as releasing tension in these contexts. In an initial music therapy session it is possible to observe this sense of individual tempo in the musical play and spontaneous movements presented by the client. As in the example of Natalie's walking, a music therapy setting provides an opportunity to support each person's tempo, to make an initial contact at that level before moving away from this focal point to explore other rhythmic and temporal experiences. This factor also adds support to the introduction of music therapy for people with gait and movement irregularities. In walking to our own comfortable tempo with musical support, for example, we are learning to synchronise a movement with a sound. At such moments the response produced occurs in synchrony with the appearance of the stimulus; this is often described as 'rhythmic entrainment'. This sets apart a synchronised musical experience from other forms of activity, as generally reactions succeed the stimulus. Anticipation of the ensuing event is crucial in synchronising a movement with a specific sound, and the temporal interval between the sounds is being used as an additional signal.[35] Observers of music therapy in action refer constantly to this immediacy of the contact. There is no delay between stimulus and response, there is an instantaneous connection. This unique blend of synchronisation and anticipation provides scope for setting up many kinds of projects. There are implications here for the use of music as a rhythmic grid to help people learn or re-acquire motor skills. How does this relate to work with people living with such disabling conditions as cerebral palsy, Parkinson's Disease or Huntington's Chorea? There are implications also for communication with people with speech and language problems.

There is a need for more systematic study of rhythm and temporal skills in music therapy both for the purposes of assessment and for establishing directions for future work. Throughout their pioneering partnership Paul Nordoff and Clive Robbins wrote a great deal about rhythmic responses. In their book *Therapy in Music for Handicapped Children* they established categories of response in relation to their experiences with over 145 children. Rhythmic responses were included in their categories because of their relationship to the vital rhythms of the organism and to both central and peripheral nervous system functions. The headings used for the rhythmic categories are:

1 Complete Rhythmic Freedom
2 Unstable Rhythmic Freedom
   (a) Psychological
   (b) Neurological
3 Limited Rhythmic Freedom
4 Compulsive Beating
5 Disordered Beating
   (a) Impulsive
   (b) Paralytic
   (c) Compulsive–Confused
   (d) Emotional–Confused
6 Evasive Beating
7 Emotional–Force Beating.
8 Chaotic–Creative Beating.[36]

Definitions are set out for each category of response: for example, 'Complete Rhythmic Freedom' is defined as 'Instantaneous sensitivity to all tempi, dynamics, rhythmic patterns and to the rhythmic structure of melodies; also the ability to beat them on the drum.'[37] These categories provide a framework for therapists trained in this specific model of working, where there is a strong emphasis on rhythmic work aiming to engage the child in a variety of flexible rhythmic interactions. Looking at the categories from the position of not being trained to use this model, there appear to be fine dividing lines between categories.

It is difficult for an outsider to separate 'impulsive' from 'compulsive' and 'compulsive–confused', for example. We could make other assumptions about the rhythmic behaviour being observed. We are making an inference about a child's inner mental state by describing evasive beating as: 'The child avoids beating in time to the music.' This may be 'due to the child's fear of the experience . . ..   Or he may avoid participation because of an emotional inability to endure contact with the therapist.'[38] There could be alternative inferences.

We have observed already that music-making takes place both synchronously and antiphonally, both modes involving elements of accent and differentiation. Such elements help us to group rhythmic patterns into manageable 'chunks' and to store such events in the short-term memory. To the elements of accent and pause we can add other variables in the grouping procedure, such as changes in pitch marking off a new rhythmic group and, in the West in particular, the larger melodic and harmonic structures.

Finally in this survey of the complex musical element of rhythm we must not overlook the emotional response, our affective responses to rhythm. Different rhythms seem to produce very different emotional responses, from the soporific and calming to the highly arousing and ecstatic. Such effects have been known for centuries: Plato advises his readers in Book 3 of *The Republic* to discover rhythms that are 'the expressions of a courageous and harmonious life'.[39] There is the hypnotic effect of repetitive and steady rhythms at the root of many lullabies. In the so-called minimalist school of composers much use is made of repetitions, with the added complexities of very subtle changes and inflection in the rhythm. Such music can sometimes produce a meditative response in the listeners. The lack of rhythmic tensions in plainsong also appears to contribute to the fluid, spiritual and almost timeless nature of this music. Conversely, we are only too familiar throughout history with the inherent dangers in the use of rigid rhythmic patterns in martial music used to drum up warlike feelings of corporate aggression. Anthony Storr has recently noted that such powerful musical rhetoric is even more dangerous when topped by the chant-like and harsh declamatory style of a tyrant such as Hitler.[40] In music therapy we would be aiming to achieve opposite responses, to explore the healing potential of rhythmic patterns. As will be noted in all the examples being described, we meet a vast range of rhythmical behaviour in our work, and here flexibility is a key factor. To a Western-trained musician used to grouping rhythms in basic patterns of two (strong, weak) or three (strong, weak, weak) working within irregular patterns of five or seven presents rhythmic challenges. Such odd-number groupings are rather common-place in other cultures.

MELODY AND INTERVAL

Short sequences of pitches can be differentiated in a young baby's crying, babbling and early turn-taking. This is not to say that the baby is intending to create melodic structures but that such potential exists. Researchers have also demonstrated that, when exposed to rigorous training, babies as young as 6 months can be programmed to match pitch and sing back short series of pitches.[41] As we shall see when we review Helmut Moog's work in the next chapter, there is a great deal of spontaneous melodic exploration in the first few years of life, an area of more immediately practical interest to the music therapist.

The pitch of self-generated songs of early childhood tends to wander a great deal. My 5-year-old son still changes pitch willy-nilly, although he uses the rhythm and contour of the melody as devices to help him keep within the formal structure. Often the contour of the melody is replicable at different pitch levels. My son is definitely aware of certain melodies as stable entities in their own right, a point noted by Dowling in the child's growing perception of melody. As children become older and hear more pre-composed songs, more of their sung melodies and intervals are true to the original pre-composed songs. I can hear this when my son sings along with my 8-year-old daughter, who is increasingly true to the original. Gradually the melodic and intervallic relationships of the prevailing musical culture become established, and in the West this means, for the most part, the relationships within the major and minor diatonic scale system. If we had been living in another country with its own musical culture, we can assume that our children would have become increasingly fluent within the intervallic relationships in that music, possibly being able to sing intervals of less than a semitone.

There seems to be agreement among researchers that the age of 5 is an approximate marker for preserving a stable tonality within a song, or at least for a large proportion of one. Zenatti found only chance-level performance of both tonal and atonal sequences with 5-year-olds, superior performance with tonal sequences occurring between 6 and 7.[42] As would be expected, children between 6 and 10 were more interested in tonal sequences and were more accurate in performing tonal rather than atonal sequences. This confirms the absorption of the diatonic system during these years of schooling. It is also between 6 and 8 that children appear to have a heightened reaction to unexpected or different aspects within the music.[43] At around 12–13 interest in atonal sequences catches up with the tonal. Perhaps children of this age are beginning to be more curious about a wider range of music, considering each new experience for its unique musical merits. Perhaps atonality and tonality are now considered as academic or arbitrary divisions. Zenatti's research relates to the debate within music therapy on the use of dissonance and the balance of dissonance and consonance when working with children and adults. If children under 5 seem to be interested in both dissonance and consonance alike, it is difficult to substantiate any specific claims on the influence of a particular series of consonances and dissonances. But this overlaps with our future discussion on harmony. Fundamentally the overall developmental sequence is from the young baby's early discrimination of gross features such as contour and pitch level, through the 5-year-old's growing awareness of tonality, to the young adult's detection of small changes in interval size.

There appears to be an importance attached to the different levels in scale systems. Some of the pitches seem to have a prime position when placed in melodic sequences, an observable feature in the music of most cultures. In his discussion on 'musical universals' John Sloboda highlights some of these 'privileged' reference points.[44] It may be that by exploring some of these features more can be found out about the cognitive processes that underpin most music and how musical we really are.[45] Sloboda notes that a 'drone', for example, is often used to delineate the principal pitch or pitches in much instrumental music of many cultures. In purely vocal melodies, such as plainsong, we note the particular occurrence of certain pitches and structural reference points. The octave seems to be one such reference point, in spite of the obvious doubling of melodies at the octave between female and male voices. The octave is the first interval in the harmonic series with a straightforward doubling of the frequency. The octave can be used to double important pitches and to mark off a new repetition of the sequence of pitches – here we start again from the 'same note' at a different pitch. The octave also supports the notions of scale and tonic. The development of fixed reference points in music, Sloboda adds, is closely linked to instruments of fixed pitch such as bells and many tuned percussion or stringed instruments, where the pitches remain fixed during a particular musical activity. These kinds of instrument are used a great deal in active music therapy work. There are other pitches that seem to be privileged, in particular intervals that approximate to the perfect fourth or fifth, which naturally when added together make up an octave. There are close links again here with the natural world of acoustics and mathematical proportion.[46]

When we examine smaller intervals we begin to add the complexities of human organisation. The falling minor third (G to E, for example) is often used as a call for gaining attention. Young children will call their mothers with it ('Mum-my') and use it as a ritual in their play. This interval at the hub of a short phrase which adds the interval of a fourth (an A in our example) is so common in children's play (G, E, A, G, E) that several commentators have become very excited about the pattern's universal nature and its link with the harmonic series. This little melodic tag became a central argument in Bernstein's strong plea in his Norton lectures for the centrality of the tonal system and links with the natural order of the harmonic series.[47] The C, E, G in our example relate to the first six harmonics of the series; but, as Storr, as one of several writers, has pointed out, the A of this little tune is the seventh harmonic, which sounds 'out of tune' to our ears accustomed to equal temperament.[48] Bernstein refers to it as a 'sort-of-A' yet continues with his all-embracing theory – which includes the central position of this pattern in the popular pentatonic scale C, D, E, G, A – based on a notion of 'sort-of'. Nordoff and Robbins have labelled this tag 'the children's tune', describing its archetypal nature as 'the three-toned phrase usually sung by children in ring games or at play'.[49] The phrase is used extensively almost as a 'calling phrase' in this music therapy approach.

The ever-popular five-note scale, the pentatonic scale (one version being a sequence that omits the fourth and seventh notes of any major diatonic scale – the black notes on a keyboard will make up this version) appears in a variety of guises, not all with only whole tones, in music from many cultures. It is the basis, for example, of much folk music from America, Scotland and Ireland. The sounds are pleasing and, if pitched at a comfortable level, are well within the range of children and even the most musically inhibited of adults. The absence of the discordant intervals of the augmented fourth, minor second and major seventh in the pentatonic scale makes this a popular scale in music therapy group work. Tuned percussion instruments such as xylophones, metallophones and glockenspiels can be 'set' for one of these pentatonic scales. All members of the group can take part in melodic exploration with satisfying results, be it a small group of six people or a large training session of over a hundred. Playing in this scale frees people from the confines of the Western diatonic system, the desire to play the 'right note' and to search for a favourite melody. This freedom is also possible when such tuned instruments are set in other scale systems, commonly known as the modes. Here each mode is made up of a particular order of semitones and tones and has a unique emotional quality. They are still called by Greek names, and any keyboard will give you the opportunity to explore within our present-day approximations (with all the semitones made 'equal') the following modes:

D,	E,	F,	G,	A,	B,	C,	D	–	Dorian
E,	F,	G,	A,	B,	C,	D,	E	–	Phrygian
F,	G,	A,	B,	C,	D,	E,	F	–	Lydian
G,	A,	B,	C,	D,	E,	F,	G	–	Mixolydian
A,	B,	C,	D,	E,	F,	G,	A	–	Aeolian
B,	C,	D,	E,	F,	G,	A,	B	–	Locrian

The next mode, C to C (Ionian), is our Western diatonic major scale, the order of tones and semitones being consistent throughout all of its transpositions. The Aeolian mode only needs a sharpening of the penultimate note, G, to become our harmonic minor scale. On a keyboard the modes outlined here can be explored solely on the white notes; when transposed the black notes will be needed to keep the same order of tones. In medieval times the modes were consistently used in their natural state, the tuning of the intervals being based on the natural harmonic series. If exploring in the Lydian mode, you may have wanted to change the fourth note, as it may have sounded 'out of tune' to our ears, accustomed as we are to the Western diatonic system. The Lydian, in its original form, I use carefully, being aware of the implied tension in the interval F–B, known in medieval times as *diabolus in musica* ('the devil in music'). I find the Locrian rather unbalanced and tense and do not use it in music therapy work.

The Greeks were aware of the emotional effects of different orders of tones in their modes. In Book 3 of *The Republic*, Plato warns against the use of their so-called Lydian mode, as it was expressive of sorrow, and of the Ionian because of its softness and indolence. The Dorian and Phrygian were proposed for their warlike qualities. They also contain 'the strain of necessity and the strain of freedom, the strain of the unfortunate and the strain of the fortunate, the strain of courage, and the strain of temperance; these, I say, leave'.[50] I have not found that our present Dorian mode generates warlike reactions, but on more than one occasion it has been very appropriate in helping group cohesion and provoking movement and dancing.

One July morning I had just arrived, jet-lagged after a long plane journey, to start working with a large group of Italian students. We began by gently singing the notes of the Dorian mode and setting up call and responses in the mode. One by one the 'set' tuned percussion were introduced. It was a large group of about forty students. At the start the members of the group explored the mode for themselves. Gradually connections were made with other melodic fragments, answers were provided to implied musical questions. The music became more focused and locked into a comfortable physical tempo. We were playing in a large hall and gradually the students began to move, get up and dance with their instruments and each other. The loudness level increased as we began both to sing and to play. The music began to subside and by the end of the improvisation we realised that the session was nearly over – we had explored the Dorian mode for over forty minutes.

Plato made bold claims for the emotional effects of the different modes, but even on a first playing of some of the present-day modes outlined here we can feel different reactions. Certain intervals and series of tones appear time and time again in similar emotional contexts. Deryck Cooke has provided an analysis, albeit highly subjective, of the connections between melodic fragments and the expression of emotions. He draws on a narrow band of Western classical music, including many vocal examples that have the additional impact and implications of the verbal text. He groups similar patterns of intervals within a tonal structure that seem to connect with our emotional responses. He found a phrase of two notes, for example – the minor sixth of the scale falling to the fifth – seemingly expressing intense anguish in music ranging from Josquin, Bach, Mozart through to Schoenberg, Stravinsky and Britten.[51] We can criticise Cooke's work for its lack of experimentation and rigour. More account also needs to be taken of ever-changing taste in musical style. A third, for example, would have been heard as highly dissonant to a composer working in the twelfth century, the interval developing two centuries later as a consonance and starting its development as a cornerstone in diatonic music.

A more open-ended, empirical approach to a study of emotional responses to music has recently been adopted by John Sloboda. Some of his early findings indicate that people can connect a specific emotional response to a particular theme or musical event. Sloboda was interested in exploring the associations between physical reactions such as crying and shivering – the commonly expressed 'tingle factor' – and intrinsic features in the music listened to and chosen by his subjects. In his analysis of the crying response, for example, he found: 'The majority of these passages contained melodic appogiaturas and melodic or harmonic sequences.'[52] Sloboda found that tears were provoked by such melodies as Albinoni's famous *Adagio for Strings*. Sloboda's work relates to the important contributions of Leonard Meyer, who connects our emotional responses to notions of expectancy and violation of expectancy within the musical structure. In describing melody, for example, Meyer would say that a melodic line had, within its very structure, implications for future musical events.[53] What Sloboda's work indicates is that there is much scope for empirical investigations through which more can be discovered about our emotional responses to music.

HARMONY

With harmony we are concerned with the way pitches are sounded together, the resultant combination of sounds often being described as consonant or dissonant by listeners. There are many overlaps between melody and harmony. There are harmonic implications in melodies, and harmony can itself generate melody. We can also perceive a series of chords as musical events in themselves without an obvious melody. Harmony can be regarded as the most complex element and as absolutely central to music. As the developmental psychologists are indicating, harmony is only mastered after melodic understanding is secure.[54]

In music therapy work with people with severe learning difficulties, a complex harmonic world may prove to be redundant. Too many changes may be unsettling. Tensions in harmonic progression and harmonic resolutions will need to take on equal importance, too much of either being counter-productive. Thus the optimal level of interest and arousal can be maintained.[55] At a very fundamental level a harmonic basis can be provided by a drone or small repeating pattern of simple chords, over which melodies can be supported or emerge.

Up to this point in our survey of sound and musical elements the implied focus has been on how clients use the elements, either receptively or actively. There is an implied emphasis on interaction. 'Through musical interaction, two people create forms that are greater than the sum of their parts, and make for themselves experiences of empathy that would be unlikely to occur in ordinary social intercourse.'[56] Some clients may be harmonically very fluent, but this is the element that can separate the musically trained therapist from clients. The therapist's harmonic fluency will depend on the individual's own style of playing and musical background. Some therapists are technically very proficient on keyboards, with a previous solid background in the harmonic structures of tonal and what is commonly referred to as atonal music. These therapists will develop skills in using a keyboard to provide a clear harmonic support to a client's musical gestures. String specialists will discover ways of using their 'cello or violin harmonically, possibly starting with the simplicity of open strings and plucked chords. Like string players, wind and brass specialists can make use of long lines and melodic shapes to support with harmonic implications their client's playing, often imparting a sense of coherent musical integration to what might otherwise appear as fragmented and disorganised sounds. It is encouraging that musicians from other backgrounds, such as jazz and the more popular forms of music, are training as therapists. These musicians will open up different harmonic potentialities for clients from those offered by a more classically trained therapist.

We are often attracted to the harmonically ambiguous in music. What seems to make a Mozart or a Haydn stand out from his contemporaries is the unpredictability of his music, the musical events that are different from what we expect. We will be surprised by the music's sudden change of direction from the implied harmonies. It was this sense of the harmonically new and unexpected that Sloboda found produced physical reactions such as shivers down the spine or goose-pimples in his respondents.[57] We can relate these moments to Meyer's notion of our expectations being either fulfilled or violated.[58] The composer provides all the necessary harmonic background and information for the implied expectation; we assume the next harmonic change must be this. On some occasions, our expectations are fulfilled, at other times they are violated – the progression did not move as expected. A careful study of harmonic implications, with all interplay of tensions, dissonances, consonances and expectations, can further the music therapist's understanding of some of the most complex processes at work.

SOME COMMENTS ON THE ORIGINS AND MEANING OF MUSIC

After listening to music some clients report very rich images; others talk of the interactions of the sounds themselves. One beautiful melody on the 'cello, for example, can create associations with the flight of birds, the sound of waves, even the very earth itself. The same melody can also be described as a series of rhythmic, melodic and harmonic tensions and resolutions. The first group of responses points to associations with the natural world, almost to a biological origin of music. When interacting vocally using non-verbal sounds, I can fantasise about similarities between these kinds of sound and the vocal signals of higher primates. However, as Sloboda is quick to point out, such animal signals seem to be involuntary and have more connections with our crying, laughing or screaming.[59] The sounds lack the organisational and motivational aspects of our arrangements of tones that we call music.

The sounds of birdsong seem to have some of the precision of our music. We can hear discrete pitches in the sounds. Some birdsong also seems to involve variation, which brings us closer to our musical use of sounds. But still not close enough – major ingredients seem to be missing. Birdsong appears for the most part to be very stereotyped and limited in the range and transposition of the sounds.[60]

We get closer to understanding more about the origins of music when we look at the dancing and chanting rituals of tribal cultures. As John Blacking points out, moving our bodies and modulating timing with speech in an organised way can create both rhythm and organised pitch in melodic and harmonic patterns.[61] In dance we can observe a stirring of the body creating an inner state of flow and resonance, which in turn is a source of musical patterning. In chanting and dancing together we have an essentially group-based activity, music being used to learn more about personal and group territory and group movements and patterns.

Music used in this way can support major group celebration and rituals. Blacking talks about knowing what a group is doing through song.[62] A sense of musical ritual seems to be fading in Western society. The composer Roger Sessions reminds us that the present-day divisions between composer, performer and listener have occurred successively throughout history. At one time:

> Music was vocal or instrumental improvisation; and while there were those who did not perform, and who therefore heard music, they were not listeners in our modern sense of the word. They heard the sounds as part of a ritual, a drama, or an epic narrative and accepted it in its purely incidental or symbolic function, subordinate to the occasion of which it was part.[63]

But there are still places where group singing and dancing are features of major celebrations. You can walk into a pub in Ireland, Scotland or other rural communities with a strong musical tradition and take part in some spontaneous music-making. Our churches may not be as frequented as in previous centuries, but at Christmas we can still recall the words of many of the favourite carols. The oppression of a television-dominated culture has distracted us a great deal from this kind of celebratory musical expression. But there still seems to be a thirst for such experiences, and music therapists can contribute in channelling some of this in a positive and creative way.

Joint action seems to be one key for understanding the organisational and temporal nature of music. Such action occurs in the communal musical activity of a religious festival; as an incitement to work, dance or play; as a prelude to love-making; or in a planned musical performance such as a concert or an opera. These musical experiences are functionally different but are shared and communal. Perhaps one of our deepest satisfactions from music results from the emotional support gained in such collective action.

Music helps us in our appreciation of the quality of life, a phrase often used to persuade any sceptics of the importance of music therapy for the elderly, for instance. As we noted when discussing duration and time, music tells us more about the quality of time than about the specific length of time. We rarely comment on the specific length of a particular musical experience but seem more preoccupied with the quality of the overall experience. As Blacking proposes, we can learn of the pertinent features of a society at any given time within the articulated forms of music.[64] Music is essentially humanly organised sound, 'sculpted sound' as a client recently beautifully put it. We find personal resonances in these musical sculptures. If we are forming some new musical patterns – be it re-creating a pre-composed piece or on-the-spot 'playing with sounds' in an improvisation – we will be working hard to give form to those inner feelings and experiences. When we are composing or playing music all our cognitive processes are being brought into the music – the cerebral processes involved in motor control, feelings, cultural experiences, social activity, intellectual activity, and so on. This helps us to differentiate my music from your music. If we begin to think of music in these terms, then music therapy could become a radical force and opportunity for change in people's lives. We may never be able really to know what different people are feeling within themselves when playing music, but we can begin to understand by observing what and how they play. Music's deep connections with our inner world of feelings helps such musical expression to become a potential manifestation of such feelings.

Today there is the paradox of our shops being filled with the latest technology for listening to recorded music of all kinds from all over the world yet of very few people calling themselves 'musical'. We can increasingly produce all kinds of synthesised sound at the push of a button. Blacking points out that the West expects people to sort out musical patterns to gain meaning as listeners but makes few claims on people to engage in active musical processes.[65] What would happen if all this recorded sound, all the musical scores and musical document- ation of the past were suddenly obliterated? Would we be able to re-capture the spirit of the Greeks and early minstrels in telling our stories once again in song? Sloboda surmises that music might then once again become a necessary tool for our survival:

> The resources that we carried around in our heads would, once again, form the mainstay of our attempts to survive. Songs and poems would become vital mnemonic and cohesive tools for the construction of a new society, and musical skill would, indeed be a skill for survival. It is not, therefore, simply a task of disinterested scientific curiosity to come to a better understanding of musical skill. Music is a fundamental human resource which has played, and may well play again, a vital role in the survival and development of humanity.[66]

Songs can be seen as major repositories of knowledge that can be passed on from one generation to the next. We in the West may be far removed from the Aborigines' deep knowledge of 'songlines' and use of music as a 'map reference' and 'memory bank', so stunningly described by Bruce Chatwin.[67] But we can work to take charge of our own music again. I feel that one of the major responsibilities of a music therapist is to attend and assist people in the discovery or re-discovery of how they can use music. Practising therapists will all have memories of moments when a child discovers a beautiful sound for the first time or when an adult makes contact again with a musical impulse and interest long since buried under the hectic strain of daily life.

In an address to the British Society for Music Therapy, the eminent psychia- trist and writer Anthony Storr pointed out that we may have similar feelings towards a piece of music when the context is clear, as, for example, in the use of slow music at funerals to heighten the feelings of grief, but that beyond such collective experiences the situation is far more complex and individually based. We know what we are supposed to be feeling at a funeral but not when ex- periencing a new piece of music. Storr suggests that music does not cause a particular emotion but induces a general sense of emotional arousal.[68] This point is echoed by Sessions:

What the music does is to animate the emotion; the music, in other words, develops and moves on a level which is essentially below the level of conscious emotion. Its realm is that of emotional energy rather than that of emotion in the specific sense.[69]

Music helps us to feel the essence of emotions; it is about feelings. We can all laugh with pleasure, for example, but perhaps music brings us closer to appreciating the essence of pleasure. It is also common for both different reactions to occur and for reactions to change on the next hearing. One day we may be feeling particularly tearful and one of our favourite pieces that provokes tears does so again. When we listen to it on the next occasion and in a very different mood we may find it hard to believe the effect caused on the previous hearing.

When we listen to music we are forming abstract, symbolic and internal representations. We need to be able to do this in order to be moved by any music. When we compose, improvise or perform music we are externalising some of these inner impulses in what the philosopher Susanne Langer calls 'significant forms': 'The real power of music lies in the fact that it can be "true" to the life of feeling in a way that language cannot; for its significant forms have that *ambivalence* of content which words cannot have.'[70] A piece of music can be regarded as a composite whole, an integrated structure binding together these inner and outer realities. As music therapists we can concentrate on this integrating nature of music to help our clients bring a sense of order and cohesion into their lives. Susanne Langer describes music as an 'analogue of the emotional life', composed of the very gestures, forms and shapes that are the everyday pattern of our emotions. We can regard music as both transformer and metaphor. Langer makes it clear that music is not direct self-expression but an expressive representation and formalisation of moods, mental tensions and resolutions.[71] As changes occur in our lives, our ideas and our emotions, these can be articulated symbolically in musical forms. We do not need to know all the details of these ideas and feelings to understand and be moved by the music. Music can act as a transformer of shared meaning.

Music does not represent objects in the way a spoken language does; it is not discursive. We cannot paraphrase a piece of music as if it were a piece of prose; we are dealing with completely different subject-matters. We cannot make assertions, propositions, suppositions or questions about the world in music. Music is very much beyond words, articulating inner forms beyond language. In spite of these fundamental differences recent developments in both linguistics and our cognitive understanding of music have indicated some grammatical and structural similarities between music and language. Sloboda provides a detailed comparison of the work of Chomsky, the linguist, and Shenker, the music analyst, in their search for meaning in both deep and surface structures within language and music. There appear to be some formal and behavioural features related to inner representations, and Sloboda discusses these links at the levels of phonology ('finite and discrete sound categories'), syntax ('units and sequences') and semantics ('the way meaning is carried by such sequences').[72]

We return finally to the notion of cultural diversity. In a very literate culture such as ours the emphasis on the written word seems to stifle some of the early spontaneity of singing and playing music as we move into adulthood. In a culture where the written word is not so highly stressed we observe an active spontaneity lasting far longer. These are rather general statements but do relate to observations of adults making music and trying to connect again with the simplicity, openness and spontaneity of the children they all once were. Such an unleashing of the creative potential to make music within us all, both able-bodied and so-called 'disabled' alike, is at the heart of much music therapy practice. We now need to look more closely at how music is used as a potential medium for both child and adult health.

Chapter 4

Music therapy and child health

INTRODUCTION

Most children develop an insatiable curiosity for sounds and sound-making during early childhood that appears almost innate. Very few children seem not to derive any pleasure from singing and making music together. The first part of this chapter concentrates on this naturally emerging response to sounds and music. In music therapy we are not concerned with musical instruction, although very often regular exposure to music does develop musical skills as an offshoot, as we shall see in several of the examples.[1]

The developmental psychology of music is a growing discipline where more is being discovered about both the growth of musical behaviour and the various psychological processes and theoretical models that may underpin such behaviour.[2] We shall survey some recent work in this field alongside examples of music therapy practice with children. The music therapy examples will then be related to processes in developmental child psychology, with particular reference to research on non-verbal child–adult interaction. A major theme of this chapter is that such early developmental processes, for example the development of turn-taking, can provide a supportive framework to much of what happens in music therapy with young children. These links between general processes in child development, the child's natural musical development and music therapy will be highlighted in the various case examples, which in turn will be backed up by research evidence in the next chapter.

THE PRENATAL MUSICAL EXPERIENCE

In his book *The Third Ear* Joachim-Ernst Berendt notes the similar shapes of the embryo and the ear, the shape of the outer ear being like 'an upturned little human being'.[3] The inner ear contains the important organ known as the organ of Corti, which develops from the skin of the embryo, our hearing apparatus being so intrinsically linked to our very early development as human beings. Our ears develop very quickly, with rudimentary forms emerging from within a few days of conception. The middle and inner ear reach nearly adult size by five months after fertilisation, with the complete auditory system becoming fully functional at about thirty weeks. Before thirty weeks sounds in the form of vibrations may be picked up. Berendt stresses: 'During the first few months of existence, the most important thing for the embryonic creature is to be able to hear for itself – to be all ears.'[4]

What does this young embryo actually hear? *In utero* there are the sounds of the maternal heartbeat, blood circulation and other nearby sounds, creating a high level of sound with a predominant rhythmic whooshing; there are also the foetus's own heartbeats and rhythmic movements of chest, body and limbs. In the 1960s Leo Salk investigated the connections between the attachment to the maternal heartbeat and the health of the foetus, proposing that the sound is imprinted on to the growing foetus.[5] There are also anecdotal accounts of singers reporting how their unborn babies are quieter when they are singing; and pregnant instrumentalists often note increases in activity during or shortly after playing, particularly during the last three months of pregnancy.[6] Such research and anecdotal accounts led to the use of tape-recordings of the heartbeat and of other womb sounds as aids to calm distressed babies. More recent research is abandoning this imprinting of the maternal heartbeat as the main stimulus. Hargreaves points out that any sound is better than no sound at all.[7] A young baby will be particularly interested in a new or different sound, being acutely aware of changes in the immediate environment. Ockelford has found that full-term babies were calmed by a rhythmic stimulus (a metronome) beating at the speed of their own heart-rate, rather than their mother's. Other research is exploring how outside sounds may reach the growing foetus: the mother's voice, her choice of music, environmental sounds, conversation. Ockelford and her colleagues, in a later study, found that young babies less than twenty-four hours old could orientate themselves to the sound of their mother's voice.[8] There are other anecdotal reports of young babies quickly turning to a source of sound such as the television, especially to their mother's favourite programmes. Research into the auditory world of the pre-term baby continues to develop, with interesting findings that are relevant to a music therapist's understanding of a child's elemental responses to sound and music. In 1980 Donald Shetler set up an inquiry into prenatal musical experience that measured foetal responses to both 'stimulative' and 'sedative' pieces of music. The study indicated differences in responses: 'a. The infant tended to respond with more sharp, rapid or agitated movement to the stimulative selection, and b. With more rolling or soft, muted motor movement to the slower "sedative" selection.'[9] Such differences led to the conclusion that awareness of tempo variation may be a very early and almost primitive musical response. Such findings support the notion that some of our appreciation of the basic ingredients of music may be innate. Other scientists stress the nurture argument, with most emphasis on musical experience developing the relevant neural pathways in the brain. A further spin-off from Shetler's seven-year study is that the children who were exposed to a lot of prenatal musical stimulation went on to develop highly organised and articulate speech.

MUSIC IN EARLY CHILDHOOD – PART I

Much listening, humming, singing and playing with sounds and instruments comprise the young child's developing musical experiences. During the first few months the newborn will react to sudden sounds with reflexive muscular contractions. Ostwald and his colleagues have spent a lot of time studying the cries of young infants, observing a typical rising-falling pattern with maximum loudness at the peak. As all mothers know, the loudness, pitch and duration (all basic 'sound elements') of the early cries are closely influenced by factors such as pain, hunger and distress. Quieter humming and cooing sounds are often associated with feeding or other pleasurable experiences. There is a great uniformity of neonatal crying relating to pain or distress observable in several studies worldwide. Such research led Ostwald to the conclusion: 'Newborn babies produce sounds that have melodic structures and rhythms which seem to be fixed by the neurophysiological and respiratory apparatus of the infant.'[10] The time of the first smile not only elicits much social interaction from the caregivers but also much vocal interaction. A real social feeling is being set up between child and caregivers. The baby begins to explore a variety of sounds, beginning with vowel sounds such as 'ah' and 'oo'. The baby becomes increasingly interested in environmental sounds and sounds made by hands, feet or the baby's entire body. Songs and lullabies are natural experiences for a young baby at this stage, having a calming effect especially when combined with rocking. The rocking need not necessarily be linked to a slow swaying tempo; one psychologist colleague reports how a rather vigorous African melody in five time was the most efficient in calming one of his children.[11] John Sloboda adds a note of caution in attaching too much significance to these early responses, noting that up to the age of six months there is very little overt behaviour that could be described as musical. Analysis of a young baby's cries and sounds tends to use an adult's preconceptions of what is musical.[12] I am not suggesting here that the young baby intends to make a musical communication with these rather reflexive movements and vocalisations.

The rather reflexive nature of a young baby's emergent response to sounds can be illustrated in the following short case study.

THE STORY OF ALEX

During Alex's time *in utero* there was a history of maternal alcohol and drug abuse, the potential label of 'foetal alcohol abuse syndrome' surrounding her birth. During her first few weeks of life she was very distressed on handling, making it difficult for her first set of foster-parents to form any close bond with her. She was referred at six weeks to the child development team at the local hospital for a full assessment. The physiotherapist was concerned about a high degree of muscle tension when handling Alex, particularly in the shoulders and upper arms. She continued to cry when being handled. The team began to be concerned that the alcohol abuse may have caused some brain damage affecting both physical and intellectual development, manifested in the early problems she had in moving her limbs freely. A series of physiotherapy exercises was introduced to help the foster-mother in her handling of Alex. I was asked to see her to see if sounds could attract her interest, distracting her from the discomfort caused by the movements. If the crying could be stopped, we would then be able to form a more accurate assessment of her development. Her new foster-mother brought Alex to a combined music therapy and physiotherapy session when she was nearly five months old. A pair of beautiful Indian bells seemed to fascinate her. Something about these bells – the colour, shape, size or sound – clearly attracted her. She turned to the source of the sound and stopped crying. When previously working with young babies in combined work with physiotherapists I had often observed that one beautifully produced sound that is very different from the surrounding environment can be attractive to babies of this age. During the first few sessions we began to evolve very simple combined techniques such as:

- a simple vocal phrase to reflect movements from lying to supported sitting, a rising 'Time to sit up', and falling 'Time to lie down'
- instruments played to both right and left side and in the central mid-line position, providing a focal point for her developing attention
- a pulse played out on a drum to support specific patterns of movements, such as the encouragement of 'saving reactions' – both her arms placed in front of the body as she falls forward
- the introduction to instruments, such as shakers, to reach out for, grasp, explore, often taking to mouth before discarding (a natural sequence mirroring the common dropping of a toy rattle from the pram with the delight in the adult retrieving the object and the repeating of the sequence)
- the encouragement of 'listening' to short melodies played on a little flute while being supported in a sitting position.

Sessions lasting up to twenty minutes occurred twice a week in these first few months of intervention. Her foster-mother would often bring her other children to the sessions. Increasingly all members of the family were able to observe Alex's growing interest and curiosity in the sounds. We filmed her at both five and six months. In the sequence when she was five months it was clear that she attended to the bells and the sound of my voice and was able to accept direct handling by the physiotherapist, with the sounds acting as a kind of reassuring and relaxing cocoon. The physiotherapist commented that the music helped her to relax, enabling her to work more efficiently. The family, who were working towards adopting Alex, began to take the simple musical ideas home to play together as part of family life.

In the video sequence when she was six months old we see Alex turning to the bells on alternate sides when two pairs are played in sequence, one to her left and one to her right. She reaches out to touch the bells with both hands together in the mid-line position. She takes the bells and other instruments to her mouth to explore. She holds a pair of bright yellow shakers and moves them for a few seconds before releasing them from her grasp. She astonishes us all with her interest in a skin-topped tambour (drum). She explores the instrument in all manner of ways, including scraping and then spontaneously tapping. Afterwards we remind ourselves of Piaget's comments about the sensori-motor stage of development, when children explore in undifferentiated ways, so that poking, scratching and reflexive banging of this tambour is very much to be encouraged and all part of a child's natural development. Alex is particularly curious about a drum in the form of a wooden box, a 'tongue drum or slit drum'. Various slits in the top of this hollowed-out box enable sounds of different but rather indiscriminate pitches to be played. What seems to attract her attention is waiting for this sound. I lift up the stick with the bright orange head and stop half-way down, whereupon Alex vocalises as if to indicate she expects to hear the sound next. She giggles or vocalises again when the drum is played but sometimes, if it is too sudden, will react with a reflexive muscular contraction. She vocalises much more during the rest of the session, particularly in response to short melodies played on a small flute. She vocalises in the gaps between phrases, as if to put in her contribution to the music. We begin to set up a turn-taking dialogue: flute–Alex–flute–Alex etc. I play a livelier phrase which elicits movements from side to side, bouncing up and down, bottom shuffles and some spontaneous movement backwards. I then end the session with a longer, quieter and slower melody to which Alex gives full attention, with much eye-contact and fewer movements.

The intervention continued with this intensity for a few more months, eventually reducing to one weekly session. Alex began to move quickly through her developmental milestones; the initial concerns about possible damage were gradually discarded. She increasingly demonstrated intelligent and very age-appropriate behaviour in the sessions. Her range of movements and vocal sounds developed and she became increasingly exploratory and relaxed in the sessions as her trust in us developed. This emerging spontaneity in vocalising, moving and interacting was fundamentally influenced by the secure and loving environment provided by her now adoptive parents and brothers and sisters. By the time of her first birthday we considered it appropriate to withdraw the physiotherapy/music therapy input, seeing that she was beginning to race so far ahead. The team at the clinic suggested monitoring the situation at longer intervals, as is the case in any normal development. We were invited to her dedication service one year later, where it was clear that Alex was functioning very well, with plans for schooling being discussed as for any other members of the family.

I have focused on this example for two main reasons:

1 It provides us with practical examples of a child's early responses to sounds and music.
2 It reinforces the importance of early intervention, integrated team-work and the fundamental connections between work in the clinic and a child's developing security in a loving and consistent home environment.

MUSIC IN EARLY CHILDHOOD – PART II

Alex was 5 and then 6 months old when we filmed the two video sequences. A group of children between 5 and 6 months was also the youngest age-group used in Helmut Moog's extensive series of pre-recorded tests played to pre-school children to observe their developing responses to music.[13]

During the earliest period of five to six months he observed a developing active response to sound, the baby stopping still and turning to the source of sound as if concentrating the listening on the sound itself. Moog then noted that movements occurred when music was heard, particularly singing and instrumental music, a few weeks after this active turning of the attention. There are repetitive patterns in these movements that we could regard as an early response to rhythm. We noted this sequence of turning and then moving in response to heard sounds in Alex's case. We also noted this emerging repeated banging. Parents are familiar with this increase in reflexive rhythmic activity. I recall both of my two children banging spoons on table-tops or any surface at around eight months. It was very tempting to rush into regarding this as intended rhythmic behaviour and fantasise about prodigious musical futures, since there does appear to be some regularity in the way one rhythmic burst follows on quickly after the previous one. It is as if one burst reinforces the next, with developing cycles of self-reinforcing activity. This behaviour gives the appearance of regularity but it lacks the subtleties of rhythmic activity, such as pause, accent, subdivision, development and repetition of rhythmic patterns, that need to be present to indicate rhythmic intention.

There is a marked increase in vocalising during the second half of the first year. Moog notes a phenomenon that we observe time and time again in music therapy, namely that vocalisations seem to start after motor movements to music have occurred. It is as if the physical excitement induced by moving to the music elicits a vocal sound. We have only to remind ourselves that we often are able to start singing spontaneously after moving, perhaps after dancing and even only then, for some people, after a few glasses of alcohol. But to return to our highly spontaneous babies. At this stage Moog distinguishes two types of vocal response: babbling as a rehearsal for speech, and what he calls 'musical babbling', which only occurs if music is sung or played. The musical babbling has an amorphous rhythmic and melodic structure, as distinct from the rehearsals for speech, which are more rhythmically formed and structured. In response to music, sounds of varied pitches are produced, either on one vowel or a few syllables, and the speech-like sounds are not practised.

Increased selectivity is noticed by nine months either in the turning-away from certain sounds, especially the noises and rhythms in Moog's tests, or in focusing on the rhythmic aspects of words. This corresponds to growing awareness of speech-sounds and the child's developing interest in what goes on behind the external events. It is no coincidence that this final part of the first year of life sees the growth of patterned and simple action songs such as peek-a-boo games. It becomes increasingly possible to share experiences and for whole sequences of non-verbal communication to be set up between child and adult. Both partners are trying to get in touch with the feelings behind the physical events, a process that is central to much music therapy work. However, we still need to be very wary of attaching too much musical significance to these developments. The baby may be demonstrating no more than an increasing awareness of changes in the auditory environment, selecting out the most pleasurable sounds. The baby begins to ascribe significance and meaning to certain sounds: the sound of mother's voice, the sounds of the everyday environment such as running water for the bath, sounds that indicate preparation of food, and the like. Moog asserts that it is the attention to the quality of the different sounds that pervades most of the baby's sound and potentially musical experiences during the first year. As noted in Chapter 3, it is this basic response to the quality of a sound that is also a fundamental part of the adult's response.

In parallel with general development there is a marked increase in motor activity in response to music during the second year. Space is used more freely as walking becomes more confident, movements in response to music becoming more frequent, more varied and of longer duration. These movements are also tried out with others, and Moog regards them as early examples of social behaviour in response to music. There is a developing need for independence; yet, as Daniel Stern has observed in describing the infant's interpersonal world, the child still seeks out close interactions.[14]

Moog confidently states that by the age of 2 every child of normal development should be able to sing. Amidst the babble are odd words or parts of words and we begin to hear more tonal and intervallic content. Before this stage the baby's babbling does not contain discrete pitches but is rather composed of highly expressive microtonal slides. Small intervals such as seconds and thirds seem to be part of the initial experimentation. A child by the second birthday begins to launch out into the world of fourths and fifths. These spontaneous songs are the most striking feature of this age, with their original mixture of microtonal slides, discrete pitches and the odd recognisable word. The songs are rhythmically very simple and Moog reports a very simple ratio of 1:2 between the basic note lengths, namely subdividing by half. This simple ratio and duple underlay can be observed in most of the nursery rhymes within the Western tradition: there are few nursery rhymes in simple three time. The sensory impression of these songs still predominates. The pitch wanders but the melodic shape (contour) is replicable, often being repeated at different pitch levels. It is as if the contour and simple rhythmic shapes are being used as formal organisational and mnemonic devices. As the second birthday approaches a child's pitch range expands and there is more imitation of sounds and words, with attempts to sing something similar to songs sung to the child. Certain melodies are recognised in their own right as stable entities. The moves from gross to more precise features occur globally in both spontaneous singing and the reproduction of heard melodies. Our daughter surprised us at eighteen months with the sudden rendition during a car journey of her own version of 'Twinkle, twinkle, little star'. It was a mixture of some approximate intervals and rhythms, the general contour, some of her own words and some correct words.

Between 2 and 3 a child will often choose to sit while listening to music. There are still difficulties in coordinating rhythm with movements but such moments continue to increase in frequency, intensity and duration. One of Moog's observations of importance to music therapists is that a child of this age will keep to a personal temporal framework while singing spontaneously but not to music heard. We cannot expect our nursery-age children to 'keep in time' to the music but we can encourage them to make all manner of spontaneous responses to music. The range of these spontaneous songs increases to just over an octave, and learned songs gain in accuracy and length. The child continues to mix snatches of learned melody with the spontaneous songs. There is more repetition of rhythmic and melodic patterns. These imaginative re-arrangements, what Moog neatly refers to as 'pot-pourris', mirror the development of imaginative play, and to some extent we can place music alongside Piaget's stage of pre-school symbolic play.

By the age of 4 children are singing more or less accurately, with some difficulty in tempo and pitch control producing idiosyncratic adjustments. Singing games and action songs are important tools for learning at this stage. Music and movements also seem to be inextricably linked. Broad distinctions between fast and slow are now being mastered and simple patterns can be produced in rhythmic and intervallic imitation. Several commentators have also observed the beginning of little musical rituals: for example, the spontaneous singing of a minor third, which, though heard earlier in short snatches, may now be extended in play (see Chapter 3 on melody).

As expected, control and accuracy develop in the later pre-school years. By the age of 5 most children can keep in tempo for short periods, sometimes following the melodic rhythm of songs. There is growing awareness of dynamics, but, as with the other parameters, there is still more coordination with spontaneous singing and playing. There is still a wide range in ability, but most children of this age can produce the rhythm, words and pitch of a song in a recognisable form. Maintaining a stable tonality and imitating the precise intervals of a song have not been fully mastered by all children by 5. Moog is convinced that children of pre-school age are unable to distinguish harmonic content, not a single child in his study showing signs of displeasure when listening to the series of discordant 'cacophonies'. Such an assertion makes almost a nonsense of some of the assumptions within some music therapy reporting, where links are proposed with a young child's response to a particular key centre or tonality, and where importance is attached to certain keys to meet and support certain moods and behaviours of the child.

Sometimes a music therapist is fortunate in working with a young child during these formative pre-school years and in charting progress during an extended period. Such is the case of M., who attended for music therapy over a period of two years between his third and fifth birthdays. His story is presented here in detail to highlight some of the points made in the previous section and to provide a link to the next section relating other processes in early child development to a music therapy intervention.

THE STORY OF M.

Referral and background

M. was referred for music therapy just after his third birthday. The referral was made by the speech therapy department of the local hospital, and the reasons listed for the referral included: problems with his expressive speech, fleeting interaction both with other children and with adults, and a developing sense of social isolation. It was stressed that his comprehension was within his age-range and that he had a passive vocabulary well ahead of his age-level. It had been difficult for the speech therapist to test his actual level of expressive speech.

His mother had doubted his hearing at 6 months when noticing him fiddling with his ears. This was dismissed as teething pains. A check at 11 months suggested some hearing loss, although this was apparently contradicted by a later test at 14 months. It was not until 24 months that his mother's original doubts were confirmed by the diagnosis of a hearing loss, resulting in surgical inter-vention to insert grommets. This undoubtedly enabled M. to hear more clearly (the consultant considered that it would account for a 50 per cent improvement), but his mother observed that it did not result in any dramatic improvements in his communication or general behaviour. When M. spoke, his speech was quiet and rapid, lacking clear distinction. He would make substitutions for sounds not heard. He became upset and frustrated when he was not understood, which also caused him to withdraw more and isolate himself. At the age of 3 he was already reading and writing. He was fascinated with mechanical objects, spending a lot of time during this first visit exploring a typewriter and other desk-top objects. He appeared to be more interested in mechanical objects and solitary play than direct communication and more interactive play. M. was not socially very aware, apparently often not acknowledging a visitor's presence, remaining quite shut off from events and people around him. His mother confirmed the speech therapist's observation that he had age-appropriate comprehension of language, pointing out that she felt him to be a highly intelligent boy.

M. is the only child of a single parent. His mother's parents lived close at hand. His mother found him to be very demanding, reporting that it was a full-time job looking after him. She herself is a highly intelligent and sensitive person who has been working through her own personal problems with the support of therapy. At the time of referral she had also been attending a group, run by a child psychiatrist, set up for mothers to meet together to discuss 'handling problems' and to gain insight from the support of the psychiatrist and the other members of the group. While his mother attended the group M. was with the other children and the nursery nurse.

Music therapy assessment and first sessions

The setting for the music therapy sessions was a pleasant, airy room with windows on two sides overlooking some grass. On another wall was a mirror, which doubled as a one-way screen for observation purposes. There was an upright piano in the room. Other tuned and untuned percussion instruments were available and stored on shelves in the room. A free-standing drum and cymbal were also available.

The picture of M. as reported by his mother and the speech therapist, and as observed during the initial visit, clearly presented itself in the first music sessions. M. made only fleeting contact with any of the instruments, seeming to be more interested in the way the instruments were made than in their sound-producing potential. If left to his own devices during these early sessions, it was apparent that he would have stayed for the whole session exploring an instrument such as a metal glockenspiel by taking off the bars and putting them back on again, often also naming the notes in his own way. He did not seem very aware of his mother or of my presence in the room, walking directly past either adult and engaging in very little sustained eye-contact. There were some fleeting moments of engagement and short little bursts of activity on instruments, usually when M. was initiating an idea. There were one or two examples during the early sessions of M. following or imitating one of my musical ideas, such as an up-and-down pattern on a xylophone. He also seemed to cut himself off and withdraw even more if I put any pressure on him to join me in any sustained musical play. There did not appear to be any growing awareness of limits or boundaries to his behaviour: he would quite often walk over an instrument he had just explored, for example. It was very hard to hear or understand any of his speech when it did occur. M. made me feel very tense and communicated a sense of nervousness and anxiety which was even picked up by some of the students who were observing through the one-way screen. During one of M.'s moments of solitary play on what appeared a favourite instrument, the glockenspiel, I spontaneously improvised some music to accompany his play. I hoped that the music would articulate some of what was happening in the room: M's apparent need to withdraw from any sustained contact with me, my feelings of not being able to provide the kind of musical stimulation to interest M., and his mother's feelings (aired at the end of one of the previous sessions) that M. was also avoiding contact with me. The resulting music had a kind of poignancy about it, yet the upward phrases of the melody were expectant of potential future contact. In fact I sang his name after a pause in the music and he turned from what he was doing and looked back towards me. Perhaps M. was aware of what was happening but was not at this stage prepared to trust me enough to make music with me. The session was taped and I managed to transcribe this music, transforming it into M.'s music. This music became a rich resource of ideas for variation and exploration in future sessions – a kind of musical calling-card or leitmotif for M.. These moments when a music therapist makes such an intuitive musical response can be potentially very creative. What is fascinating is that the personal and musical make-up of each therapist would respond differently to each and every situation. This music I improvised for M. at this moment would be different from music improvised by other colleagues. Yet I would imagine that there would be certain features of attentive listening, seeking for a genuine, accepting and warm response to the situation, common to many of these responses.

It became quickly clear to me that M. needed a great deal of space, both physically and musically, with as little overt pressure from me to play as possible and an emphasis away from verbal communication. He began to feel more comfortable towards the end of the initial period of work and we had the first signs that musical interaction could become an area where much could be explored. Two examples illustrate this development. The first was when his interest in mechanical objects was transferred into a musical game. During one session he became fascinated by the clips on the piano's music-stand. I took up his idea by playing the notes directly under each of these clips. M. became very animated, repeated the two-note pattern on each note and moved up and down in his chair. As we observed in the brief survey of a pre-school child's musical development, it is the spontaneous initiation of ideas by the child that seems to be very important at this stage. M. initiated this idea and seemed excited that I had picked up his idea and incorporated it into our joint activity. The second example was when we began to explore two tambours, sitting on the floor together. M. had his own drum and I had mine. We built up a little musical game – playing on Leslie's drum, playing on M.'s drum, etc. Once this simple pattern had been established I paused before naming my drum, providing an opportunity for M. to indicate the next turn. He indicated the next turn by nodding, looking at me and smiling – one of his most direct communications to date. This simple technique of waiting and using silence is an example of building up expectations in a musical form and causing curiosity and interest in confounding expectations. As was discussed in Chapter 3, such is the stuff of much musical communication.

Development of the relationship and early work

It was apparent to all involved that music therapy could be a useful medium for M. to begin to develop a relationship with an adult over a period of time and to begin to explore some of his problems non-verbally. The first stage of this process was the building-up of various activities that became secure and predictable. M.'s apparent excitement in anticipating musical patterns and sequences led into structures using a variety of instruments: for example, alternating on drum and cymbal; building up imitative and turn-taking sequences on drum, cymbal and xylophone. He began to explore the musical parameters of fast/slow and soft/loud with increasing control and ensuing confidence. All this work enabled M. to sustain his attention for ever longer bursts of activity. His sensitivity to mood changes became apparent and active music-making, such as his playing on the drum and cymbal while being supported by me on the piano, would alternate with moments of almost private reflection and listening. It is hard to be sure if a child or adult is listening, but over a period of weeks it becomes possible to observe subtle changes in posture or mood that seem to indicate listening. In M.'s case, he would often demonstrate this by resting his sticks on the drum and looking towards me while I continued to play in a softer and more lyrical vein. We were now well into our third month of weekly sessions and it was clear that trust was developing. I was respectful of M.'s musical ideas and incorporated them into our joint music-making. M. began to take up some of my ideas and tolerate some of my direction. In effect M. was beginning to tolerate more turn-taking, more playful exchanges of musical ideas. Some of these exchanges appeared to carry over from one week to the next. At the end of one session I said 'Goodbye', M. returning to the drum and producing a musical version of 'Goodbye' with a two-beat pattern. We built up a rhythmic exchange of one-, two- and three-beat short phrases, sometimes soft, sometimes loud. The next week M. went straight to the drum and opened the session with a two-note pattern which I transformed into 'Hello', before engaging again in a similar exchange of rhythmic ideas. It was as if the music had provided the link from one session to the next, the last sounds from one being almost identical to the first sounds of the next, a week later.

M. was becoming more engaged in the music and was demonstrating a highly imaginative, creative and intelligent use of the instruments. As we moved into the fourth and fifth months of sessions he began to resist some of this contact. He would play for a large majority of the session before taking 'time out' by moving over to sit in a chair in the corner of the room. I would continue to play to him. This need to sit in his chair began to occur at earlier points during the next few sessions, moving closer to the start of the session. The result was that one week he entered the room crying 'No music today', repeating 'No'. He needed a great deal of calming before any contact could be established and during this session only tolerated some gentle singing. There still seemed to be a problem over becoming too involved, in spite of a growing sense of confidence and trust in the music.

After these rather difficult sessions we returned to less demanding and confrontational musical activities, with more side-by-side playing on the tuned percussion instruments. This appeared to reduce some of the upset and was a period of consolidation before a new period of work. To support M.'s start at a local nursery we then arranged for M. to have a series of five joint sessions with another child and her music therapist. We aimed to see if M. could tolerate more sharing and to develop some social awareness by extending some of the turn-taking already achieved in the adult–child context. At first M. seemed only to tolerate activities on his own terms and of his own choice. Gradually he began to respect some of the needs of the other child and responded to a more directive approach deliberately adopted by the adults. At times M. would vocalise while playing, and he was beginning to show some awareness of singing the melodic rhythm. We were given an anecdotal account of M. making use of his musical interest at the nursery. The nursery nurse reported that M. would show the other children how to play the piano with one or two fingers as an alternative to a random banging of the notes. Perhaps this is an example of taking some of the processes evolved during his music therapy outside the sessions and using them to communicate with other children. Music therapy in isolation with me could be regarded as rather redundant if M. was not able to make use of the sessions in other areas of his life.

The middle stage of the work

After a three-month summer break M. returned to a further period of individual work; it was now ten months after the initial referral. The main aim of this period of work was firmly to establish this reciprocal sharing in the individual activities. There was a balance between improvised music and more clearly structured music and activities. He began to use some of his earlier interest in numbers, letters, shapes and taking instruments apart in a more communicative way. A song incorporating a part for M. on a reed horn extended his interest in counting, as we enjoyed exchanging different numbers of sounds on the horn and piano. Our music-making became very extended, with long piano dialogues and xylophone/metallophone exchanges. There were moments of synchronous musical play and interactive antiphonal exchanges when M. seemed to delight in setting up musical question-and-answer routines. His playing became increasingly flexible and sensitive, with awareness of changes in speed, mood, loudness, and even more complex recognition of phrase lengths, pauses and melodic and rhythmic shape. Nowhere was this more clearly demonstrated than in a lengthy exchange at the keyboard where there was full mutual interplay of musical ideas that demonstrated immense flexibility to the rhythmic and melodic structures. Such an interaction was free of the tension and sense of isolation that had influenced our earlier music-making.

'The Cat Song'

This free expressive playing coexisted with the demands of more structured music. One example of a piece of composed music is 'The Cat Song'. At around the time of his fourth birthday M. brought along some of his soft toy cats to a session, letting me know their names. We built up over the weeks an extended song with many verses, where these and other imaginary cats would be taken out on various excursions – to the park, to the shops, and the like. We established a routine over the weeks that M. would choose the location for the next verse and the instruments he wanted to depict the scene. I would return with some new music the next week. If he was in the mood for the next verse, we would then add this new verse to the music already learned. In this way M. was building up a memory for a whole series of musical events, showing an almost prodigious ability in retaining the details of the song and predicting the next event. This song not only helped him to imbue the instruments with a more representative and at times symbolic meaning but also provided much opportunity for spontaneous talk. He had known me for over a year and was able, on days when he was most relaxed, to come into the room talking. He was now able to string together quite complex sentences, although his speech was still unclear at times and tended still to be rapid and quiet.

The absence of his mother from the sessions meant that M. could return to her and tell her about the various activities. After the first few early sessions his mother had withdrawn from the sessions, watching through the one-way screen. When she felt more comfortable she was invited to wait for M. in the room opposite, so that she would learn all about the session directly from M. himself, providing him with as much space as possible.

M. began to attend the nursery more regularly and this was considered to be the top priority in providing as much contact with other children as possible. We arranged for a three-month break from the music therapy.

The final period

The final period of work culminated in the build-up to his starting primary school at the time of his fifth birthday. The work continued with this balance of pre-composed and improvised music. A new watch song was composed to build on M.'s developing interest in present, past and future time, M. being able to predict accurately the time and date of the next session. I had to resist the tendency to compose material for him and build on this very positive aspect of our work. There was a danger that I might have relied too much on composed material, to the detriment of more improvised and freer music. On some days it was clear that M. wanted to improvise for all the session and that any new song or pre-composed music was not what was wanted, even if I had been up the night before writing some new music for him. An example from near the end of our work demonstrates this need to continue to explore improvised music. I had written a song about the move to the new school and as a preparation for the end of the music therapy sessions. He did not want to play or hear this new song. Instead he asked for two cymbals and the drum, playing with loud sounds to a 'Goodbye' song using the drums for my name and the cymbals for himself. During the ensuing weeks he used the same structure, sometimes choosing to play a quiet ending, sometimes with apparent difficulty in actually leaving the session. He seemed to be working through his way of bringing the work and our relationship to a natural ending. In fact the final two sessions were very light-hearted, with a retrospective look at all our favourite material. M. asked for the new school song on repeated occasions during these last two sessions, singing and playing the drum to it.

Postscript

M. started primary school at the age of 5. His educational psychologist assessed a reading age of over 8, although there were still some communication difficulties and problems in socialising. It is clear that music therapy had been a medium where M. was able to develop a certain level of positive self-achievement. He was able to learn several non-verbal coping strategies that he could put to use outside the sessions. His speech had developed over the period of intervention and, although there are the obvious maturational factors and outside influences such as the nursery school to consider, it does seem possible that increased organisation and clarity in his music-making could have contributed to this development. His mother commented that he was always in a noticeably good mood after a session. We are still left with a picture of a child with a complex range of emotions and problems, but music therapy had begun to enable M. to find some outlet for expressing and exploring some of these areas. He was able to play for extended periods of time and tolerate better the limits set by an adult. There were fewer moments of isolated play, the music therapy being able both to support such moments and to extend them outwards into more reciprocal and interactive activity.

M. now attends a local secondary school. He is flourishing academically, as we might have predicted, but there are still some problems with socialising. His mother reports that he continues to be very interested in music but not as a means of personal expression. This early creative curiosity, observed so clearly in the music, has now developed into an interest in writing. His mother has recently provided an example of this interest, a poem M. wrote during the final period of his music therapy, when he was 3 years 9 months:

> Today's over,
> The night climbed down from step to step.
> Oh Sunlight, talk to me.
> I am cold in the moon,
> I am cold and pale,
> Dim under evening star,
> Cold am I.
>
> Sadly the sun went down
> Till night dropped stars around.

MUSIC THERAPY AND LINKS WITH PROCESSES IN CHILD DEVELOPMENT

The story of M. can be viewed from the perspective of an emergent curiosity in all things musical, in particular a growing interest in inventing musical ideas. On a different level we can also observe features relating to interactive and developmental processes that are at the heart of many of the early processes in child development. Listening to music and music-making can be linked to processes in physical, intellectual, emotional and social development. Such processes include the development of imitation skills, turn-taking, vocalisations, looking behaviour, attention, motor skills, social skills and other aspects of non-verbal communication, especially the all-embracing concept recently proposed by Stern of 'affect attunement',[15] what I like to translate as 'tuning in to the child'. A study of these early processes can provide a workable framework in which to describe and monitor changes in music therapy sessions with young children. The music therapy sessions with children described in this book are based very much within such an interactive, transactional and developmental framework. There is always an emphasis on building up a relationship with the child through the music, at whatever level of contact. We are always adapting the music to meet the needs of the child, possibly concentrating during part of the work on a specific non-musical need. What is becoming increasingly clear is that there is a great deal of common ground between processes in the music therapy described here and a 'normative' developmental pattern. For example, such central clinical issues as the establishment of trust, the notion of the attendant, listening therapist, empathy, facilitating and supporting independence are common to both child and adult work throughout the life-span.

Since the late 1960s there has been a growing interest in the early skills of the competently emergent infant, with a great deal of research concentrating on the developing interactions between mother and child in particular. Detailed analysis, using sophisticated monitoring devices, of the minutiae of behaviour – for example research into looking behaviour, turn-taking, pre-verbal vocal interactions – are providing researchers with rich data which can help us understand a lot about a child's future development.[16] The child is no longer considered to be a *tabula rasa* on which experiences are drawn and imprinted, but the child brings to the immediate environment from birth onwards a higher degree of competence than previously recognised, although we can assume that parents have known this long before it became fashionable within the field of psychological theory-building. Work by Bower and his colleagues has produced an array of evidence for the complexity of skills manifested by the young infant on arrival into the world.[17] Trevarthen is another researcher who has observed how babies communicate very efficiently with their mothers, and indirectly with objects, from a very early age.[18] The effects of the behaviour of the adult on the child also began to be more carefully researched.[19] The child's skills are developed within a social relationship well before any words are used to signify meaning. The child's emerging repertoire of behaviours is increasingly being considered to be part of 'action dialogue in which joint undertakings are being regulated by infant and adult'.[20] It is as if the child and adult develop their relationship through interlocking transactions, both partners being an essential part of the child's development. A synthesis of the experimental work in this field and recent developments in psychoanalysis, for example the work of Winnicott and the British school of object-relations, provides a potential working framework for describing much of what happens in music therapy. Concepts such as 'action dialogue', 'transactions', 'intersubjectivity' and 'joint undertakings' can be applied as well-needed reference points in beginning to understand some of the complexities of the interactions between adult and child while making music. It was very clear with M. that we developed over the months together a highly fluid way of negotiating a whole range of joint actions together.

We have previously noted that it is possible to make sense of what is happening while playing music together. Music-making offers the opportunity for both synchronous and antiphonal interaction, making it a very adaptable medium for building up these series of interlocking 'transactions' with a child. Within interaction studies attention has been drawn to self-synchrony between patterns of movement and speech: we talk as much with our bodies as with our voices.[21] There is also striking evidence of common temporal frameworks that unite different behaviours (to discover how difficult it is to go against this, try to rub your stomach in a circular motion in one tempo with one hand while tapping your head with the other hand *at a different tempo*). The young infant is also able from quite early on to recognise common temporal frameworks even across different modalities, such as visual and auditory.[22] What is also of interest to the music therapist is the research on difficulties in synchronising, referred to as 'dysfunctional behaviour'. Condon's work also included children with autistic tendencies and learning difficulties. What may appear to us as the bizarre and random body movements of an autistic child, for example, may have meaning within the perceptual framework of that particular child. Condon found that such a child would often respond to sounds multiple times. By slowing down films of children responding to sounds and matching the movements with the sounds, he found close correlations with the earlier sound sequences. It was as if the child was responding to the sounds within a different framework, which may contribute to the difficulties we have in trying to contact children with these very complex patterns of behaviour. We may have to develop a different way of observing such a child's responses in order to begin to understand the child's unique time framework. Perhaps the music is too arousing for a child that may be already over-aroused. I have observed many children who appear to respond to musical stimulation with an outpouring of loud sounds, often with accompanying bizarre movements, while looking away at the same time. One assumption could be that the child is making a meaningful musical connection with the therapist. An alternative assumption could be that the child is using the music as a barrier to hide behind, thus preventing any sustained contact. Perhaps the increases in aural stimulation are contributing to the high degree of over-arousal; the child may have passed an optimum level of excitation and the excitement be overflowing into the movements and general avoidance behaviour.

The evolving two-way nature of the interactions during the work with M. was clearly apparent. We can observe such two-way interactions between child and adult in any park. Intelligence develops within this interpersonal process and partners are needed in order for this natural process to develop. The adult not only allows space for the child's turn in the verbal or non-verbal conversation but is also very adept at pointing up behaviours that are relevant and socially significant. It is unlikely that a mother would be imitating behaviours of her young baby that she feels are socially inappropriate. Kaye's term for the child's role in this evolving social system is 'apprentice'. The young child has almost a predisposition to be social. Kaye organises this period of apprenticeship into four stages:

(a) shared rhythms from birth to about 3 months, when dialogue is built up around inborn patterns of sucking, attention and arousal
(b) shared intentions, when the adult guesses at the baby's intentions, often investing them with more meaning than can be observed externally – rather like getting in touch with the feelings behind the physical event
(c) more two-way sharing, by 8 months, when aspects such as expectation of and reliance on memory of activities or experiences come into play – the adult often helping to regulate with great subtlety the infant's own behaviour; and
(d) the period of shared language when the child begins at first social discourse leading to internal discourse.[23]

What is clear throughout this 'apprenticeship' is that not only does the child influence the adult but the adult is constantly drawing the child into higher levels of interaction than the child is actually capable of at that stage – in musical terms a process rather akin to 'theme and variation' form. Kaye's analysis of adult frames of reference and adaptability are interesting to the developmental music therapist who works within the inherent form and shapes in music to provide frameworks for the evolving relationship. This two-way process where meanings are jointly negotiated can provide a working framework to help us unwrap something of what happens during a period of music therapy.

Imitation

Imitation is very often used as an immediate way of establishing some contact with a child, especially at the start of the work. In M.'s story we saw in the early part how I was able to pick up on his musical ideas by imitating them, which resulted in M. taking up the ideas and/or elaborating on them. The process also occurred later in the work the other way around, with M. imitating my musical ideas. In her research Pawlby found this pattern to be a natural one. Early in infancy a mother tends to imitate the child more frequently, with the child imitating the mother as age increases. The kinds of behaviour Pawlby observed being imitated are interesting: vowel-like sounds, bangs and consonant sounds were the three most frequently imitated behaviours in her sample of mother–child pairs.[24] Pawlby also noted that indirect observation via object increased as the child got older. This pattern often occurs in music therapy when a direct interest in the therapist's music (a more passive response on the part of the child) predates a more indirect (active) use of instruments. Pawlby stresses the importance of imitative behaviour in the development of language and the building-up of understanding of the meaning of joint action. She uses the example of the child attempting to reproduce the exact motor movements of his mother's drum-playing. The child attempts to imitate the action, to relate hand to drum, and begins to understand the action and share the meaning with the mother.

Turn-taking and vocal behaviour

Turn-taking has already been discussed as part of a symmetrical arrangement between adult and child, with the adult being sensitive to the child's patterns, fitting in alongside the child and gradually providing a frame and semblance of dialogue. Likewise, the infant develops skills at communicating intentions to the adult and in responding to the adult's expressed intent.

Very often a music therapist will be working with children who find vocalising difficult owing to some cognitive impairment or problem. Here encouraging and stimulating all kinds of vocal activity through musical interaction becomes an important feature. M. would vocalise freely when relaxed and over the course of the work began to synchronise his vocalising with the rhythmic patterns he was playing, either in improvised or in pre-composed music. Synchronous vocal interaction with a young child often employs silences, switch-over points and other non-verbal cues that break up the sustained stream of vocal play into antiphonal turn-taking. The relaxed and child-centred setting of much music therapy with this age-group often fosters playful exploration of vocal sounds. Timing is a crucial feature in vocalising. So often we can observe a mother overriding her baby's distress by exaggerating her vocalising, increasing her tempo and loudness level before gradually slowing down both her vocalisations and accompanying movements as the baby calms. Stern uses other musical vocabulary to describe these early, playful vocal interactions, referring to their rhythmic content, the dynamics, speed, pauses and orchestration of the activities.[25] Bullowa also uses musical parallels in summarising the early play between mother and child: 'Movement, sound and rhythm make up much of the common experience infant and parent bring to their meeting – patterns of synchrony and potential patterns of counterpoint and syncopation.'[26]

Tuning in to the child

This emphasis on the establishment of non-verbal codes via imitation, vocalising, turn-taking and mutual attention and understanding can help us understand some of the levels of an interactive music therapy session. Such unified exploration seems even more important when working with a non-verbal child. The sequence of musical gestures or messages becomes part of the evolving history between the adult and child, taking on a significant meaning that is attended to, shared and potentially understood by both. But how can we be sure that we understand the feelings that lie behind the musical gesture? A child makes a series of sounds, for example on a drum – physical events in time and space. If I repeat these sounds directly, I am only imitating the sounds. I may not be getting behind the sounds to make contact with the child's world of feelings. I need cues to help me understand the child's feeling world and to guarantee that I am on the appropriate track, all without words to confirm my musical responses. Clearly a series of imitative mirrorings of instrumental or vocal sounds is not going to indicate to the child that I have understood the whole picture. It is not going to help me to communicate that I have really understood the subjective world of the child, the same world of feelings as inhabited by the child. At this point we can turn for guidance to Daniel Stern's label of 'affect attunement'. In order for there to be a satisfactory 'intersubjective exchange' (a mutual exchange of feeling states) Stern considers that there need to be several processes at work. The adult needs to find some way of 'reading' the child's feeling state from the external behaviour (in our example the playing on the drum). The adult then demonstrates some understanding of the child's behaviour by providing something that is more than an imitation of that behaviour, yet bears some similarity to it. In the example of the drumming, the therapist may take up the similar tempo and loudness level of the child's drumming as part of the musical response, which would include the therapist's own ideas. The therapist may even articulate such ideas on a different instrument. The child then needs to read this corresponding adult behaviour as being connected to the child's original behaviour. The connection is read not simply as an imitation but as a real attempt to connect with the child's feelings.[27] If we look at a vocal interaction, the process could be similar. The child vocalises and the therapist vocalises back, perhaps with the support of another instrument, as if summoned into action by the child. This is not an exact imitation of the child's vocalising but contains features of it. The adult incorporates some of the child's ideas and extends them, introducing individual variations. This may then lead to the child's second response, which is again taken up and elaborated upon by the adult. A whole chain of reciprocal vocal turn-taking with instrumental support can then be set up. Once again the musical form of theme-and-variations is an appropriate analogy for such a flowing dialogue. Stern considers the various characteristics of attunements to be: the impression that some kind of imitation has happened, with some form of matching which is not an exact copy; that the matching can take place across different modes – for example, a child's physical movements can be matched by a series of adult vocalisations either in synchrony with the tempo and loudness of the movements or as an antiphonal response; that the matching is an attempt to reflect the feelings behind the external behaviour. As Stern states: 'We appear to be dealing with behaviour as expression rather than as sign or symbol, and the vehicles of transfer are metaphor and analogue.'[28]

Looking behaviour

Music therapists share with other developmental therapists an interest in encouraging children to look both at the objects of play (in our case a whole range of beautiful instruments not only to look at but to touch, feel and hold) and at the adult or other children if working in a group. Following the line of vision and visual fixation are acts that are normally under the control of the infant, becoming an early means of expressing attention – 'Can I play with that now, Mum?' Unlike the ears, the eyes can be turned off to regulate input. Averting the gaze, closing the eyelids or dilating the pupils are strong regulators in this on–off system.[29] Direct eye-to-eye contact between child and adult is a rich source for communication, as it remains during adulthood. Such contact, often linked in with much smiling, considerably enriches the attachment process, mothers often naturally addressing their children in the *en face* position – a position often favoured, when accepted by the child, in early intervention in music therapy work.

At times a more indirect contact via an instrument may feel more natural for both child and therapist. Here the instrument is the common point of visual attention. Often a mother is led by the infant's visual attention to an object; she will then verbalise about it, elaborating to make the act more significant and meaningful for them both. Very often the adult will predict the direction of the child's gaze.[30] Scaife and Bruner were also interested in the child's developing curiosity in tracking the changes in the adult's direction of vision. They suggest that orientating to another's perspective is evidence of less egocentricity on the child's part.[31]

Developmental delay can cause problems with the development of visual attention. Miranda and Fantz, for example, have indicated some of the problems children with Down's syndrome have in demonstrating their visual preferences when compared to a group with no developmental delay.[32] In observing autistic children approaching adults, Hutt and Ounsted noted normal approach gestures but with averted gaze: for example, an approach with outstretched arms but with face held down. Here gaze aversion is being used as a regulator, Hutt and Ounsted suggesting that the rich source of stimulation from the eyes is too arousing for the autistic child.[33] The implications of such research can aid music therapists in their attempts to make contact with children with autism. Often when working with a child with autism or autistic features an *en face* position is too arousing and a side-by-side position may be more comfortable for the child. When working in this position emphasis can be put on indirect communication and visual attention via the instruments. It is also of note that where visual attention is impossible, as in the case of blind children, normal speech can develop if there is sufficient alternative auditory and tactile turn-taking experience.[34] The responses of blind people to music are strong indicators that music can be understood without visual or even active participation.

Other aspects of non-verbal communication

We have observed that music can be regarded in its own right as a prime example of a non-verbal communication system. It is obvious to any observer of music therapy in action that musical interaction embraces many aspects of non-verbal communication, all with their own levels of meaning. Such features as music-making's relationship with proximity, posture, facial expressions, gestures, head-nods and other non-verbal and subtle systems of communication could generate studies in their own right. As in vocal behaviour and music's links with language and speech, much stressing, pausing, repetition and differing durations are observable in these systems, and we can apply musical terminology to describe many of the non-verbal communications and dance-like patterns that take place between people.

Children with a whole range of learning disabilities often have difficulties in certain features of non-verbal communication. We have noted the approach-avoidance behaviour of the autistic child. There may be difficulties defined by specific motor and neurological problems. Cues from the non-verbal systems are even more vital when the child (or adult) lacks the ability to speak, for whatever reason. Often timing of social responses is confused, and there may be problems in recognising and coding non-verbal communication and in choosing the appropriate framework for replying. Anticipation of events is sometimes difficult, this leading to what may appear to an observer as jerky and unclear patterns of interaction. Once again, a musical interaction provides a rhythmic and time-based grid that enables the child or adult to explore, re-acquire, learn or practise a wide range of non-verbal communication.

Music-making as an aspect of developmental play

Making music with children shares many features with a developmental view of play. I often refer to working with pre-school children, in particular, as 'playing with sounds'. As Leonard Bernstein says:

> 'Play' is the very stuff and activity of music; we *play* music on our instruments just as the composer *plays* with notes in the act of inventing it. He *juggles* sound-formations, he *toys* with dynamics, he *glides* and *skips* and *somersaults* through rhythms and colors – in short, he indulges in what Stravinsky called 'Le Jeu de Notes.' The Game of Notes: a striking concept of what music is.[35]

The child will often delight in vocal play even before instruments are introduced. Sounds will be explored, imitated and played with for their own sake. Here, as in play, there are no strict rules. The child discovers that a sound can have an immediate effect on the adult, who in turn will be encouraged to reply, thus building up the beginnings of a close system of interactions. It may take some time for a child with a learning problem to make these connections. A music therapy intervention can certainly facilitate this process, even if several months may be needed for the child to begin to understand. The rewards definitely outweigh the effort of waiting.

Some children may have physical difficulties in handling the instruments or understanding how the instruments sound. There may be spatial or perceptual difficulties. Gradually the child can be supported in exploring an instrument and practising the behaviours, which may not be totally instinctive in the first instance. The child plays with the concept of cause and effect, being responsible for making something beautiful happen. There is often much playful repetition, particularly as the reward is such a rich and pleasurable experience. Much joy is often felt and observed in recognising that 'I' am responsible for that action and for influencing the adult. Such pleasure can also arrive for the most economical of means: a slight movement towards a suspended bell, or a small scrape on the skin of a drum. Even at a receptive level a child can be helped to understand that 'I' have influenced the adult to make that sound by smiling, vocalising or turning to the source of the sound, for example. Such curiosity and playful enjoyment of the most elemental of sounds are not just confined to children. Once we can reassure a group of adults that we are not concerned with musical standards time and time again there is a spontaneous release of pleasure in exploring instruments. When working with adults it is as if a music therapy experience allows the child within to have complete freedom of playful expression.

Making music is a complete experience, based in time and space, with a definite feeling of beginning and end. We are concerned here with processes of gesture and intentionality. The play can be carried through to its conclusion even at the simple level of the placing of one sound or the grouping together of two sounds. Even here there are processes of organisation and integration at work. There is very little time lost in the execution of a musical gesture – for example, between picking up a stick and playing the drum – with the result that children often attend to music for a considerable time. It is not only a complete experience in itself but also playfully appeals to all of the senses. This integrated aspect of music has led some therapists to explore the concepts of sensory integration where the auditory and visual aspects of music can be linked to the development of other areas such as perceptual and motor skills.[36]

Emotionally, play in music can be a means of exploring a whole range of feelings. In many ways a musical instrument can be regarded as taking on, to use Winnicott's terminology, the properties of a 'transitional object'.[37] How can an instrument be a similar source of comfort as a child's security blanket? Alvin notes that instruments could be regarded as prolongations of the body through contact, for example, with hands or mouth, through which feelings of both protection and projection can be explored.[38] A child can look at, touch and even smell an instrument. The object/instrument can be charged with all manner of private feelings by the player yet also used as a means of communication with another person. It can bridge a gap. The child can hear the sounds being immediately reflected back and also experience the play of the adult. The child can begin to explore all the boundaries of self and other. Alvin describes how instruments resist action, however slight, and in so doing provide the player with a sense of mastery and control (this concept is parallel to the psychoanalytical notion of mastering). An instrument will not retaliate, will not speak back; music cannot be hurt, the child (and adult) soon learning that music can sustain a vast range of feelings, even those destructive feelings too frightening to verbalise. Instruments are also consistent objects, which is an important factor when working with insecure children who may need that sense of sameness in their surroundings. Instruments can be invested with special qualities. They can take on specific characteristics or become imaginary figures.

Martin, aged 10, is a child with some physical problems (moderate athetosis) and complex emotional difficulties. His parents were having a crisis in their relationship. Martin used the instruments in his music therapy sessions as part of a kind of 'psycho-opera'. He invested three instruments with the characteristics of his mother, his father and himself. As the weeks progressed Martin was able to use the sessions to explore his feelings and reactions to what was happening in his home life. He sang the statements made by his father to his mother and himself in a deep voice. The responses of his mother were represented by another instrument and with a higher voice. He placed his instrument centrally and sang using his normal voice. All his feelings and reactions were contained within the musical structures that evolved during the therapy. He was able to invest the instruments with a vast array of feelings and explore the various connections and processes of integration.

The processes of Martin's music therapy were carefully supervised and are a clear example of the powerful way in which instruments can take on the profoundest of meanings for a child. An instrument is being used as a bridge – the field of play – between the inner and outer worlds of the child and between the child and the adult.

THE EVIDENCE FOR A DEVELOPMENTAL SEQUENCE: MUSIC IN LATER CHILDHOOD

Until the last example we have been concerned with music and music therapy for young children. What happens to a child's spontaneous music-making during school years? What are some of the other influencing factors? We shall explore such questions in this section and include summaries of music therapy work with older children. As I have noted, there are some observable commonalities within the sequence of a child's musical development alongside the more specific individual differences. One common base for all children, irrespective of any additional musical training, is the influence of the range of musical experiences within their own culture. In the Western musical tradition this has tended to be children's songs and general instrumental activity, although the sustained development of practical music-making in schools is becoming increasingly a staffing, financial and ultimately political issue. Nowadays we need also to add the influence of television, radio and the popular music of the day, with all the shifts, close links to fashion and other interacting influences on the growing child and young adult. It is clear that any sequence of musical development involves a web of complex influences from home, school, the general environment and what each child contributes from their own genetic make-up.

Some commentators have looked to existing theories of child development to understand this sequence. Goodman is one who suggests that musical development could pass through similar phases to those outlined by Piaget.[39] The

Piagetian concept of conservation, the understanding of the invariance of a factor through changes of state, is one area that has attracted much interest from musical psychologists. Pflederer, for example, has done extensive research into the area of conservation and musical development. In one of her projects she found that 8-year-olds were able to attend to more than one musical event simultaneously and far more so than 5-year-olds.[40] Rider has worked on conservation tasks as a means of assessment of cognitive level through musical perception. In one study he set up two auditory conservation tasks, rhythm and tempo, with developmentally delayed children between the ages of 7 and 13. The order of the tasks achieved placed rhythm and tempo at either end of the scale, and Rider concludes that, regardless of developmental delay, conservation of rhythm precedes that of tempo. In a second study he used fifteen musical tasks and there were clear correlations with age, adding support to the use of such tasks in the assessment of cognitive skills.[41] Funk and Whiteside argue that, unlike the classic conservation of objects experiments, a musical equivalent needs to be varied before presentation to a child. The child does not actually witness the transformation process itself.[42] Whether or not musical developments are due to musical conservation may only be one interpretation. Hargreaves notes that results could be influenced by increased memory, attention and perceptual skills and more competent verbal expressiveness among other developing behaviours.[43] Perhaps we could talk more of a discerning musical discrimination than of musical conservation.

Other developmental models have been proposed as bases for a study of musical development. Gardner proposes three stages of artistic development: a pre-symbolic first year or so of life; a development of the use of symbols up to around 7; and a later stage during which earlier processes are being refined.[44] Shuter-Dyson and Gabriel refer to the flexible work of Bruner, who observes that the child is also able to return to re-assess an earlier stage as development goes forward, like the form of a spiral.[45] This link with a spiral is most persuasive and is at the basis of a substantial piece of research recently conducted by June Tillman. She recorded and analysed over 700 compositions of children from age 3 upwards, evolving a sequence of musical development on the figuration of a spiral. Her model is an integration of some of the classic research previously discussed, in particular the work of Moog and Piaget. Tillman noted, as I have done, that most previous work on the developmental musical sequence had concentrated on what a child did in response to sounds. What daily confronts a music therapist working with children is also the musical play of children, what Tillman calls a 'composition' or 'musical offering', by which she stresses the spontaneity of the musical process rather than a rehearsed musical product. She has collaborated with her supervisor, Professor Keith Swanwick, in publishing the results of her work, and Professor Swanwick refers to this study in his book *Music, Mind and Education*.[46] Swanwick and Tillman summarise a sequence of development 'through the stages of Mastery, Imitation and Imaginative play'.[47]

The spiral configuration evolving from Tillman's research presents a carefully constructed model for beginning to understand the complexities of the musical gestures presented by children in music therapy sessions (see Figure 4.1). The model is very flexible, with both vertical two-way movement and right-and-left sideways movement. A child may need to dip down through the spiral to an earlier stage in the sequence as a new stage is assimilated, a feature also common in the adult learning profile. The left side of the spiral seems to represent more individual and the right more social features. Swanwick and Tillman have

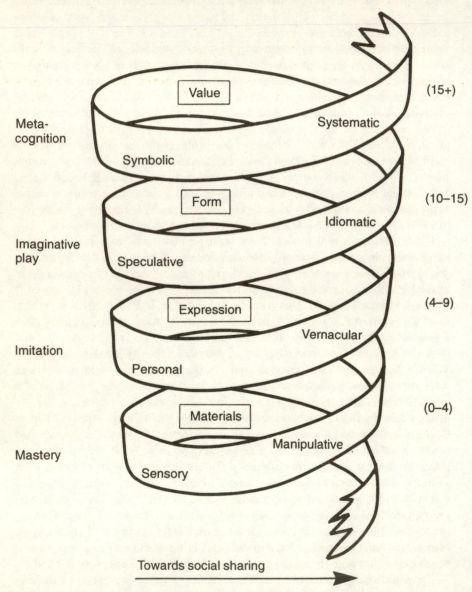

Figure 4.1 The spiral of musical development (Swanwick and Tillman, 1986)

described the various developmental modes, from sensory to systematic, and the themes of mastery, imitation, imaginative play and meta-cognition in very clear detail. I cannot do justice to the significance of this work in a short description of each stage, and readers are strongly recommended to consult the source material for themselves. Practical illustrations of the various modes will be included in the following examples of music therapy work with older children.

MUSIC THERAPY WITH OLDER CHILDREN

In the two following examples we shall try to provide practical illustrations of some of the main theoretical themes outlined in this chapter. By bringing the words 'music' and 'therapy' together we are able to synthesise the two worlds of music and of child psychology.

The story of Julia

Referral and assessment

Julia was 9 years 5 months when referred to music therapy. She had severe language and speech problems both in understanding the content of language and in expressing herself. She was reluctant to initiate any verbal interactions, with resulting isolation from her peers. The speech therapist assessed her verbal comprehension as having the characteristics of that of a child of 3 years 7 months and her expression as that of 2 years 4 months. There were some autistic characteristics in her behaviour such as ritualistic and repetitive play but the language problem was considered by the multi-disciplinary team to be the central root of her difficulties, with the attendant emotional problems. She was attending a language unit, where she was seen for music therapy.

Julia was very responsive to music, a child who by all reports 'loved music'. She adapted immediately with sensitivity to the tempo, levels of loudness and different moods of the music. She followed with almost uncanny accuracy the minute changes and fluctuations within the musical form, pausing and ending phrases in synchrony with me. She appeared to have very flexible rhythmic mobility and could imitate quite complex patterns accurately. She was most secure when she was imitating, which could be seen as a reflection of her language difficulties and the rather 'patterned' nature of her behaviour. She tended to use all the instruments for their rhythmic potential, setting up patterns that she would repeat for the length of an improvisation. If we look at Swanwick and Tillman's spiral, we can assume that she had passed through the 'sensory' mode, with the emphasis on a fascination with the quality of sounds and the extremes of loudness levels. She had developed 'mastery' over the control of a steady pulse and how to manipulate the instruments, the 'manipulative mode'. Her playing was quite impeccable when she was imitating the music she was hearing. On one level she was beginning to understand and assimilate into her playing the rhythmic patterns that were part of the musical conventions surrounding her, the 'vernacular' mode. Although we can see from using the spiral that, to some extent, Julia's music-making is very much age-appropriate, on another level the structures of the musical conventions of rhythmic patterning were contributing to her sense of being 'musically stuck'. At the start of the work she found it almost impossible to initiate even the most simple of musical ideas. Her melodic sense was also not well developed; she imitated some vocal sounds but with few spontaneous sounds. She would sometimes sing favourite songs with rhythmic accuracy but as if the words did not mean much to her. She also spoke quickly and rhythmically accurately but with little vocal shape or modulation. If we look at the spiral again, we might conclude that Julia needed to dip back into earlier modes to explore a more spontaneous reaction to sounds and to be encouraged to be less rhythmically controlled and conventionally ordered. It was very tempting to make quite complex music with Julia as the sessions, again on one level, were musically stimulating and satisfying. But to what extent was this kind of reliance on imitation, on supporting her almost complete rhythmic intelligence, helping her development? There was the danger that this rhythmic emphasis would only increase echolalia (reiterating words and phrases automatically), reinforcing some of her prime difficulties. She would often repeat words after people, and there was a potential trap that her great interest in music would contribute more to this problem. If we were able to encourage a more playful and spontaneous sound-making, there might also be carry-overs into helping her expressive speech. Understandably, she resisted change to this apparently secure world of order and became very frustrated if her needs were not met immediately. Any changes to the security provided by her music would need to be very carefully introduced. It was within her musical behaviour that we could observe some of her most developed skills and at the same time persistent problems.

The early work

The music therapy sessions began by trying to build on this sense of security and trust. A greeting song was composed that encouraged her to extend her rhythmic fluency by adding to and varying the patterns within a pulse framework. Her memory for the detail of this song was apparent, even after one hearing and a Christmas break. To avoid any rhythmic rigidity setting in, I encouraged her to add a rhythmic variation to any already-established pattern. This began to happen in a short Spanish dance that became a feature of our early sessions. She sometimes varied the rhythmic pattern once it had been well established and also began to vocalise spontaneously on vowel sounds in the middle slow section. At the end of this opening period of music therapy – a period of twice-weekly sessions for five months – she was beginning to make the first tentative moves in starting a rhythmic or melodic pattern or activity.

The middle period

During this period we began to encourage her to initiate even the simplest of musical ideas. This meant a return to some of the earliest of sound experiences, inviting Julia, in the first instance, to play one sound. She began tentatively to explore one then two sounds on chime bars, for example. She began to sing the sounds she produced, with increasing accuracy as the weeks progressed. Meanwhile I was aiming to show her that I could imitate her sounds and would try to 'tune in' to the sounds she gave me, first by imitating the sound and then by elaborating on her idea by using it as a basis for a short improvisation. She began to develop more confidence in initiating the activities. After the opening greeting song she would often ask for the chime bars and work hard to give me some simple sounds without becoming too fixed on them. We always returned to more safe musical territory after this more difficult part of the sessions.

Julia would not always tolerate these more difficult parts of the session. On such occasions she would not accept any invitation to start an activity, and this would result in behaviour such as banging the piano keys and rejecting the more melodic instruments. During one such rejection I responded musically to her banging of the piano keys, to which she replied 'very naughty' and indicated a wish to return to a more familiar song. I took a risk by not complying with her wish and continued to play. She began to vocalise with the kind of sounds I had never heard in her sessions. The sounds and the music we made together felt very spontaneous and personally very expressive. I felt that she was trying to share with me some of the difficulties she was facing in this more stressful part of our work together. We worked through this moment and were able to return to such similar spontaneity on future occasions. She began to initiate melodic and rhythmic patterns of more than two sounds. By the end of this six-month middle period she was becoming adept at inventing new patterns, working hard to find variations. This part of the work was still hard for her and during some sessions she would ask for the 'Goodbye' song if she was finding the initiation of ideas difficult. At other times she would leave the room or say a firm 'No'. This resistance was a complete reversal of the earlier instantaneous delight that greeted me on her being introduced to music. In discussing this work both in supervision and with other members of the team it became clearer that Julia was finding it increasingly difficult that the once very safe world of music and rhythmic dependency was becoming another area where some of her problems were being encountered. We felt that it was important to continue to keep working through this resistance with as much support and flexibility as possible.

The final period

We had a final six-month period of weekly music therapy sessions to consolidate some of the progress she had made during the work. It was very clear that her sense of spontaneous and initiative play had developed. We had dipped back through Swanwick and Tillman's spiral to the early sensory mode, with fascination with the quality of simple sounds. We had eased some of her over-fixated reliance on rhythmic imitation. She was beginning to initiate musical gestures by changing the tempo or loudness level herself or by playing deliberately against my music to suit her needs. I recall one beautiful moment when she continued to play after I had finished, laughing as she did so. She had not come to the end of her music – something she would have found very hard to express at the beginning of the work. She was able to pitch with increasing accuracy and could locate and reproduce accurately up to five different pitches in a variety of sequences.

She was able to stay with the more stressful part of the sessions and would tolerate more changes to the expected order of the events in any session. At the end of a total of over sixty sessions her speech therapist commented: 'Music Therapy was particularly helpful with one child (J) in getting her away from a very rigid attitude of mind – helpful in relaxing this attitude to learning (self-imposed).' It was apparent to other observers of the overall period of the work that music therapy had been an appropriate medium for Julia and had made a contribution to her general development over a period of eighteen months. She had used the sessions to move from the very safe areas of rhythmic imitation to the more risky and vulnerable world of flexible interaction with developing responsibility for initiating musical ideas. According to Swanwick and Tillman, we could assume that she had dipped down through the spiral to reassess her spontaneous reactions to sound and that she was now able to be musically and personally more expressive. In some ways she was using her imagination to deviate more from the established 'vernacular' patterns and begin to be more exploratory and 'speculative', a mode Swanwick and Tillman observed in the spontaneous music-making of many 10-year-olds.

Robert and Julian

Referral and assessment

Robert was 9 years 8 months and Julian 9 years 4 months at the time of referral. Both children were attending a school for children with moderate learning difficulties. Both had specific speech problems: Robert – immature speech with articulation problems; Julian – delayed speech with a severe stammer. Such problems resulted in both boys being rather socially isolated from their peer-group. They were good readers but had poor numeracy and drawing skills. In addition Robert often appeared confused and frustrated and Julian had very little confidence and was hypersensitive.

Robert's spontaneous music was very fast and showed no apparent ability to sustain a consistent tempo. There was more semblance of organisation when he was invited to play slower. During the assessment period he began to understand the concept of rhythmic imitation, laughing if his sounds were imitated. He was very reticent in singing, needing a slow tempo and much space for the words to be accurately formed. When he was encouraged to sing louder and support himself rhythmically the words became clearer. He enjoyed the sense of getting louder and was interested in extremely loud and extremely soft music. His musical play appears to match the 'sensory' mode as described by Swanwick and Tillman, with the early signs of some 'mastery' and control in the 'manipulative' mode. Four initial aims were proposed for an opening stage of two weekly music-therapy sessions:

1 for the music to release some of the frustrations he felt in verbal communication, vocalising in music being a kind of bypass
2 to help develop auditory awareness and memory
3 to develop his self-esteem
4 to help develop his ability to share.

Julian's spontaneous music was both slow and fast. Most organisation was in the mid-range of tempi, with confusion and erratic playing at the faster end of the spectrum. He tried hard to follow changes in speed and melodic rhythm and was able to imitate simple rhythmic patterns. He responded to turn-taking and could be engaged in improvisation. At first his playing was very quiet and he would apologise if he felt he had played out of turn or the 'wrong' sort of music. There seemed to be connections between his level of frustration and the degree of stammering and auditory attention. During one of the assessment sessions there was a stream of 'Sorrys' which resulted in an improvisation based on 'Sorry is a funny name'. He found this amusing and even during this one session he became steadily louder in his playing, singing 'Goodbye' at a higher pitch than before. His musical play seemed to show some sense of control ('manipulative mode'), with certain signs of early 'personal expressiveness' according to the Swanwick and Tillman spiral. The aims for the first period of work were:

1 to develop his confidence and sense of initiative
2 to reduce some of his frustrated and fearful behaviour, with an emphasis on
   developing enjoyable and positive experiences
3 to take attention off verbal communication by encouraging a lot of singing –
   spontaneously, of well-known and of specially composed songs.

As there were some similar aims for the two boys, we decided to work towards a stage when joint sessions could be arranged.

The early work

An initial period of twenty individual sessions helped to develop each child's sense of trust in the music therapy setting. Songs and instrumental activities were developed in relation to the needs of each. Robert's 'special song' gave him sufficient time to form the words well, ending with loud and fast music. Julian's song included a chance for him to choose between a loud or a soft version; I recall the memorable day when he asked for the loud version. Robert became increasingly interested in singing songs and would bring song books to the session. He would often invent his own actions for the songs. His playing became less confused and more sustained. He had a particular interest in strumming the guitar while singing, and his singing became louder and more focused. His memory for words increased and he was beginning to listen and interact for longer periods, although playing and singing together for any length of time was difficult for him.

Julian began to request particular instrumental activities and songs with increasing confidence. His rhythmic skills became more controlled, particularly his sensitivity in following the melodic rhythm of songs. He sang with increasing vigour, loudness and confidence. He became less distractable and would sustain concentration throughout a twenty-five-minute session. Towards the end of this first four-month period of music therapy his teacher commented anecdotally that since the intervention of the music therapy he had become more organised and confident in class, with more general awareness of his environment. I recall being moved in observing how the music offered opportunities for his personality to unfold and blossom. There were hardly any 'Sorrys' towards the end of this first stage of the work.

Joint sessions

The first six months of joint sessions focused on the following five areas:

1   Vocal activity

Each child's 'special song' helped to give him a unique musical identity. Songs were played for and to each other, developing an early sense of mutual listening and respect. Other songs were jointly developed and each child was offered a chance to choose.

Each child developed increasing sensitivity to each other's specific speech problems and would allow space to wait for the choice to be articulated. Singing became louder and freer, each child supporting and encouraging the other. We worked on spontaneous vowel and consonant sounds and aimed for increased modulation and vocal inflection. These developments were aided by developing musical fantasies, for example a long car journey up and down hills.

2   Auditory awareness and memory

Both developed further in their memory of details, especially of the words of songs. Robert still had some difficulty in following tempi and Julian was less organised if he became tense or his attention was diverted.

3   Self-organisation

It was interesting to observe how each child developed increasing self-organisation and how this reflected on the other. Sometimes the occasional immature piece of behaviour from one child would be commented on by the other and eventually changed. The two boys themselves evolved their own system for waiting their turn, choice-making and organising how the session would develop. The pattern of interactions between adult and child in the individual session was beginning to be transferred outwards to child and child.

4   Spontaneity

We began to improvise more together once each child was more aware of the other musically, emotionally and spatially. There was a lot of initial over-excitement and playing together, with the inevitable retreat into disorganisation and chaos. Gradually we began to explore such musical parameters as soft/loud, slow/fast. At times Julian would appear very upset by Robert's loud playing, although he had no difficulty at this stage in playing loudly himself. They began to enjoy dancing to each other's music.

5   Reducing frustrations and fearful behaviour

Both boys appeared to develop more confidence and a consistently positive attitude during the sessions. They became more sensitive to each other and tolerant of each other's needs. Rather than withdrawing, they both appeared to be more able to confront difficult and frustrating areas and externalise their feelings. Sometimes this resulted in a refusal of the other's choice, as opposed to passive acceptance, and a moment of healthy negotiation. During this period Julian's teacher reported that he would often shout across the classroom and, for the first time, she had to ask him to speak quieter. His mother also reported that she linked his spurt in confidence and self-assertion to the music therapy. He had sung his 'special drumming song' at home, surprising his family, as he had always been very frightened of loud sounds. Loud sounds became increasingly tolerated in the street. Both of Robert's parents noted he was becoming less withdrawn and more positive. There was an associated improvement in his speech. He was using music more at home, singing to his records.

The final period

There was a final period of six months of joint sessions, supported by the occasional individual session if there was a need to focus attention or build confidence during a difficult patch. During this final stage it was clear that Robert's musical organisation and interest were still closely linked to his mood of the moment. He was clearly now able to accept Julian's needs, listening more, sharing and turn-taking. Julian continued to develop his personal musical expressiveness, finding much support from the music therapy. He began to bring issues that were worrying him to the sessions and was able to verbalise about them.

In order to extend this transference of roles, an older boy from their class was introduced (he had specific speech problems and had also experienced a period of individual music therapy). A music therapy student was also introduced to the group. The new older boy provided a boost to Robert and Julian's musical and social behaviour. He also helped them to tolerate the intrusion of the student. Towards the end of this period both Robert and Julian had developed sufficient confidence to direct the group, including the student, in group improvisations.

CONCLUDING POINTS

Robert and Julian have shown that work can develop from individual therapy to pairing together to small-group work. This follows a natural developmental pattern with the transference of roles from adult and child through to child and other members of the peer group.

All the case examples have reported changes anecdotally. It is clear that the musical behaviour changed as each child progressed through the therapy, and we have seen how this can be loosely described using such tools as the Swanwick and Tillman spiral. The developmental changes have been observed by other colleagues such as speech therapists and teachers; they are not solely the subjective observations of the music therapist. What is grossly lacking from such examples is any controlled measurement of change. The development of measures to observe changes of behaviour in music therapy with children will be the focus of the next chapter.

Chapter 5

Music therapy and child health – a survey of research

INTRODUCTION

When I started out as a music therapy researcher in England in the late 1970s it soon became apparent that much clearer descriptive evidence needed to be collated in order to move on from some of the earlier, more anecdotal, albeit pioneering, summaries of work with children published in the 1960s and the early to mid-1970s.[1] There was mounting pressure from funding agencies and other professionals – especially from doctors and psychologists – to relate practice to eventual outcome and to organise descriptive evidence from within clearer operational and experimental frameworks. In the survey of the *British Journal of Music Therapy* (see Chapter 1) we found that 16 per cent of the surveyed articles concentrated on work with children with wide-ranging disabilities and problems.[2] Of these some discussed the uses of music therapy with children with special needs,[3] others focused on specific conditions: for example, autism, deafness, emotional disturbance, blindness and physical disability.[4] Elaine Streeter used a descriptive case study as the model to discuss the role of the music therapist in the assessment and treatment of a pre-school child with language problems. She pointed out how music therapy is a useful medium for children with such problems and where a mixture of emotional disturbance and or delayed development makes assessment difficult.[5] Of the five British papers categorised in the research group in this *BJMT* survey, three are concerned with children. Campbell McQueen, a music educationalist, devised a test to see if the child's ability to recognise everyday objects improved with a period of music therapy by comparison with a control group. Percentage improvement in scores was discussed without any substantial commentary.[6] John Chesney, a musical clinical psychologist, designed a system to analyse the musical preferences of a group of children with Down's Syndrome.[7] The third paper was a description of the Hammersmith intervention study described below.[8]

A survey of 164 American music therapists highlighted the still commonly held goals of many therapists working with children with learning difficulties. These included development of: attention span; cooperation with peers and adults; eye contact; eye–hand coordination; appropriate use of language; auditory discrimination; and active participation.[9] It is only a small step to organising such goals into question format and more research-based interventions. One such study, as yet unpublished, was carried out in the early 1970s at Goldie Leigh Hospital, south London, on the effects of music therapy on two groups of children with profound disabilities. A period of music therapy was compared with a similar period of attention from a teacher. The study used a standardised developmental test and rating scales to record each child's level of solitary play and interaction with the adult before and after music therapy. The study, although producing inconclusive results, drew attention to the sensitivity needed in devising new measures to record the often very small behavioural changes with the children and the problems involved in using standardised tests.[10]

Two scales were developed by Paul Nordoff and Clive Robbins: 'Child-Therapists Relationship in Musical Activity' and 'Musical Communicativeness', for use in their work with children.[11] These scales are used as assessment tools for therapists trained within this model of working. Their use outside this particular model is hampered by the apparent lack of reliability checks on the definitions used.

Ethologists make detailed descriptions of both animal and human behaviour. Their approach can be helpful to the music therapy researcher attempting to find simple and clear levels of description and to develop a rigorous style of investigation. According to the ethologists, every new discipline needs to carry out extensive periods of direct observation, with the building-up of clear descriptions and systems of classification.[12] From direct observation, categories can be selected and more specific questions asked. If such categories are to be of generalisable use, high levels of inter-observer reliability need to be set. More general and speculative inferences can then flow from the clearly formulated and reliable descriptions. In moving towards a clear description of interpersonal relationships ethologists do not exclude the use of evidence of a more inward-looking nature to establish a sense of meaning.[13] More supportive and subjective data have their place besides the more reliable and quantitative data. For a music therapy researcher also involved in the practice of music therapy a totally strict ethological approach, with the researcher in the role of passive observer, is difficult. The use of video as a recording device can compensate to some extent, since video film can be viewed on more than one playing, with specific questions being asked in sequence. Strong time-based measures can be constructed for video analysis. Such duration and frequency measures as 'total time looking' can attain far higher levels of reliability than the more general bi-polar ratings such as 'relaxed–tense'.

I carried out a series of interlocked projects between 1978 and 1985 that corresponded with this need to develop simpler and stronger methods of describing interactive music therapy with young children with a wide range of disabilities and problems. These projects are summarised below in report format; readers interested in reading material with a less research-based content could now pass to the summary of this chapter.

THE HAMMERSMITH PROJECT (1978–80)

This was an intervention study aimed at assessing the role of music therapy for children with learning difficulties in the district of South Hammersmith, London. By collating observations of children in music therapy we could begin to discover some of the areas where music therapy appeared to be effective. Two research strategies were devised: (a) to assess the benefits of music therapy for the children referred to the project; and (b) to discover the attitudes to the intervention of the staff involved.[14]

During the project eighty children (out of a potential population of 302) were referred to music therapy from the district's four special schools and a pre-school nursery unit for children with special needs. After an assessment period each child was seen individually (see Figure 5.1 for an example of a music therapy assessment sheet). The assessment procedures included detailed observations of the child's behaviour both in music therapy and in the classroom; the teacher's or nursery nurse's observation of a music therapy session; discussions with parents and any other members of the para-medical team; and reference to medical records. Over half of the children were able, at some stage in the project, to be seen in pairs or small groups.

Simple evaluation procedures in the form of questionnaires were used. We wanted to discover if the staff could observe any indications of change in the children that may have been linked to music therapy intervention, and also to explore some of the staff's attitudes to the music therapy intervention. The results from these questionnaires could then become a focus for more rigorous studies in the future.

'Pilot' questionnaire

The first questionnaire was 'pilot' in nature and was designed for use at the nursery to assess the contributions of music therapy after the first eight months of the project. The questionnaire was divided into five main sections: physical skills; perceptual skills and attention; motivation; communication skills; and social behaviour. The two nursery nurses and the music therapist completed questionnaires on the seven children attending the unit. The results were obtained by percentaging the number of 'Yes' responses to whether each observable item of behaviour – for example, 'imitates vocal sounds', 'initiates gestures', 'takes turns' – was 'more than before' the music therapy intervention. The results provided supportive findings to the many intuitive observations. The areas where the staff felt the children responded well in music therapy were highlighted in the results for each child. One 3-year-old boy, for example, had developed over the eight months from being rather quiet and unmotivated in his play (both of instruments and with toys in the nursery) to a livelier, louder and what was inferred to be a generally more confident little boy. In the music therapy sessions he began to vocalise with increasing loudness and to use clear gestures to indicate

Name . . . .

Date . . . .

Rhythmic behaviour/tempo
presence of pulse
organisation of beating
tempo
tempo flexibility
awareness of therapist's tempo
imitation/initiation of rhythmic patterns

Vocal sounds
when
what
spontaneous/imitative

Use of blowing instruments

Reactions to changes
loud/soft: aware   follows
pitch
timbre
particular interests

Problems reflected in the musical behaviour
Motor
gross
fine
Perceptual
initial focusing
concentration
Communication
understanding
expression
Motivation
Emotional behaviour

Additional comments

Figure 5.1 Music therapy assessment sheet

choices – behaviours that staff began to observe in the nursery. His nursery nurse wrote:

> Tom shows a keen interest and enthusiasm for the instruments and indeed the whole music therapy session, tending to 'wake up' at music time. He is much more aware of people and objects about him. He will actually get up from a chair and fetch something to play with – a radical development for Tom. He will share and is much better at taking turns. He defends his own things and makes it clear what he wants.[15]

The results from the questionnaire were also useful as a developmental profile of each child; the children with severe physical disabilities, for example, were not expected during such a short period of time to indicate major changes in physical control. Areas where each child had shown any signs of change or not could then be fed into the future aims. The two overall aims linking all these children – (1) to help focus attention and increase concentration span; (2) to increase and sustain vocal sounds – were interestingly ranked at the top of their respective sections when the results were considered as a whole. At the other end of the ranking of sections was the area of social behaviour, where any development for these very young children was expected to be slow. One very positive spin-off of the questionnaire was that there was more understanding about the particular needs of each child on the part of both the nursery staff and the visiting music therapist.

Children-based questionnaire

The second questionnaire evolved from the 'pilot' and we asked whether the staff at both the nursery unit and the schools considered that music therapy had contributed in any way to the child's general development over the eighteen-month period of intervention. The same main sections were included as in the 'pilot', with an additional section on emotional behaviour. Questions from the previous questionnaire were altered or omitted and additional ones added. The contributory nature was stressed, since the many overlapping and uncontrolled influences in a child's life made it difficult to generalise outwards from the music therapy. A seven-point scale was used, ranging from 1 (definite improvement) to 7 (definite deterioration). Fifteen staff completed questionnaires on thirty-seven of the children under 12 who had regularly attended music therapy throughout the project. The main points from this questionnaire can be grouped as follows.

Progress of the children in music therapy

The spectrum of overall mean scores for each child involved in music therapy ranged from 1.36 to 4.12 (where 4 was equal to 'no effect'). Comments from the same teacher about the two children at either end of this spectrum support such figures:

Child A (very positive overall score of 1.36).
'After an initially reluctant start she rapidly developed an enthusiastic approach to her music therapy. The positive attitude she displayed towards these activities was certainly sustained on her return to class and became responsible for a greater development of self-confidence and a marked improvement in her relationship with her peers and teachers.' (Class Teacher)

The head teacher at this school referred to this child in his general comment at the end of the attitude questionnaire (see below).

Child B ('no effect' of music therapy with a lean to the more negative side of the scale – 4.12).
'He confounded all my expectations that he would benefit from music therapy by using the sessions as an opportunity for regressive, infantile behaviour intended to manipulate the therapist and myself. Whilst this behaviour did not persist between sessions, it was, I felt, sufficiently disturbing to warrant re-evaluation of his involvement in the activity.'

The work with Child B is an example of music's highly arousing nature: even the calmest of musical endings to a session was not sufficient to help him with his over-excitement, the very reason for his referral to music therapy. The session was followed by classroom work, and not a period of outdoor play, where some of the remaining excitement might have been more readily dispelled.

There was a very positive trend to the results from the children who had been part of the music therapy group. This may be related to a possible desire of the staff to provide positive feedback about the work and to please the researcher, what psychologists label the 'social desirability effect'. A consistent result, as with the 'pilot' questionnaire, was the supportive evidence from the staff who knew the children well corroborating the more intuitive observations of the music therapist. There were many instances of items highlighted on an individual questionnaire matching the objectives for the music therapy – detailed objectives not necessarily very familiar to the staff. One teacher wrote about an 11-year-old boy:

I feel that D. was an intelligent but very disturbed child. The therapy he has undergone with the music therapist has almost eliminated this disturbance and consequently his attitude, behaviour and achievement have massively improved. I was delighted to explain all this to his parents at a recent parents' meeting and we look forward to a good school career for D.

During the course of the two-year project D. had sixty-two individual music therapy sessions and seven joint sessions with one of his classmates. He presented as a child with much rigidity and resistance to ideas other than those he initiated himself. For the first part of the therapy he would only respond when he was in charge of the music we made (note the opposite position in Julia's story, described in Chapter 4) and he would set up quite complex patterns and a specific order to the instruments. He began very slowly to listen to my music and follow changes, this resulted in a time, well into the work, when he began to accept and follow my musical ideas, in one session playing a free improvisation for an unbroken period of thirty minutes. We had hoped that he would be able to develop this interactive sharing with a classmate but it proved too difficult for him and we stayed with the individual work. In the later stages of the work he was able to bring very personal issues to the sessions and would freely improvise and work through some of his very confused and isolated feelings. He would create musical journeys and fantasies and accompany himself with his own 'orchestra' of instruments. He was able towards the end of the work to tolerate the extra presence of a music therapy student. When his teacher completed D.'s questionnaire she rated 1 – definite improvement – in the areas 'Development of':

- control of movements
- fine motor skills
- awareness of movement in space
- positive expectation of the music therapist
- motivation to work on return to class
- general verbal understanding
- relationships with adults
- relationships with other children
- awareness of others' needs
- confidence and self-esteem.

and 'Decrease in':

- hyperactivity and impulsiveness
- level of frustration
- negative behaviour.

The list links closely with the recommendations for this child's therapy, which at the outset included:

- to provide a consistent and relaxed setting where he can begin to explore two-way interaction and a sense of sharing at his own pace
- to develop his sense of confidence and trust in the musical relationship prior to involvement in paired and small-group work
- to provide a supportive outlet for his sense of frustration and acute isolation.

Both the aims for therapy and the teacher's final assessment contained factors relating to confidence, awareness, relationship, understanding, isolation, frustration and control. His parents also reported that he was more relaxed at home and that there were fewer temper tantrums than at the start of the music therapy.

Ranking of the main developmental areas

When we analysed the overall scores per section this order emerged:

- motivation (2.54)
- physical skills (2.61)
- perceptual skills and attention (2.68)
- social behaviour and play (2.94)
- communication skills (2.98)
- emotional behaviour (3.12).

There is only a small difference in the overall scores across this ranking, the level 3 still indicating 'slight improvement'.

Music therapy appears from this survey to be a highly motivating medium for these children. Figure 5.2 shows a ranking of the individual statements in the questionnaire according to the priority of each statement given by the staff. The items at the head of each section, such as control of movement, positive expectation of the music, listening, development of self-esteem, corresponded to some of the broad aims of the music therapy intervention.

The range of problems

The thirty-seven children were grouped into eight smaller sub-groups: for example, children with physical disabilities, children with hearing impairments. The results were tested to see if there was any significant difference in scores between the groups.[16] No significant difference was found, confirming no one group had more positive scores. Such a result supported the commonly held notion implying the effective use of music therapy as an efficient therapy able to adapt to the needs of children over a wide range of problems and disabilities.

Difficulties with the questionnaire

It was evident that certain areas were easier for the staff to evaluate than others. Staff expressed problems in attempting to score statements involving references to inner mental states such as anxiety or frustration. Future descriptions needed to be much simpler. The extra attention given to the children in the music therapy group could well have accounted for any of the differences in scores.

Staff-attitude questionnaire

A third questionnaire was used to assess the attitudes of the staff to the intervention. Twenty-five staff (head teachers, teachers, therapists and nursery nurses) completed this attitude questionnaire, which was administered by a student not directly involved in the intervention.

Statistical analysis of the results indicated that the therapists had a significantly more positive overall attitude than the teachers/nursery nurses, with the head teachers in third place. This was an expected result, since the music therapist was working as part of a para-medical team and had most contact with fellow therapists, the intervention being viewed as a therapeutic one.

As one occupational therapist wrote:

Music therapy is a subtle form of therapy and very appropriate for 'difficult' children . . . . The child finds a way of expressing him/herself, enabling the therapist to establish rapport with the child and understand those inner feelings which the child cannot or may not want to verbalise.

1		*Development of positive expectation of music*
2		Development of positive expectation of music therapist
3		*Development of listening ability*
4	" "	*sustaining of concentration*
5	" "	*control of movements*
6=	" "	*confidence and self-esteem*
6=	" "	motivation on immediate return to class
8	" "	focusing of attention
9	" "	organised rhythmic movements
10	" "	*ability to listen and be still*
11	" "	initiation of vocalisations
12=	" "	auditory memory
12=	" "	relationship with adults
12=	" "	ability to initiate an activity
15	" "	bi-manual skills
16=	" "	gross motor movements
16=	" "	fine motor movements
16=	" "	hand/eye coordination
19	" "	alertness
20	" "	reaching out
21	" "	initiation of eye contact
22=	" "	awareness of movement in space
22=	" "	sense of independence
24	" "	body image
25=	" "	sustained interest on return to classroom activity
25=	" "	initiation of gestures
27	" "	relationship with other children
28	" "	imitative play
29		Sustaining a positive attitude and mood
30		Decrease in negative behaviour
31		Development in general verbal behaviour
32		Decrease in fear, tension and anxiety
33=		Development of sense of constructive exploration
33=		Decrease in level of frustration
35=		Development of ability to share
35=	" "	motivation to creativity
37	" "	symbolic play
38	" "	activity to cope with distraction
39=	" "	non-verbal expression of needs
39=	" "	awareness of others' needs
41=		Decrease in hyperactivity and impulsiveness
41=		Decrease in obsessive mannerisms
43		Development of make-believe play
44		Decrease in resistance and aggressive behaviour
45		Development of an alternative mode of communication
46	" "	articulation of speech
47	" "	rhythmic fluency of speech

Figure 5.2 Ranking of Statements

Note: Statements in italics are the first to appear from each of the six sections of the questionnaire.

Financial responsibilities tended to dampen slightly what was still, however, a positive response from the heads of schools and units. One head teacher wrote:

> Although we have not had the time or resources to use any specific measurements the teachers and I have noticed marked changes in behaviour, academic attitudes and social interaction, 99 per cent of which we feel is positive. The detailed and comprehensive music therapy reports added new insights about the children, a valuable and much appreciated contribution . . .. I think of one child in particular [Child A above] who was painfully introverted and could not hold eye contact at all. Now I see her ordering her partner about (almost bullying), this partner being described by most teachers as 'difficult'. She will now hold eye contact with me for about five seconds and return a smile. I feel music therapy has been the main agent in effecting this change . . .. I would like to see music therapy continued at this school with a limited and specific number of children.

There was a general increase in a positive attitude towards music therapy as the project progressed and more was understood about the work. The staff felt that music therapy had a wide range of applications and that it need not be linked specifically to any particular problem or disability (a result that added weight to the finding from the children-based questionnaire). The staff were clear as to the differences between music therapy and music teaching and stated that discussions with the therapist and reading reports had furthered their understanding of the children. The music therapist was able to provide a helpful view of the individual needs of the children from a different perspective. The staff welcomed more permanent intervention. Unlike in the previous questionnaire, where no specific smaller sub-group appeared to benefit most, the staff in this questionnaire itemised their priorities for music therapy work with children in the order:

- children with emotional disturbances
- children with severe language disorders
- children labelled as 'clumsy'
- children with visual impairments
- children with profound learning difficulties
- children with mild learning difficulties
- children with physical disabilities
- children with hearing impairments.

The high positions given to children with emotional problems and severe language disorders parallel commonly expressed views about where music therapy is most appropriate for children. In the second questionnaire many changes relating to the children with hearing impairments were credited to the music therapy intervention. When it came to this 'attitude' questionnaire we found a more widely held view questioning the immediate relevance of music to children with hearing impairments. For the teachers not so closely involved with this group of children the connection between music and the child with a hearing impairment was not so obvious. However, where the staff had an understanding of this potential there was strong support for more music therapy input:

> As a speech therapist I feel music therapy can contribute enormously to the speech and language development of a child especially with emphasis on pitch, rhythm and stress, all vital for speech and language.[17]

The staff concluded their questionnaires with strong agreement that music therapy is a necessary addition to community childcare services and to all types of Special School and Special Care Units. A head physiotherapist wrote: 'I feel that all units catering for handicapped children should be able to call on the expertise of a trained music therapist.' There was a very positive estimate of the benefit of the music therapy intervention to the children referred. Such a positive response occurred despite attempts to balance positively and negatively phrased questions and to randomise the order, the staff tending to reply as positively as with the previous questionnaire about the children involved. In addition to answering the specific questions, nineteen of the staff added their own written comments, some of which have been quoted. Two colleagues and the music therapist coded the various comments, choosing one main theme around which the comments clustered. The following themes were ranked thus:

(a) Music therapy is a necessary part of any team concerned with the care of a child with a disability (seven comments).
(b) Positive changes have been observed due to the intervention of music therapy (four comments).
(c) Music therapy provides further insights into the children's problems (three comments).
(d) Music therapy contributes to general speech and language development (three comments).
(e) Music therapy contributes to general physical coordination (one comment).
(f) Music therapy contributes to social interaction (one comment).

At the end of the project it was also possible to make practical recommendations concerning the number of children seen in one working day. Naturally this number closely relates to the nature of the individual problems of the children and the personal style of each therapist. During this project there was a balance of individual and small-group work, with never more than eight sessions per day; six was more common, with three sessions before and three after lunch. A maximum of eight children made up any group for music therapy. Most sessions were up to a maximum of one hour.

We can criticise this project, with hindsight, for the use of retrospective questionnaires, for the lack of any systematic controls and for the large number of questions presented to the staff both in the attitude and the children-centred questionnaires. Nevertheless it provided a rich body of information that could become a focus for the next project. A final comment from one of the teachers involved summarises what was a very positive intervention study and experience:

Music therapy offers a unique opportunity to a handicapped child to uncover/discover an ability previously not recognised. This can foster communication and build relationships with adults and peers.

THE ISLINGTON/HARINGEY PROJECT (1980)

The previous two-year intervention project raised many questions. We decided to move forward by posing a limited number of very simple and straightforward questions concerning the effectiveness of music therapy with young children. Given that the staff in the previous project indicated the very general effects of music therapy on children with learning difficulties, we now wanted to focus on a few of the key itemised areas. All consultations, particularly with psychologist colleagues, pointed to the need to attempt some way of recording what music therapy offered, if anything at all, over and above natural processes of maturation. We can assume that as children develop changes occur, albeit in some instances at a much slower rate than the norm. Was there any link between the intervention of music therapy and the itemised outcome? Could we find some way of recording that a period of music therapy might contribute significantly to the development of vocalisations, for example?

This project began by formulating three basic questions:

(1) Are there any changes that can be clearly observed in a period of music therapy?
(2) How can any such changes be recorded and analysed?
(3) Are any such changes significantly different from a similar period of general development without exposure to music therapy?[18]

We decided to develop time-based measures and to use video as the main recording tool. This was in line with the work of the ethologists, who pointed out the strong reliability of time-based measures as compared to the more subjective and qualitative measures used in the questionnaires in the previous project. Filming enabled the work to be viewed on more than one occasion in order to ask different questions, the films also being able to be viewed by more than one observer.

Eighteen pre-school children with wide-ranging problems were matched as far as possible, and in spite of the problems involved, for chronological age, developmental age and sex, for inclusion in two groups (see Figure 5.3). Each group had a period of twelve weekly individual sessions and an equal period of time without music therapy, the children therefore acting as their own controls in this basic cross-over research design. There was a similar range of problems in each group. Each child was filmed with the music therapist at strategic points during the project (marked with an asterisk in Figure 5.3). We recorded the first two minutes of play on each of five simple instruments: tambour, chime bar, glockenspiel, maracas and Chinese pipe.

The evaluation passed through various stages.

Group	n.	CA	DA	Sex	Jan.	Mar.	Jul.
1	9	38	18.6	5b, 4g	* ... MT .... * .... *		
2	9	38.4	18.5	5b, 4g	* .... * ... MT .... *		

Figure 5.3 Project design

Notes:

n.   = number in group
CA = chronological age (months)
DA = developmental age (months) – from developmental tests
b, g = boy, girl
*   = first 2 minutes filmed with 5 instruments
MT = music therapy period

Evaluation – stage 1

First, in order to discover if there were any clearly observable changes (question 1), twenty-one students were presented with two thirty-second segments of each child's early and late film from the music therapy part of the project. The presented order of both the segment and the instrument chosen for it was randomly organised. A short fifteen-second gap between each of fourteen pairs of segments provided time for a quick answer to the question: 'Which segment (A or B) comes at the end of the music therapy period?' The students were accurate with their decisions for 81 per cent of the time. This was a strong initial indication that clear changes can be observed in music therapy even with a random order of presentation and instrument used and after only twelve weeks of intervention. We felt that, since the period of twelve weeks was so short, major developmental changes could not be regarded as the main factors in influencing the results. This was confirmed by asking the students to list the criteria they used in reaching their decision. These included: increased eye contact, more social interaction, more general sense of arousal; increases in vocalisations, playing time and reaching out.

Evaluation – stage 2

We decided to explore further the criteria itemised by the students. These were very similar to areas itemised by the staff in the previous project. A standard time-sample of one minute with each instrument at the different stages was examined per child (question 2). Time and frequency measures were used to record changes in the frequency, mean length and time spent in the five areas of:

(a) making the instrument sound (a measure of playing time)
(b) vocalising
(c) looking at the instrument
(d) looking at the adult
(e) looking away.

All the measures reached an acceptable inter-reliability level of over 80 per cent agreement. Over seven hours of video film were analysed in this way.

Evaluation – stage 3

Owing to the equal amounts of time in music therapy and not in music therapy, and the fact that the groups were well matched, it was possible to submit the results to a battery of statistical tests.[19] We were thus able to begin to address our third question relating to significant differences between a period in and one not in music therapy. Analysis of the results indicated significant differences across all the instruments. Such differences were also noted when each instrument was analysed in turn. After this project we were able to make the tentative conclusion that a period of music therapy (even as short as twelve weeks) created changes in behaviour within these sessional measures that were not so apparent in a period without music therapy.

What also interests us here is the practical implication of such time-based results and any potential links with the general processes of developmental psychology outlined in the previous chapter.

The very basic nature of the drum (tambour) and the maracas seemed to produce a marked effect on the children, stimulating a lot of playing and attention from them. Response to such instruments can be regarded as motoric, reflexive or elemental. The durational and rhythmic potential of the drum and the tactile and sound quality of the maracas seemed to make a direct appeal to the children. The sustained and highly melodic nature of the pitched instruments, the pipe and glockenspiel, provoked much looking at the adult. The rather complex chime bar and beater, sometimes needing a two-handed organisation of both bar and beater, was not as successful with the children as had been expected.

The playing measure (making the instrument sound) was useful in a general sense provided that in future the different levels of organisation within such a measure could be itemised. The two groups followed the hypothesised trend, with longer contact with the instruments at the end of the music therapy period. An increase in total time playing an instrument is not wholly congruent with a more developed use of the instrument and musical ideas. A child may play for a longer period, but that play may be random and disorganised. A child playing fewer sounds for a shorter total time may use the instrument in a more developed way. Nevertheless what this increase in time may indicate is an increased motivation to explore and make contact with an instrument which has become more familiar over time. Owing to the short attention manifested by most of the children in the project, this very crude measure can still be regarded as a basic indicator of change.

The vocalisation measure produced the most significant changes across all the instruments. The time-based results were backed up by sessional notes and intuitive observations by the music therapist, who noted that the children vocalised for increasing lengths of time as the music therapy sessions evolved. The support and encouragement of vocal sounds were a major aim for most of the children, many being at a pre-verbal stage. Making music and being surrounded by musical sounds appeared to stimulate such spontaneous vocalising. As in the playing measure, this change may be closely related to the growing trust developed between child and therapist, with the child feeling increasingly comfortable in freely exploring vocal sounds with the therapist. As with the playing measure, the next project needed to provide some more qualitative support on the levels of organisation within the more global time-based measures. At this stage we can say that the vocalisation results reinforce the use of music therapy as a stimulus and a support for spontaneous vocalising when working non-verbally. There are clear parallels with the areas of non-verbal behaviour discussed earlier: the beginning and ending of sounds, intonation, turn-taking, imitation, initiation, length of sounds, number of sounds, timing and phrasing. The development of vocal activity is an area where music therapy has an important contribution to make to a child's development, linking with speech therapy where appropriate.

The looking measures are closely interlinked. Music therapy appears to be able to reduce the amount of looking away and conversely to focus the looking at the instrument and the adult therapist. We can link these measures to a simple assessment of part of a child's attentive behaviour. Looking at all five instruments seemed to be well focused at the start of the intervention. Instruments do seem to attract a child's immediate curiosity and interest. The chime bar, maracas and drum increased the amount of looking at the instrument during the music therapy period. As mentioned before, the melodic instruments seemed to produce the most looking at the adult. There are wide individual differences with these looking measures, and the situation is far more complicated than such a basic analysis suggests. It is quite possible, for example, to attend to music while looking away from the source of sound – how often do we find ourselves closing our eyes when listening to music? Nevertheless, given the fact that many children in this project were finding major problems in looking at both objects and even familiar adults, the results of these looking measures are further positive indicators of the relevance of music therapy for this age-group.

The results of this project also highlighted the need for a longer period of intervention to see if any of the observed changes in behaviour could be sustained. There was often a marked fall-off effect after the period of music therapy, when the children were not having the weekly intervention. Coming back to film the children in a music therapy context after twelve weeks of no intervention also posed ethical and methodological questions.

In conclusion we can state that music therapy does appear to have a marked influence on the selected range of developmental behaviours when observed and analysed within sessions and when compared to a period of general development without music therapy. We were able to give positive answers to the three opening questions. The time-based measures used were very basic, specifically selected as the result of observations from other observers. In no way does this project begin to concentrate on any of the inner processes that many therapists consider to be at the heart of music therapy.

As in the Hammersmith project, where some funding for sessions was set aside, a further positive outcome of this short period of intervention was that at two of the three units involved funding was found for half-day sessions so that other therapists could continue to develop the work.

THE HACKNEY PROJECT (1981)

The fundamental challenge to emerge from the previous short period of intervention was whether the changes resulted simply because of the amount of sustained attention. Would similar changes have resulted from a different kind of attention: for example, a walk to the park or individual play with other objects? What is so special about music, and what are the processes common to other forms of intervention? To begin to answer these more complex questions a longer project was set up in one special school in Hackney, with individual play with the classroom teacher or assistant being used as a further baseline for comparison. It was predicted that music therapy might have certain features in common with developmental play and that such comparisons would also indicate some of the qualities specific to music therapy. A longer intervention over three school terms would also enable more note to be made of any fall-off effect as observed in the previous shorter period of intervention. With the three conditions of music therapy, no music therapy, and individual play it might also be possible to begin to look at the difficult issue of generalisation from any changes.[20]

No attempt was made to match groups in this project. After consultations with staff and parents, a random allocation of children from the special care unit, the nursery and two junior classrooms resulted in two balanced groups of eight children, the average age being 7½. None of the children had any recognisable speech.

The cross-over design of the previous project was extended to include the additional filming of each child's play with the familiar adult. Two complete music therapy sessions were also filmed at the specific cross-over points. There were no restraints on filming or on kinds of instruments used; a piano was also available for this project.

The same time-based measures were used as in the previous project, to see if the earlier significant results were replicated over a more extended period of time. The same measures were applied to the play sessions, 'instrument' being replaced by 'toy'. The total time of each session was analysed, with percentages of the total time used in the comparisons. This resulted in a great amount of video to analyse – over six and a half hours of play sessions and twenty-seven and a half hours of music therapy.

A series of six attempts was also made, with the help of a patient group of music therapy students, at constructing a rating scale that would analyse some of the more qualitative material, discussed in relation to the results from the previous project. The final version (see Figure 5.4) only contained descriptions that reached over 80 per cent inter-observer reliability. A standard sample of the first five minutes of each play and music-therapy film was divided into twenty fifteen-second intervals. A fifteen-second gap was allowed between each segment for the observers to make the rating.

Evaluation

A more complex battery of statistical tests using repeated measures was used for this project, which involved computer analysis.[21] The major findings from the time-based measures were:

- On average a longer time was spent playing with the toys than with the musical instruments.
- There were very significant differences in the amount of vocal activity between music therapy, play and no music therapy, with the music therapy clearly effecting changes – a major finding, replicating earlier evidence.
- There was a tendency to look more at the objects in the play sessions than in the music sessions, although most of the looking in the music therapy occurred towards the end of the intervention for both groups.
- There was more looking at the adult, on average, in the music therapy sessions than in the play sessions.
- Although there was more looking away, on average, in the music therapy than in the play sessions, the amount of looking away was reduced at the end of the music therapy period, as compared to a more static profile in the play.
- There was not the degree of fall-off effect at the end of the no-music therapy period for the first music group that had been observed in the previous project, indicating that some progress was beginning to be sustained.

With the rating scale there was an expected developmental progress within the changes in the level of organisation in the children's playing across all the results during the duration of the project, most changes occurring within the music therapy periods. Other general findings were:

(a) The mirroring of some changes in the music therapy within the play sessions indicates that there may be links between the introduction of music therapy and general changes outside music therapy.
(b) Music therapy appears to share with play the ability to effect and sustain changes in the amount of activity that is related to the context, with an increase in related and decrease in unrelated activity in both play and music as the project evolved: for example, a child would play more instruments or vocalise in the music therapy, and play with the toys more effectively, as the project developed and the child became more accustomed to the setting.
(c) There were trends suggesting that music therapy was able to reduce the amount of interruptive behaviour within the sessions, with some evidence that this was beginning to transfer from the music therapy.

Section A
Motor activity (playing)

0 – no observable activity

1 – activity is disorganised, e.g. out of control, chaotic

2 – activity tends towards being disorganised

3 – not sure, neither disorganised nor organised

4 – tends towards being organised

5 – activity is organised, e.g. clear, definite

Score: 0–5

Is the activity related (R) / unrelated (U) to context?
Code: R or U
Does the child make any interruptive movements, e.g. head-banging,
hand-flapping, throwing of objects?
Code: M for Yes or X for No

Section B
Vocal activity

0 – no vocal activity

1 – the child vocalises in a free sing-song manner, i.e. without using
recognisable consonants

2 – the child vocalises using clear single or double syllables, e.g. da, goo,
ah-da, etc.

3 – the child vocalises in a continuous stream (i.e. more than two syllables)
of clear, recognisable syllables, e.g. da da ba-da oo-ah . . . .

4 – the child uses a recognisable word

5 – the child uses two or more recognisable words together

Score: 0–5 Score the highest level reached during the interval sampled: do not
include crying, sighing, laughing or effort noises.

Is the activity related (R) or unrelated (U) to context?
Code: R or U

Section C
Levels of activity

Is the activity *sustained* or not?
Code: S for Yes or X for No

Does the child *imitate* the adult or not? This implies a one-to-one
correspondence between the child's imitation of the adult's act – gesture,
sound, etc.
Code: 1 for Yes or X for No.

Does the child *begin* a new activity or not? This implies that the child starts a
new activity or changes the direction within an activity.
Code: B for Yes or X for No

Is the child's activity *mostly* :

- child-centred (C), i.e. self-centred activities such as sucking or mouthing
  toys, brushing own hair;
- object-centred (O), i.e. manipulation, exploring or playing with the objects;
- adult-related (A), i.e. incorporating the adult into the activity; touching,
  looking at or reaching out to the adult?

Code: C, O or A

Section D
Modes of interaction (please note most prevalent mode with *)

Is the *adult supporting* the child's activity or not, e.g. imitating the child or
following the child's ideas?
Code: AS for Yes or X for No

Is the *adult directing* the child's activity or not, e.g. encouraging the child to
imitate or choosing an activity for the child?
Code: AD for Yes or X for No

Is there any *turn-taking* or not, i.e. both adult and child taking a share in the
direction and running of the activity?
Code: TT for Yes or X for No

Figure 5.4 Rating scale for qualitative analysis

(d) There was significantly less vocal activity unrelated to context in the music therapy sessions than in the play. Most related vocal activity seemed to appear at the end of the music therapy period.

(e) Over time it appears that a period of music therapy can contribute to a child's increasing ability to sustain and initiate activities and to imitate the adult.

(f) Developmental trends were observed, with more object-centred and adult-related behaviour as the children became older during the project. There was less child-centred activity throughout the project as a whole, with less in the music therapy than in the play sessions.

(g) There were very significant differences between the level of active adult support in the music therapy and the play sessions. There was much more adult support in the music therapy, particularly at the start of the project. The pattern changed, with more adult direction and turn-taking as the children became familiar with the music and the music therapist. Such patterns are consistent with the approach adopted during the project, a high level of child-centred focus at the start moving towards more reciprocal interaction and sense of partnership. Conversely, there was more adult direction in the play sessions than in the music therapy.

(h) One of the major findings of this project is that music therapy can contribute significantly to the development of turn-taking. There are many opportunities within music-making for a child with problems to build up a repertoire of shared events and meanings with the therapist. This flexible and reciprocal interacting is a central theme of this work with children, with its emphasis on linking with natural processes in child development that appear to run parallel in musical interaction. An intuitive hunch about such a parallel can now be substantiated by evidence from practice.

Summary

In spite of the maturational changes over a longer period of intervention, it is clear that the results of this project indicate that music therapy can effect changes over a wide range of behaviours. Some of these changes share features with patterns in a play setting, but others, such as vocalisations and turn-taking, appear to be more specific to music therapy. What is now needed is for developmentally based music therapists to run even longer projects, with a return after a period of six months to a year to chart whether any of the changes have been sustained and used as building-blocks to even more changes in behaviour. As in all research of this kind, one series of questions leads systematically on to the next and there always appears to be another set of ideas resulting from the previous work.

CONCLUDING POINTS

It is clear from these three inter-linked projects that music therapy has a specific role to play in child health. We can look to our understanding of a child's developing use of music to understand some of the processes involved. The three projects also highlighted the proposed links that can be made with processes in early child development. These links can contribute to an academic base to music therapy and add to its increasing validity as a para-medical discipline providing a coherent service for children with all kinds of problems and difficulties. We are now also at the stage when more descriptive evidence from work with children can further our understanding of the music therapy process. We can then begin to link the process of music therapy to the therapeutic outcome and to develop research that integrates both of these important facets.

What was lacking from all three studies was any carefully researched attempt to link individual aims to outcome. The Hammersmith study provided some information in the form of individual results from the questionnaires. Much interesting information is lost in examining trends in group-based studies. One appropriate model could be more single-case studies with careful preparation of baseline measures and questions. With the general kind of research reported in this chapter there is the problem of reducing a highly complex stream of events and information to a very basic level. Whole projects, for example, could be devoted to the quantity and quality of the vocalisations that spontaneously emerge during music-making. We have indicated that changes do occur in such an area, and now more complex questions can be addressed. Other areas that are open to extensive music therapy research include:

- the process of imitation
- the process of initiation of ideas
- any links between rhythmic patterning and the development of both language and motor skills
- the phrasing and timing of responses between child and therapist
- the emotional responses of children to music
- music-making as a form of play
- the notion of the musical instrument becoming an intermediary or transitional object
- motivation in music-making
- the development of physical skills
- improvisation and the links with fantasy and make-believe.

Such a list focuses mostly on the processes of music therapy. There are also further outcome-based questions to be asked. We could develop whole surveys of the relevance of music therapy to different conditions: for example, the use of music therapy for children with cerebral palsy, cancer or severe language disorders, to list only three areas. We could look at the most efficient strategies for intervention. In work with pre-school children, research may help us discover, for example, whether an optimum use of a music therapist's time and skills is in supporting the parents and other carers by providing ideas for child-centred music-making rather than in a course of weekly individual music therapy in an isolated room. None of the projects described in this chapter examined the interactions between the daily carers and the child, although information was constantly being fed back to the important adults in the child's life. Some recent research is beginning to address this issue. Auriel Warwick and Pierette Muller have recently carried out some research into music therapy with autistic children and their mothers. Part of the research focused on the mother's involvement in the interactions. Sessions took place in the children's homes, and all the children in the project were seen for both individual music therapy and joint sessions with their mothers. The researchers feel there is a real need for music therapy in the family, and Auriel Warwick writes:

> Music has its place for all of us as a solitary and passive experience but I am convinced that its great worth is in sharing and communicating feeling that, especially within the family, may be too difficult or elusive to express in words.[22]

Chapter 6

Music therapy and adult health

INTRODUCTION

Music plays an important part in most people's lives. A sequence of musical development relating to childhood and young adulthood was outlined in Chapter 4. Are there further developments in the older adult's musical profile? What are the relationships between an adult's personal history and musical preferences? Links between processes in music therapy and child development were proposed in the last two chapters. Are there significant features of the entire life-span's development that can relate to music therapy? In this chapter we shall explore some of the links between music therapy and a life-span approach to development. We shall examine the key part improvisation plays in music therapy. The main clinical focus of the chapter will be a summary of project work within the field of mental health and at a centre for cancer care. In the next chapter other uses of music therapy, for example for adults with learning difficulties, will be summarised.

THE ADULT MUSICAL PROFILE

Most of us will be able to recall a favourite tune, sing it or tap out its rhythm. People can remember the shapes and patterns of music. Singing in church or a 'sing-song' in the pub, nowadays more likely to be singing to a pre-recorded backing track, are examples of a more public musical expression. But, as discussed in Chapter 3, the de-ritualization of present Western culture provides fewer opportunities for such joint musical celebrations. This pattern increases a division between people who listen to music, the passive receivers, and those who take an active part, the musical players. One result is the adulation of prodigious musical skills, be they of a Jimi Hendrix, Alfred Brendel, Maria Callas or Miles Davis.

We are all exposed to the surrounding musical culture with its wide range of musical styles. To some extent we all share in this musical tradition. If we take the musical element of melody, for example, we observe that there are similar adult and childhood profiles. On one level we all know of people who have problems pitching notes; on another level there are people who can keep to a melodic shape within a given tonality but who make an occasional slip with the size of a musical interval.[1] A preference for tonal melodies is also a feature of this adult melodic profile, with more interest in well-known melodies and superior discrimination of tonal rather than more atonal sequences.

The influence of musical training

Musical training is likely to be the main area that causes the separation between the musician and the so-called non-musician, a term that can only contribute further to the lack of confidence often expressed by the musically untrained. Yet the trained and the untrained musician can have similar fundamental emotional responses to the same piece of music. The untrained musician may use analogy and metaphor to describe the experience: the trained musician may do likewise but add additional musical descriptors. Repeated hearings may enable both to explore more of the music at a deeper level. What seems to separate the trained musician from the casual listener is the degree of information retained. A casual listener may only recall the important details in the foreground of the music, for example the main themes, whereas the trained musician would be able to relate this information to the underlying background processes and larger musical forms. It is a question of both the focus and the degree of attention. The division is relative when the most seasoned professional musician is likely to be out-classed in listening abilities by the skills of a genius such as Mozart or Britten. As a conductor I can focus my attention and be aware of mistakes and problems in ensemble, making corrections over repeated hearings. Such awareness pales in comparison with the attentive listening of a great conductor of the calibre of Boulez, who can locate, according to reports, such details as a tuning error made by a specific player in complex orchestral music.

A relative degree of skill is also found in the ability to read music. On the one hand some people find it extremely difficult to grasp even the basics of musical notation. On the other hand there are some trained musicians who can sit down to read a new musical score as if reading a novel, with an accurate and internal hearing of the complex relationships between the sounds. Such a musician may also be hearing the relative, or even absolute, pitch of the sounds. Whether or not people can read music to any degree does not prevent them becoming actively engaged in musical performance. There are many adults who use their musical memories to learn by rote. My work as a conductor brings me in contact with people at all stages of musical training and specialisation. What continues to move me is the commitment to music-making shown by people who find reading music difficult. Members of an amateur chorus will work between rehearsals with a friend to learn the music from the previous week. Once fully internalised, the music, mistakes and all, becomes well fixed. Notation hardly surfaces as an issue in more tribal uses of music where complex musical patterns are passed down through the generations as cultural mainsprings of the society. Here there are fewer divisions between specialists and generalists; the culture considers everybody to be part of the human expressions of music and dance, many cultures not even having a word for music.

Learning a musical instrument involves a most sophisticated range of physical skills. The old maxim 'it's never too late to learn' applies to some extent to the learning of an instrument. We are witnessing a very healthy interest in adult education: practical musical instruction on a variety of musical instruments is becoming increasingly popular. A child starting to play an instrument at an early age will have opportunities to develop the physical dexterity required to play an instrument. Obviously in later life we can build on a strong motivation to learn, but there may be a plateau level we can reach as regards instrumental and physical dexterity. But, like the singer, we are still able to take part as a musical performer in a general sense.

As we shall discover in the examples later, adults referred for either individual or group music therapy will have very different personal musical histories. The range of musical tastes will vary; some people will have had music lessons as children; some people will be able to read music, others not. There are degrees to which people feel comfortable singing and playing musical instruments. At the start of a music therapy group or a staff workshop we are often met with comments such as: 'I'm not musical'; 'I was never good at music at school'; or 'I can't sing.' People who have had some degree of musical training are often encouraged by other members of the group to perform or 'show us how it's done'. Very often though it is the people with the musical training who find it difficult to improvise and free themselves from the constraints of the musical strait-jacketing that pervades some of the more formal and exam-ridden traditional musical teaching. Later in life, as adults, we often have to search long and hard to rediscover a child's more open spontaneity, to free ourselves from the fears, doubts and competitive attitudes that beset us while singing or making music – and this can happen at all levels of music-making.

The relationship of musical training and personal history to free musical exploration presents a challenge to music therapists in supporting people as they discover or re-discover their potential for making music. It also has implications for the kinds of music presented to adults, one example being the debate amongst music therapists of the balance of improvised and pre-composed music – especially old-time songs – when working with the elderly.

THE USE OF IMPROVISATION IN ADULT MUSIC THERAPY

A group of music therapists began to explore their feelings that emerged when taking part in an improvisation workshop as part of a two-day conference held in Bristol in 1986. Most of the therapists had experience facilitating groups, specifically in the adult mental health field. Several relevant themes emerged and they are grouped here in three ways: themes relating mainly to (a) the music; (b) the group process; and (c) the overlap between (a) and (b).

(a) The music

- playing new instruments is a mixture of both enjoyment and anxiety
- people need time to get used to their instrument and to explore some of its potential
- the initial improvisations were very fragmented, some people finding this quite disorientating
- the choice of instruments and why
- rhythm is a key element for organising and changing the musical nature of the group
- the dominance of certain instruments
- listening to others and choosing when and when not to play, choosing not to play having a strong effect on the group
- an emphasis on aural awareness and sensitivity to musical cues, without the constant need for eye contact
- the use of open-ended structures that can lead to more imposed structures if the group wishes, with boundaries and ground rules understood and agreed by the group, for example permission to play loudly, chaotically and arhythmically
- the safety of the musical structures and how they are developed: for/by the group or for/by the therapist
- perhaps it is not what you play but how you play.

(b) The group process

- trust needs to be established with other members of the group before feelings can be shared
- issues surrounding leadership: not leading or wanting to lead, the group identifying a leader and giving or not giving permission for this person to lead
- giving space for other members of the group.

(c) Overlapping themes

- the pleasing feelings of playing for oneself, taking care of oneself
- the developing feelings of self-identification through the music: 'my sound' or 'my instrument'
- the relief of working through issues musically without the need for words
- the portrayal of group processes in the musical processes
- getting to know other people through making music together
- music providing opportunities to feel more relaxed and to share in a common activity
- the respect for the silence after the music and the delicacy of what was then said
- the balance of verbal and musical content, for some people words are very necessary where for others they get in the way of the feelings experienced in the music.[2]

Some of the goals of improvisation in music therapy

There is a great deal of discussion among music therapists concerning the central position of improvisation in both individual and group work and for both child and adult alike. Is improvisation a means of helping people contact some of their deepest feelings? Is the expression an authentic reflection of self? Is it possible to hide behind the music, to use music as a defence or even be untruthful in music? As discussed in Chapter 3, it is evident that the forms of music have been invested for centuries with some of our deepest feelings and impulses. In music therapy people talk of music helping them to release a feeling, to articulate in a musical gesture a feeling for which they find words inadequate. At the end of such musical experiences it is as if we are temporarily suspended in a different time framework when the problems associated with finding meaningful connections in words are often insurmountable, a kind of transcendental experience. People can articulate in musical form feelings and impulses that in other forms could be quite alarming, destructive or even harmful. This could go towards explaining why we can tolerate listening to the ritualistic frenzy of Stravinsky's *Rite of Spring* or the implied incestuous coupling at the end of the first act of Wagner's *Die Walküre*. In musical improvisations people can find release of a wide range of emotions and often some resolution of what is hurting and painful.

There is such a diverse range to the styles of improvisation in music therapy that a leading American music therapist, Kenneth Bruscia, has recently compiled a comprehensive text, *Improvisational Models in Music Therapy*. In his chapter on definitions Bruscia refers to the 'inventive, spontaneous, extemporaneous, resourceful' nature of improvising in music therapy: 'It involves creating and playing simultaneously.'[3] Sometimes the end-result of an improvisation may be more akin to what Bruscia describes as simple 'sound forms', where the emphasis is on the process rather than the final artistic musical product. Music therapists are trained to work at the highest musical levels yet can adapt to a vast range of sound and musical forms that make up the improvisations created by clients of all ages. I am reminded of one of the practical mottoes of my teacher Margaret Percival: 'adapt or perish' seems a very appropriate maxim to keep in mind while responding to the sound and musical gestures which we meet while encouraging people to improvise.

Bruscia lists the general goals of improvisational music therapy as:

- awareness of self, physically, emotionally, intellectually and socially
- awareness of physical environment
- awareness of others, including significant persons in the family, peers and groups
- perception and discrimination in sensorimotor areas
- insight about self, others and the environment
- self-expression
- interpersonal communication
- integration of self (sensorimotor experiences, levels of consciousness, parts of self, time, roles etc.)

- interpersonal relationships with significant others, peers, and groups
- personal and interpersonal freedom.[4]

Dr Bruscia discusses the use of improvisation in assessment, treatment and evaluation.[5] Active and receptive issues concern him, as does the debate relating to the balance of musical and verbal content within sessions. He adds weight to a main theme of this book, namely the relationship of the approach to improvisation and the therapist's underlying philosophy and treatment method. Bruscia also observes that there are two basic groupings to the various improvisational models and to running sessions. On the one hand there is an emphasis on structured activities, usually directed by the therapist, and on the other a more free-floating approach. We could also describe the models as part of a continuum ranging from a directive to a non-directive approach, with all the subtle moves between the two extremes. A structured or directed session seems to have a clear beginning, middle and end with moves towards and away from a central focus. This was the format of the group session described in Chapter 2. In the other kind of free-floating or non-directive session the emphasis appears to be more client-centred, with fluctuating changes of direction moment by moment. This was the format of the individual session described in Chapter 2. Bruscia confirms that there is a general tendency for group practice to favour a more structured approach, and individual practice a more free-floating one.

MUSIC THERAPY AND ADULT MENTAL HEALTH

In Chapter 1 we saw how music therapy has been used throughout history as a general diversion in alleviating mental strain and distress and that only recently has its full potential as a therapy for adult health begun to be recognised and studied. Within the psychiatric services in this country music therapy departments began to be set up within the large institutions for adults with mental health problems. Music therapists have developed services across the whole range of ages and problems: long-stay work with chronically ill people; short-stay acute work; specific work with young people or the elderly. In line with the present resettlement plans, music therapists are also beginning to develop services in small day hospitals, community-based centres and hostels. The work described in this section is project work based at both a large institution and a smaller unit of a general hospital.

A tradition of a very musically active approach has evolved in the UK, with clients being encouraged to create or listen to live music. A wide range of musical styles is employed, with an emphasis on music being improvised with the clients. Pre-composed music has its place and again the range is wide: folk music, classical, jazz, traditional songs and current popular music. Interaction through the music, both between members of the group and with the therapist, is stressed. This emphasis on a wide musical base has led to the British pattern of therapists requiring a strong musical background before training. The dependence on live over recorded music and the development of interactions with the therapist are highlighted in Helen Odell's review of her music therapy approach in mental health work.[6] In the UK there tends to be a predominance of group work, although individual referrals do come through consultants and other members of the clinical teams, the balance being dependent on the approach of the particular unit or hospital and the therapist's orientation.

In Chapter 2 we surveyed some of the connections between psychoanalytical theory and music, with the conclusion that at present there is no clear psychodynamic meaning of music. However, some music therapists do relate their work to processes in psychoanalytical theory. The most widely known and internationally respected British therapist in this field is Mary Priestley. In her specialised form of 'Exploratory Music Therapy' (originally called 'Analytical Music Therapy') the client is encouraged to talk through the issues being brought to the session, as in a normal analytical session, before exploring the issues in the musical improvisation. Very often the therapist and client will adopt a particular musical stance. If, for example, the client presented difficulties in expressing anger, during the first section of the improvisation the client may choose to play out some angry feelings with the therapist representing the more controlling side of the client's personality; in the second section the roles might be reversed. In order for the two split parts to be heard and integrated, Mary Priestley plays back a tape-recording of the improvisation. The client hears all the sections of the music and is helped to recognise all the component parts of the whole improvisation. The final discussion is then an opportunity for some of these musical insights to be processed verbally. We read in Priestley's descriptions of her work that much of what takes place in the musical interaction can be regarded as a reflection or analogue of various internal processes.[7] Helen Odell also refers to a psychodynamic approach in her work, distinguishing between this approach which includes all relationship issues – self, family, friends – and an organic more physiologically based approach: 'the music therapy group focuses on what is happening within and between members of the group, and this can be heard in the music, and worked with in a dynamic way to help clients understand more about themselves'.[8]

There is no typical session, but in general a group session may begin with a warm-up period in the form of some listening, exploration of the instruments or rhythmic work. Out of this opening period may emerge a musical idea, issue or theme that can be explored in an improvisation. Emotional reactions to the improvised music may help to focus an individual's problem and lead to further improvisation. Some common themes may emerge that resonate with many members of the group, and such themes often develop into longer improvisations. The improvisations may spark off some verbal discussion on the feelings created by making or listening to the music. Sometimes the music is recorded and played back to the group. The group members may gain further insights about their responses, their behaviour in the group, their relationships with each other and the therapist. Either an individual's problem or an aspect of the life of the group can be addressed musically. There may or may not be some form of summing-up or winding-down to form a close to the session. In her breakdown of what may happen in a group session Odell also adds:

- silence, owing to resistance, preparation, relaxation, 'stuckness', sadness, thoughtfulness
- movement in order to generate energy
- role-play of a particular situation.[9]

Groups tend to run for at least an hour. The size of the group is related to the particular therapeutic style; a group of up to eight clients is not uncommon. Reference is continually being made to the use of high-quality tuned and untuned instruments, a range of instruments that is challenging to a group of adults with wide-ranging musical preferences and histories.

Project 1: music therapy in a large institution

In 1984 I set up, with music therapist colleague Alison Levinge, an exploratory project at a large psychiatric hospital.[10] The aim of the project was to explore how music therapy could be beneficial for people diagnosed as schizophrenic. We were advised to focus on two groups of people in this large institution: people living in the long-stay and those in the shorter-stay rehabilitation wards. We asked the consultants for referrals from these two areas. Members of the project's steering committee suggested an upper age of 60. Referrals were made if a diagnosis of schizophrenia was written in the medical notes; people with other diagnoses, such as affective disorder or brain damage, were excluded even if a superimposed diagnosis of schizophrenia had been made. A total of twenty-one people with chronic schizophrenia were referred from the long-stay wards and twenty-nine from the shorter-stay.

In the early 'pilot' exploratory sessions for people from both of these areas of the hospital we observed that members of all the groups had problems in making choices. We had wanted to adopt a very non-directive approach, with the clients being supported in their uses of the instruments and music. With people from the long-stay area such an approach was met by a feeling of lethargy and confusion. We felt that this may have been a reaction stemming from the effects of institutionalisation. We needed to adopt a slightly more directive approach.

When Jack (long-stay area) was invited to choose an instrument he became rather overwhelmed by the choice. He was presented with two small instruments to play his music to the group. Instead of playing he would hold the beaters in a rigid pattern and repeat stereotyped and 'out of context' verbal phrases. After some gentle persuasion we were able to help him play some sounds, turning his attention away from the stream of words to the musical sounds.

We were told by the nursing staff that John (shorter-stay area) enjoyed listening to music. As part of a more directive approach at the start of the session we would often pass a large instrument such as a xylophone around the group for each member of the group to play some opening music supported by one of the music therapists at the keyboard. On more than one occasion when it came to his turn, John would take up a very rigid position, holding the beaters in a fixed position, high over the instrument. During one of these moments he commented, 'I'm stuck, I'm stuck.' As I was holding the instrument quite close in front of him I felt that my presence was contributing to his sense of being overwhelmed and stuck. I moved away. The piano music may have been overpowering, and my colleague played shorter phrases with many gaps in the music. John began to respond slowly to these supportive calls from the keyboard. We tried to communicate that we understood how he felt stuck, and he was invited to reply to the piano and vocal ideas. He tried out a few fragments of melody and began to search for the pitch of the sounds he was hearing. After a few experiments he found the sounds and began to imitate the therapist's melodic fragments. He visibly relaxed, with less tension in his posture and movements. He indicated to us that he had a marked ability to imitate with accuracy short scalic passages and intervals of up to a fifth. At the end of this opening period of imitative interaction – piano/singing voice and xylophone/speaking voice – we heard him say, 'Good, wasn't I?'

The apparent need for a more directed approach was pointed out by Alison Levinge from the very first sessions:

> For example, when I first sat with a rehabilitation group during the improvi-
> sation piece, the overall feeling was one of utter chaos and disintegration. No
> one related to anyone else; there was all manner of tempo, rhythmic patterns
> and dynamic. It left one feeling drained and quite isolated. These feelings can
> be seen as a reflection of the images of the patients' experience of being
> themselves in this group. There was no leader, no ego, no direction and no
> purpose as yet discernible. By providing rhythmic exercises it enabled the
> groups to begin to integrate and provided an opportunity for the individual
> musical personalities to emerge. Rhythm seemed to provide a safe musical
> structure the patient needed, that corresponded in feeling to containment.[11]

Evaluation

From the list of referrals we were able to form two 'project groups' of eight people with an equal number of men and women from each area. As expected, the age-ranges were different: 42–60 years old (average: 52) for the long-stay group, and 27–47 (average: 36) for the short-stay group. We met with the clinical psychologist to work out a simple evaluation procedure for these groups. We decided on a simple time-sample observation procedure. Each member of the groups was observed at two randomly chosen points during each session, one from the tenth minute of the session and one from the thirty-fifth minute. Each member was observed for ten seconds, and the observation sheet was then completed. This time-sampling procedure provided a sense of randomness over what was specifically observed at each point. The nature of the procedure restricted observations to the very basic: in/out of the room; 'on/off task';

movements of hands and feet; eye direction; general observations on posture and the group task. A music therapy student on an extended placement carried out the observations.

The observations were made over a period of eight sessions for the shorter-stay group and seven sessions for the long-stay group. We would have preferred a longer period but the availability of the consistent observer prevented this. The following results are based on the weekly observations of six regular members in each group:

1   IN ROOM (this measure achieved 100 per cent inter-observer reliability) – see Table 6.1

There was a high level of attendance in both groups. The measure is rather basic but indicated that members of both groups were motivated sufficiently to attend throughout the course of sessions and that a large majority stayed throughout the sessions. With only small numbers in the group even one person leaving the room – and invariably one member of the shorter-stay group would do so about half-way through the session – would alter the figures quite substantially.

Table 6.1 In Room: Average % of group over the sessions

Group	Early in session	Later in session
Shorter-stay	81	73
Long-stay	88	75

Note: This measure had 100% inter-observer reliability.

Roger (short-stay group) would often start a rhythmic drumming improvisation, developing an interest in changing the patterns as the weeks progressed. 'As the group became more united and it became obvious that he was leading, he suddenly broke off, stopped and would physically leave the group.'[12]

This very basic quantitative attendance result was persuasive in setting up a part-time post at this hospital.

2   'ON TASK'/'OFF TASK' – see Table 6.2

When three observers were asked to judge whether a ten-second period of behaviour was for the most part 'on task'/'off task' 100 per cent inter-observer reliability was obtained. With the more detailed breakdown our predictions for lower reliability levels were confirmed, the two highest levels being 'apparently listening' – 71 per cent and 'playing an instrument' – 60 per cent. The details are nevertheless included in Table 6.2. It was appreciated by members of the steering

Table 6.2 On/off task

	Shorter-stay		Long-stay
		ON TASK	
	76% of total time		66% of total time
details:-			
playing an instrument	47%		43%
apparently listening	35%		36%
talking	18%		14%
singing/vocalising	–		7%
		OFF TASK	
	24% of total time		34% of total time
details:-			
left room	40%		25%
not apparently listening	25%		60%
smoking	15%		5%
reading	15%		–
talking	5%		5%
playing (off task)	–		5%

Note: Results collated across the sessions, two observations per person per session.

committee that music therapy could engage these groups for a high proportion of the time. Some of the points that we highlighted in the presentation to the committee included:

– When 'on task' and engaged in the group the highest percentage of time was spent in playing an instrument (both groups).
– There were similar amounts of 'apparently' listening and talking in both groups when 'on task'.
– The small amount of singing in the long-stay group was related to the fact that more opportunities for singing were provided for this group.
– There was more passivity with the longer-stay and older group, with a higher amount of 'not apparently listening' or being involved, a result reflected in our general observations of this group.
– There was more sense of restlessness – leaving the room, reading and smoking in the younger, shorter-stay group.

This 'on task'/'off task' division is rather naive. There may have been a high degree of 'on task' behaviour in both groups with much playing of instruments. However, it is very possible to play an instrument in a completely uninvolved and disconnected fashion. As we noted in Chapter 5, a quantitative analysis can be supported by more qualitative information. For example, Susan's music was organised within itself but she was quite unable to enter into any meaningful connections in group improvisations. Referring to the quality of her playing, my co-therapist, Alison Levinge, wrote:

> She had a tune which she called the 'Cobbler Tune', which had a clear melodic line and an appropriate sense of timing, but often she would return to this within a group free improvisation. S. held on to her music when it seemed to her a potentially chaotic musical setting.[13]

3   EYE DIRECTION – see Table 6.3

Between the three observers there was an 83 per cent agreement on eye direction towards other(s), 60 per cent towards an instrument and no agreement towards other directions. These very general figures indicate more looking towards the instruments and others than anywhere else in both groups. As we found in the project work with children (Chapter 5), music-making does provide opportunities for focused attention. In this project there was slightly more looking towards other members of the group in the shorter-stay group, exploring how music therapy could help this aspect of a group's development being an overall objective. Could we link such a measure to a growing awareness of each other? When we looked at the pattern across the weeks there was a definite trend in more looking at the instruments as the weeks progressed in both groups. Can we infer from this that the music and musical instruments contributed to a general increase in the level of attention and awareness? An alternative assumption could be that there was more familiarity with the instruments and the situation.

Table 6.3 Eye direction

Direction	Shorter-stay	Long-stay
Towards instrument	32%	38%
Towards other members	36%	31%
Towards other directions	32%	31%

Note: Totals across sessions.

Graham was a regular member of the shorter-stay group. During the first few sessions he sat at the side of the group reading his paper, not looking at the other members of the group nor at the instruments we invited him to explore. Gradually he felt more able to sit within the group and try out some of the instruments. Towards the end of this series of sessions, when he came in, even if late, he started off by sitting with the group, looking at the instruments and the other members and quickly joining in the music. He did not need to read his paper or sit at the side of the group. In his own time, with only the gentlest of invitations, he had decided to join in and become an active member of the group.

4 POSTURE

These bi-polar ratings were too unreliable to be used in the presentation, not reaching an acceptable level of inter-observer reliability. We looked briefly at an early and late session to observe any possible patterns or trends:

- With the shorter-stay group there appeared to be a general lessening of tension over the weeks with more relaxation being observed. There was very little observable change in the other ratings: active–passive; open–closed; interested–bored.
- With the long-stay group there was a slight increase in tension observed, a similar level of passivity (with generally more passivity than the shorter-stay group) and small increases in the amount of openness and interest being expressed.

We began to look at more detailed qualitative questions and summarised our experiences with both these groups in a framework that brought together some of the social and musical processes we had observed taking place in the groups. We looked at both the social and musical processes as a movement from relationship to the self, through an object and interactive processes (the instruments and therapeutic processes) to a stage of adult-to-adult expressive communication. At one end of the spectrum a member of a group could leave the group and the room. At the other end a member could take active responsibility for the direction and development of the group. Musical illustrations could complement the under-lying social processes at work. It is obvious that people can behave at more than one level at any one time, and the image of a spiral returns. For example, it is possible for people to explore an instrument in a totally self-absorbed fashion, before connecting with it and using it communicatively.

Other wards at the hospital began to hear of the music therapy project and requested some input. Some sessions began on an acute ward and in the day hospital.

Peter, a successful business man in his early fifties, was very depressed and anxious. He attended an open session on the acute ward. His posture seemed very tense. He chose to play the large metallophone and began to play music with many clashing intervals, major and minor seconds in particular. I tried to reflect the feelings behind these strong musical gestures with strident and loud discords, using the piano very percussively. Our music-making became less tense and fragments of more flowing melodies began to emerge. The music changed and developed a less tense quality, with open chords supporting his melodic explor-ations. At the end of this rather intense meeting in the music Peter commented that he had now discovered what he had been searching for in an earlier verbal encounter with his doctor. He connected this moment of insight to the change from the tense to the more melodic part of the improvisation. The musical patterns and forms had provided a framework enabling him to feel more able to discuss a difficult issue. He left the session planning to discuss this issue with his doctor as soon as possible.

We learned many lessons during this project. One recurring lesson was connected with what might appear on one level to be a very passive response to a session but on another is highly involved:

Martin came to some of the eight sessions for the acute ward. He sat by himself, away from the group, for the duration of each session. He did not want to play any of the instruments. At the end of the period of sessions we asked for some feedback on the positive and negative aspects of the experience. Contrary to our expectations, Martin commented that he found the sessions very helpful, using the memory of the sounds at other times of the week when needing to relax. He wrote: 'I like the sounds of the different instruments. The noises mixing in my head relax me. It is a relief at times of stress to listen and play music.'

At the end of the project our findings were presented at a conference and to the steering committee. We tried to merge both quantitative and qualitative aspects of the work. The hospital authorities agreed to fund two days of sessions so that the music therapy could continue.

Project 2: music therapy in a general hospital

Part I

We now trace the evolution of some work at a small psychiatric unit within a general hospital.[14] The unit incorporated acute residential and day hospital services. The request for an initial trial period of eight music therapy sessions came from the unit's head occupational therapist in 1986.[15] Obviously this is too short a period for work of long-standing influence to develop, but it was felt that an intense exposure to the music therapy process would be an indicator of any potential effect and use for the unit. The sessions were to be closely monitored.

The age-range of the six regular members referred to the group was 24–38, four women and two men. The problems presented by members of the group were acute: severe depression, anxiety, personality difficulties, and problems in relating to others and forming relationships. One member had a previous diagnosis of schizophrenia and another of manic-depressive psychosis. The occupational therapist, who acted as co-therapist, and the music therapist held an initial meeting with each potential member of the group and the discussion highlighted overall needs, namely:

- to communicate intentions and to relate to others
- to take part in a non-verbal group with the emphasis on creative expression
- to help the development of trust and relationships in a non-threatening group setting
- to encourage spontaneity in a relaxed setting
- to help members of the group take responsibility for actions and to become more confident in making choices and decisions
- to make a commitment to attend the eight sessions at the same time each week.

A student occupational therapist regularly attended the group and there was one extra rotating place for other members of the clinical team. The group never rose above a total of ten.

The occupational therapist kept an attendance record and collated the weekly descriptive notes. During the sessions there were many spontaneous comments made by the staff members about the usefulness of the music therapy. We asked the clinical psychologist to help in forming a simple questionnaire for use by both staff and clients. This was open-ended and could be answered as fully or briefly as required:

(1)   What aspects did you not like? Why?
(2)   What aspects did you like? Why?
(3)   What could have been included that wasn't? Why?
(4)   Is there any part of it that you would like less of? Why?
(5)   Is there any part of it you would like more of? Why?
(6a) What effect has it had on you – if any?
(6b) What effect do you observe it has had? (Staff question.)

Although this questionnaire was retrospective and not ideal in its reliance on memory, we felt that it could provide a crude analysis of positive and negative feedback and help generate future questions.

As with the earlier mental health project, there was a high attendance record of 73 per cent, with appropriate reasons provided for non-attendance with the exception of one instance. A total of thirteen questionnaires (six clients, seven staff) were completed within a week of the last session and returned to the psychologist. The individual statements were grouped into:

– positive (anything liked) – question 2
– negative (anything not liked or where less preferred) – questions 1 and 4
– suggestions – questions 3 and 5
– effects – question 6.

The statements relating to effects were subdivided further into positive, negative and ambivalent, with the ambivalent division being used if the three raters were not in 100 per cent agreement. The content analysis (see Table 6.4) indicates that positive comments dramatically outweigh negative ones (92 per cent positive – questions 2 and 6 – against 8 per cent negative – questions 1 and 4).

We wanted the comments from members of the group to speak for themselves, and the following is an example of additional statements written by one of the group. For me these comments bring together beautifully some of the unique features of music therapy:

For me, Music Therapy has provided an alternative avenue to the areas of my personality and social interaction closed off, mainly through fear of disapproval. The first cracks in my outward protective shell occurred before coming into the unit. In the unit, a 'safe' place was provided for the old shell

Table 6.4 Content analysis of statements

	Negative (Qs. 1&4)	Positive (Q.2)	Suggestions (Qs. 3&5)	Effects (Q.6)		
				pos.	amb.	neg.
Clients	3	11	9	7	2	0
Staff	2	22	11	18	0	0
TOTALS:	5	33	20	25	2	0

to be shed, and by talking to doctors, nurses and other patients the absence of need for a new shell was slowly established. Group therapy, art therapy and music therapy have each provided contributions to reestablish a true self-image. The unique contributions of Music Therapy are:

1) Co-operation within a group. All efforts of equal value.
2) Contributions towards a unique creation.
3) Other members of the group, staff as well as other patients, having equal problems mastering instrumental technique.
4) Sense of achievement proportional to one's involvement.
5) Aural access to closed-off, 'un-safe' areas of inspiration.
6) Ability to get used to doing something for fun and enjoyment initially and with less unsettling analysis (cf. art therapy).
7) 'Safe' interaction with a group.[16]

One negative comment from a client referred to difficulties in arriving on time for the group. The other negative comments related to the shortness of the period of sessions: 'I was just getting confident with the instruments and involved when the eight weeks ended. The last piece created being the least inhibited.' In many ways the request for a longer period of intervention can be viewed as a positive statement. A request for more sessions was a main feature of the clients' positive comments alongside a general sense of enthusiasm for the group. We could argue that the respondents were commenting positively in order to help the staff running the group rather than reflecting what actually happened in the group. The magnitude and quality of the positive responses does seem to outweigh this tendency.

The positive aspects of the group highlighted by the staff were linked closely to the original aims of the group and included, in no particular ranking order:

– making music together and becoming a team
– group cohesiveness
– exploring aspects of non-verbal communication
– spontaneity
– using instruments as a means of communication

- providing opportunity to develop imagination
- people becoming more relaxed and trusting as the group developed
- friendly, non-threatening group
- expression of emotions through non-habitual methods
- breaking patterns of behaviour
- releasing laughter and joy.

The staff also observed the positive effects of:

- opportunities for unassertive people to experience control
- non-communicative people seeing effects of their silence
- less withdrawal and inhibition
- building of confidence
- helping quieter people to express themselves
- encouraging participation of every member.

There were two negative comments from the staff:

- people with stronger personalities taking the lead
- having to stay in one seat throughout.

Although it is difficult to assess the contributions this intervention made to each individual's therapeutic progress, music therapy undoubtedly helped mood. There was an observable change of mood within the sessions for most members of the group. We concluded that a second series of sessions would be worth developing and extending when more specific questions relating to these changes in mood could be asked. After a brief presentation to the clinical team, based on the easily accessible results from the questionnaire, and a report to the funding group, agreement was made to fund a further series of sessions. Further funds were also made available to purchase the unit's own supply of musical instruments.

Part II

The first project at the large institution collected quantitative data on a period of intervention with the additional qualitative evidence from the notes made by the music therapists and self-reports from clients. The second project at the general hospital concentrated, with the exception of the attendance record, on more subjective self-reporting as a main indicator of possible effect. Such self-reporting adds richness to some of the colder figures. In the next project we wanted to discover more about how music therapy contributed to a general change in mood.

During the next, longer period of ten sessions at the unit we wanted to discover if there were any significant short-term changes in state of relaxation, feelings of 'happiness' and sense of self-worth within sessions. We were not interested in any cumulative changes over the whole period, being very aware of many confounding influences, such as changes in personal circumstances, medication and other therapy, that can affect such patterns. Nine people were referred to this new group. Staff now had an experience of what a music therapy group could offer and were able to make more specific referrals. Staff interviewed each potential member, explaining the nature of the project group and the need for commitment. In consultation with each client a joint assessment was made of their main problems. The range of the acute problems presented was as in the previous project, and some members had histories of psychotic episodes. In addition to the initial interview an attempt was made to use a standard Kelly Repertory Grid technique.[17] Clients were invited to generate a list of key elements: for example, 'Me now', and personal constructs relating to their own perceptions of these elements, such as the continuum 'isolated–involved'. This proved too overwhelming a task for this particular group, tending to increase levels of anxiety and withdrawal. The attempt was abandoned.

We wanted to look at changes within each session, and each member of the group was invited to complete some questions at the beginning and end of each session. The first group of questions focused on the three dimensions relaxation, happiness and feeling worthwhile. A simple seven-point scale was used from 1 – 'worst I have ever been' – to 7 – 'best I have ever been'. A second series of questions focused on attempting to identify the locus of the client's perceived changes (if any) through: other members of the group, the instruments, the group facilitator. These dimensions were rated on a standard seven-point scale. As before, space was provided on the question sheet for additional comments to be made. Each member of the group completed a separate beginning and end of session rating form, the forms were collected and results collated by two university psychology students and the unit's senior clinical psychologist.

The null hypotheses to the first series of questions (relaxation, happiness, feeling worthwhile) were that there would be no changes in the scores across each session. There were changes, with a greater number of higher scores at the end, as compared to the beginning, of each session. Statistical tests confirmed the direction of the findings and level of significance.[18] In all three dimensions there was a very significant subjective shift to the positive over the course of a music therapy session. People tended to feel more relaxed, happier and more worthwhile at the end of a music therapy session than at the beginning, rating themselves on average approximately half a point up the scale on all three dimensions. When we looked at the results in more detail we saw that this pattern was consistent over all of the sessions. There was room to move both upwards and downwards in nearly all of the ratings, so we concluded that no ceiling effect was operating to distort the ratings. The ratings seemed to reflect a genuine, and reliable, increase in positive mood-change over each session.

We carried out a simple evaluation of the results relating to the possible locus on any changes. The average rating on each dimension over the period of weeks was compared to the middle point of the scale (rating 4) for each member of the group. Some general points emerged:

- No one member rated all three dimensions the same; therefore we can assume that there was some discrimination between the scales.
- On the whole most scores were above 4, indicating a positive rating on all three scales.
- It seems that playing the instruments contributed the most to the levels of change.
- In relation to scores of 5 or over: three people felt the group contributed, six the instruments and three the group facilitator.
- In relation to scores of 3 and below: one person felt the group did not contribute, one the group facilitator; nobody felt the instruments detracted.

The positive contribution of the musical instruments occurred in spite of an initial reluctance shown by some members to explore and handle the instruments. For some people the group contributed, for others not, with a similar picture regarding the music therapist. These results indicated that the group members were able to make effective use of the instruments and other members of the group to influence changes within themselves during the sessions. The personality of the facilitator was not a dominating influence. This pattern also reflects the very client-centred nature of the music therapy approach adopted at this unit.

The results indicate a clear and definite effect relating music therapy to temporary lifting of mood. This was supported by the additional spoken or written comments made by members of the group. We concluded that music therapy has a positive contribution to make to mental health care services both as a therapeutic intervention in its own right and as an adjunctive therapy to other approaches. A positive mood shift within one music therapy session could enable group members to go on and utilise other interventions advantageously. The question is raised as to whether more regular, or even daily, exposure to at least an hour of music therapy could be considered as an alternative in some situations to an intensive drug regime to improve mood. If we were able to construct such a project in the future, then we might have stronger evidence to support the case that music therapy appears to be a reliable means of producing these positive effects over a considerable period of time, with good acceptability by clients and with no side-effects.

In both projects at this unit we were aware that the positive outcome could relate to the weekly attention and the supportive and listening approach adopted by the therapists. But the overwhelming nature of the positive reactions to the intervention seem to outweigh this tendency. As always, each project leads to further questioning. Could personal construct grids be created as a means of charting individual changes over a period of therapy? How would we begin to analyse the interactions between a joint counselling and music therapy intervention, for example? What is the nature of the specific music therapy processes by which such general outcomes and changes are reached? How do we relate how people use the music therapy sessions to their personal musical profiles and histories?

MUSIC THERAPY AND THE ELDERLY MENTALLY ILL

Helen Odell has carried out a research project examining the efficacy of music therapy with regular groups of elderly mentally ill (EMI) clients. This term has been changed recently to 'elderly – continuing care'. During her project she compared the therapeutic periods of music therapy with periods within a more verbally based kind of group, namely reminiscence therapy. In the first part of her project eight sessions of both music and reminiscence therapy took place in a random order over a sixteen-week period. In the second part she ran twelve music therapy sessions in sequence. Odell constructed time-based measures to record changes in the levels of 'engagement' both between music and reminiscence therapies in the first part and cumulatively within the music in the second part. She broke up the term 'engagement' into smaller and observable criteria: eye direction; verbalising; use of materials (both in the music and talking/reminiscence sessions); smiling; sleep or absence. Observations were also carried out after the music therapy and on no-music days. In listing the conclusions and summarising her findings, she wrote:

1. Regular sustained music therapy sessions increase engagement for E.M.I. people significantly more than when music therapy sessions are intermittent.
2. Music therapy is an effective treatment for E.M.I. people.
3. Music therapy increases levels of engagement for E.M.I. people more than when there is no planned activity, and also more than at meal times.
4. Constancy of therapist and group members within safe boundaries (i.e. regular time, place and approach) are important in achieving therapeutic benefits for E.M.I. people.
5. Relationships between therapist, assistants and group members built up over a period of time help to achieve benefits for E.M.I people.
6. Music therapy using methods involving improvisation within group interactions is successful in achieving therapeutic benefits for E.M.I. people.
7. Diagnosis and background are important factors in determining how to help E.M.I. clients through music therapy.[19]

Odell also indicated that all the people involved in the project had improved or maintained levels of engagement by the end of the study. There was also a generally higher level of engagement during the music therapy – more awareness, interaction, and so on – than during no session at all. The results, as expected, were more sustained and consistent during the second part of her project. She noted that these changes occurred in spite of her emphasis on improvisation. Traditionally there has been a common use of old-time songs with this population, causing confusions, at times, between a music therapy session and an entertaining 'sing-along' session. Odell's approach is not unique in demonstrating how such songs can have their place in music therapy. They can be used in their entirety, or parts of the songs can be used as musical springboards for interactive improvisation. She cites many examples of how music is used in this free way to vent feelings. She describes supportive work with one old man, for example, who used a large tambour very effectively and loudly to voice his feelings of frustration and confusion. He had no speech. After he had articulated his feelings in this way she observed him becoming visibly more relaxed, able to join more interactively with other members of the group in small-group musical exchanges and improvisations.

MUSIC THERAPY AT THE BRISTOL CANCER HELP CENTRE

Music therapy is part of the weekly residential programme available to clients attending the internationally recognised Bristol Cancer Help Centre. The centre runs on holistic principles, providing clients with opportunities to explore the emotional and psychological difficulties alongside the more physical aspects of their disease. The music therapy is part of a group of complementary therapies aiming to improve the quality of life of the residents.

The session is for an hour and a half, mid-way through the programme, on the Wednesday morning. The group takes place in the relaxation room, a beautiful and comfortable ground-floor room. The Centre has purchased a range of tuned and untuned percussion. The session is coordinated by the music therapist, supported by the resident counsellor. We begin with a general introduction to the instruments for both the residents and their supporters. After this short opening phase the supporters leave and we focus for the rest of the time on work with the residents. The supporters have an opportunity for their own group later in the morning. The number of residents attending the centre during any one week is usually between eight and ten.

Evaluation

After the first few sessions we decided to begin to evaluate the contribution that music therapy was making to the residential programme at the Centre. The evaluation was carried out by an external assessor. This colleague is a psychologist in the final stages of training as a counsellor.[20] We looked at six sessions with three main aims:

1 to look at what was happening in the music therapy sessions in the context of the overall evaluation of all the therapy input at the Centre as requested by the management
2 to enable us to look at some of the features of the music therapy input with a view to improving the service
3 to begin to compare processes in music therapy and counselling.

Questions and method

Our overall general question was to discover how the residents viewed the music therapy session. There were three other groups of questions:

1 In terms of the developing group relationship, and the therapeutic programme, was the positioning of the music therapy session on Wednesday morning at the most appropriate time?
2 What did the session achieve in terms of the overall aims of the Centre? Did, for instance, the music therapy help the residents to express, relieve or gain access to feelings that could then be worked with further in counselling or through the other therapies?
3 Should there be any changes of the format and length of the sessions? What is the optimum or maximum group size?

To begin to answer these questions the following very basic procedures were adopted:

(a) Before and after each music therapy session the assessor did a quick 'brainstorm' with the group on the subject 'music and us'. She invited the group to give words and phrases which described both positive and negative aspects of music.
(b) The assessor observed the sessions as a participant observer and collected impressions of the process and effects of the music therapy, from the point of view both of the residents and of the music therapist.
(c) The assessor collected comments about the sessions from the residents, the music therapist and the counsellor. This was done by means of informal discussions and some semi-structured interviews.

Analysis

The 'brainstorms' from the six sessions generated lists of words and phrases that needed sorting and grouping. There were various key concepts that grouped many of the spontaneous comments; these were labelled 'constructs'. The assessor then analysed these so-called constructs with a measure of frequency. She defined frequency as the number of times a certain word or group of words was used by one of the six groups, not the total number of times by all the groups (see Tables 6.5 and 6.6).

Observations relating to the analysis of the constructs

1 In general there appears to be a shift from words which describe the effect of music on the individual, such as energising, relaxing, depressing and sad, to words which describe the effect on the group, and what it felt like playing together, such as communication, togetherness and harmony. The two most frequently found constructs before the sessions were 'energising' and

Table 6.5 Pre-session constructs

Construct		Frequency (out of 6)
a.	energising/stimulating	6
b.	relaxing/calming	5
c.	fun/enjoyment	5
d.	harmony/spiritual/inner peace	4
e.	depression/sadness	4
f.	discord/irritation	3
g.	sociable/sharing	3
h.	expressive/meaning/wordless	2
i.	sound/rhythm	2
j.	nostalgia/recall of images/mood	2
k.	therapeutic	2
l.	spontaneity	1
m.	beauty	1

'relaxing'; at the end of the sessions these were 'communication' and 'group togetherness'.

2 There appears to be a movement from words which describe the passive feelings evoked in individuals by music, such as enjoyment, calmness, sadness, to those which refer to the individuals' active experience or use of the music, such as strengthening, positive, connections, understanding, focus.

3 There appears to be a marked shift of energy. The words after the sessions tend to be more dynamic and often refer to relaxation of tension and release of feelings via catharsis, loss of inhibition and spontaneity.

4 There were some negative post-session constructs, such as difficult, frustrating, retreat, inhibition.

5 The words used after the sessions seem to be more focused and specific. For example, the third group had the words sociable/sharing at the start; afterwards members of the group talked about interaction, unity, cooperation and the desire to be in harmony.

6 Some constructs appear both before and after the sessions, notably enjoyment, nostalgia or reminiscence, sociable/sharing, energising and group togetherness.

7 Some constructs appear before and not afterwards, notably depression/ sadness and beauty; others such as discord/irritation, spiritual/peace, therapeutic, do not appear as such but are reflected in other, usually more specific, constructs afterwards.

8 A number of constructs appear afterwards and not before, and the number of words and different constructs used afterwards was higher. Some of these

Table 6.6 Post-session constructs

Construct	Frequency (out of 6)
a. communication	5
b. group togetherness/harmony	5
c. enjoyment/fun	5
d. spontaneity/immediacy	4
e. catharsis/release	4
f. noisy/loud	4
g. concentration/attention	3
h. frustrating/difficult	2
i. connections/understanding	2
j. strengthening/positive	2
k. sensitivity/gentleness	2
l. focus/tuning in to inner rhythm	2
m. reminiscence	1
n. energising	1
o. discover potential	1
p. near to nature	1
q. retreat/inhibition	1
r. exhaustion	1
s. tension	1
t. desire for form and shape	1
u. ambiguous	1
v. individuality	1
w. interpretation	1
x. passion/drama	1
y. trial/experimentation	1

reflected totally new ideas, such as discovery of potential/unknown talents, desire to be in harmony (with the group as opposed to individually), nearness to nature, catharsis/emotional release, tuning in to (our) inner rhythm, sensitivity/gentleness (with ourselves).

Discussion

Such an analysis is consistent with intuitive feelings and expectations of such a before-and-after-session procedure. Each group was asked to comment on the notion of 'music and us' in a cold way, as it were, at the start of the session and again at the end. It is not surprising that the words move from the rather general at the start to the more specific afterwards. The residents had experienced a session where there was an emphasis on active involvement in music-making. A rise in energy was predicted. But the contrasts in the before and after constructs do tell us something about the process of the music therapy and how those attending the sessions construed the experience.

There are a number of important points. It seems that for most groups (five out of the six) a sense of togetherness and desire to be in harmony with each other has been aided by their experience of making music together. This has implications for the development of the group culture and identity and is very much part of the therapeutic value of the week at the Centre. Half of the groups mentioned sharing/sociability beforehand, but afterwards communication and group to-getherness head the list.

For many of the groups some members found the experience cathartic. Although before the sessions the constructs reflect the common belief that music can be energising or relaxing, afterwards there is a more specific reference to more active constructs such as emotional release, catharsis, loss or overcoming of inhibitions and breaking down of barriers. Spontaneous comments such as 'I didn't know I had that in me', 'It's a good way to get that feeling off my chest', 'That was very primitive, I enjoyed that' were common.

There is a similar contrast on the negative side. The depression and sadness induced by music, mentioned at the start of the session (four out of the six groups), did not appear again afterwards. Instead there are more active constructs such as frustrating/difficult; retreat/inhibition; exhaustion; and even consternation.

The importance of music for accessing memories and the feelings associated with them is also reflected in these constructs, although surprisingly not to the extent that the experience of the sessions had indicated. Before the session two groups mentioned nostalgia, or the ability of music to stir up images and memories. Afterwards only one group specifically mentioned reminiscence in the 'brainstorm', but others mentioned previous experiences and private connections which had to do with past memories and feelings.

The post-session constructs also reflect the ability of music therapy to relieve the residents, temporarily at least, from their preoccupation with their pain, illness and problems. Many spontaneous comments related to being out of yourself, side-stepping the problems, being able to look at yourself and laugh, tuning in to your inner rhythm and focusing.

There is also the mention in the constructs of a key philosophy of the Centre, namely for the residents to look after themselves by giving priority to their real needs. We can see this in the references to sensitivity and gentleness (with ourselves), to strengthening and being positive.

The post-session constructs reflect the experience of several of the residents who discovered, or rediscovered, a talent for making music. There was mention of unknown talents, discovering potential and increased confidence after having played in the session. For some residents there was an unexpected pleasure in finding that they could play the instruments they had explored in the session; for others it reminded them of music-making they had taken part in in the past. Some residents stated that they now intended to take up music again.

The following are supportive points arising from the interviews and observations during the sessions. There were many personal insights gained by the residents during the music therapy:

Resident A felt frustrated when playing the drum; she lived with a professional musician and she herself had stopped playing the violin. She was able to ask herself why she stopped playing, commenting that something positive had come out of the frustration.

Resident B mentioned in her interview that she had felt nervous before the session, with a 'problem with music'. During the session she realised that since her discovery of her illness she had suppressed a love of music. She also had the insight during the session that this 'shutting-down' to music was mirrored in the way she did not listen to her own body, putting off attending to her developing problems. The music acted as a trigger to many of these feelings, enabling her to continue to open up and talk to other staff at the Centre.

Resident C found that music was a very direct way to contact her emotions. She cried when she heard the sounds of one of the pitched instruments, which reminded her of the time when her son played the same instrument at school. It was at this time that she was nursing her own mother. She talked with insight of the innocence of the sounds, which reminded her of the warm contact she had with her son at that time. She was able to use this powerful experience as a focus in the later visualisation work and was able to develop the insights further in her painting and other experiences at the Centre.

Summary of the evaluation

The evaluation of the processes and effects of the music therapy input at the Centre consisted of the gathering of information from all involved. We used a combination of before-and-after-session 'brainstorming', participant observation and semi-structured interviews. We also gathered information on how the residents viewed the music therapy interacting with other therapies at the Centre, and the timing of the session.

This one session during the programme indicates some of the potential of music therapy for this client group. At present the residents are just beginning to become familiar with the instruments when it is time to break. We often have some of the profoundest experiences towards the end of the session, as often in a therapeutic situation. In order to explore more work relating to individual needs – for example, opportunities for playing individual 'life journeys' on the instruments with the support of the other members of the group and the therapists – more time is needed for the developing trust to be carried forward.

There was a very positive reaction to the timing of the music therapy. It is in the right place in the week. The group know each other sufficiently well for a sense of group trust and entity to have built up. The music therapy session helps to consolidate this sense of cohesion and enables the residents to explore feelings that they can then take forward into the rest of the week.

THE USES OF MUSIC THROUGHOUT THE LIFE-SPAN: THE IMAGE OF THE SPIRAL

Psychologists have traditionally spent a great deal of their time and energies in charting the physical, intellectual, social and emotional development of children. When we turn to the longest period of life, adulthood, we note that until recently there has been a dearth of any sustained research. The most discussed model seems to be the eight stages of psychosocial development proposed by Erik Erikson.[21] His model demonstrates how an individual adapts to the various challenges from society as life develops. He describes how a crisis arises at each crucial stage. A new 'virtue' or 'vital strength' develops from the resolution of each crisis. For example, Erikson views the crisis of young adulthood (from approximately 20 to 35) as being between the polar opposites of intimacy and isolation. The young adult has formed some sense of self and is able to risk becoming intimate with another person. Erikson regards love as the new 'virtue' to resolve this apparent crisis. If forming intimate relationships is too risky, then the young adult becomes increasingly isolated. The adult develops through these stages in relationship both to others and to the environment as a whole.

Bronfenbrenner has shown how different levels 'nest' one within the other. He describes the first level as a 'microsystem' – the relations in the immediate environment: home, work, personal relationships. A 'mesosystem' is a grouping of 'microsystems': for example, how work relates to home. An 'exosystem' contains the previous levels and is a system that influences them: for example, the effect of the job market. The fourth level is the 'macrosystem' which is the way in which the underlying values of the society are reflected in the other three levels.[22]

It is clear that any life-span view of development is multi-dimensional and multi-directional. There is no fixed route; we all have the potential to change and grow. An individual moves through the adult years with a shifting perspective on self, on others and on the surrounding society. For all of us there are recurring themes and physical ups and downs that interact with life events. We all have our personal stories that constantly change and re-form as we respond differently to events around us.[23] Some authors write about these processes from within a hierarchical framework: for example, Maslow's work on processes of 'self-actualization', the life goal for which we are all striving when all our talents and potentialities reach their full flowering. His hierarchy of needs moves through physiological well-being, safety, love and belonging, self-esteem, to eventual self-actualization. Maslow's identification of the processes through these stages and the characteristics of self-actualising people has been very influential in the humanistic psychology movement.[24]

Poets and playwrights have used many metaphors to describe this process.

Images from the natural world have been used to describe the journey: for example, the flow of a river, the daily movement of the sun, the changing seasons. Music can be used at different stages of life to suit different needs and I would like to conclude this chapter with some thoughts on possible connections between important moments in our lives and our uses of music. In Chapter 4 we referred to the image of a spiral as proposed by Tillman and Swanwick as a model for a developmental profile. I would like to propose that this image is still valid for the adult's musical profile.

Music is in constant ebb and flow, with vibration at its source. As discussed in Chapter 3, we make the connections between the elements of the physical world of sound to produce melody, harmony and rhythm, which are the flowing and interacting elements of what we call music. Music therapists are able to observe children and adults creating all kinds of musical gestures. An adult may be very familiar with the basic parameters of music but in free improvisation may dip back through the spiral to capture again some of the early sensuous delight in the sounds. This is observable in the sessions at the Cancer Help Centre. This may also be happening to the highly trained musician when trying to develop skills in improvising.

We seem to need different kinds of musical experiences at different times of life. We may not even understand certain music at certain stages. My piano teacher was rather alarmed to see his 15-year-old pupil with a score of Sibelius' fifth symphony – I was not meant to understand such a complex work at such a tender age. I remember being confused by this remark as the piece was a particular favourite. On reflection I assume that my teacher considered that some of the background musical features of the piece were beyond my intellectual and emotional grasp at the time. Beethoven is an example of a composer who offers opportunities for a life-span development. If we just look at the string quartets we can see how the various changes throughout the series can meet our needs as we get older. There is a great deal written about the last quartets, for example, as the culmination of a life dedicated to composing, works full of the wisdom and spiritual insight of old age. Yet this wisdom also has the feel of the rapt innocence of childhood, with song-like melodies of the utmost simplicity. In later years we may find the youthful energy of the early quartets invigorating and inspiring. The very fact that people with dementia can often recall more of their childhood than of recent events may be part of this whole cyclical process of the interconnections between beginnings and endings. Long-term memory still remains intact. Our sense of hearing is both the first to develop and, very often, the last to leave us.

We express both our personal and our group identity through music at different stages in our lives. This is very clear when we look back and connect various pieces of music with significant life events. Music from our adolescence creates a lasting impression, having very much contributed to the identity of an individual's peer group. Some of our elderly clients have lived through the upheavals of two world wars. Songs played a very important part in providing a sense of cohesion during those troubled times. The songs can be used again to evoke memories of the emotional context of these times. Memories of loved ones are often associated with a particular song or piece of music, what John Booth Davies aptly labels the 'Darling, They're Playing Our Tune' theory.[25] I assume that the words on their own would not create such an immediate recall. So at a time when we are preparing for the end of our lives, music can help us to review earlier stages in our life and re-live the full impact of those emotional moments.

Much therapy focuses on the re-enactment of past events in the present moment in order to gain clarity and re-adjustment. Music therapy is no different. A piece of music can be improvised as an articulation of a present feeling or group of feelings. We can externalise aspects of our inner emotional lives in the music we make. In this way music can be an articulation on the level of Bronfenbrenner's 'microsystem'. On a different level the music of the day, be it popular or so-called serious music, can be an articulation of the issues that the society holds to be important at any one time; we move through the levels to the notion of 'macrosystem'.

Music is multi-dimensional and multi-directional. How we use music can be beautifully represented in this image of the spiral, a shape so fundamental to life. There are so many variations: the homes of snails and other sea creatures, our inner organs of hearing, the natural forms of whirlpools and hurricanes, even the building-material of our genes, the DNA molecule, which has the form of a double spiral.[26]

At one and the same time music can represent individual and group needs. Music therapy can help adults to take risks, confront changes, reconcile crises and move forward. Adults in a music therapy group can use the music to explore present issues from a different perspective and to re-assess earlier problems as if going back to go forward. This creative flexibility contributes to music therapy's increasing relevance as a resource for adult health and well-being.

Chapter 7

Music therapy as a resource for the community

INTRODUCTION

The way in which music and music therapy can build links is a key theme of this chapter. In Chapter 1 we observed that much of the early work of the professional music therapist began in the large institutions for mentally handicapped and mentally ill people, to use the terminology of the day. Only forty years later we are currently witnessing major changes in the way in which society is adapting to people with such problems. The terminology is shifting, with the current terms 'learning difficulties' and 'mental health problems' replacing the older ones. A further radical change is the closing-down of these large institutions and their replacement by more community-based day centres, small units and hostels. We are currently living through the difficult implementation stages, with the concomitant implications of additional human and financial resources. The start of the 1990s has also seen an increase in unemployment, homelessness and further strain on our probation and prison service. What is the music therapist's response to all these changes? The profession is working hard to develop an effective service outside the security of a hospital department. We are only a small profession, and today's market is stressing a supply-and-demand, purchaser-and-provider model. We shall need to organise our small resources to meet the enormous demand and challenges in a fashion that will gain the support of the funding bodies. Otherwise there is the real danger of the profession losing some of the momentum it has gained over the last few decades as it struggles again to find a new identity, indicate its efficacy and hold its own in the open market-place.

As technology increases our ability to travel and contact each other in all corners of the globe we are learning more about different cultures and discovering more common links than differences between people from many backgrounds. We are hearing more music from different cultures and meeting more musicians fluent in non-Western traditions. It is now possible to attend musical events such as the WOMAD festival and to hear and see performers from all over the world. Such opportunities were only available to intrepid musical explorers until a very few years ago. Pioneering spirits such as Peter Gabriel are bringing musicians from many traditions together to play music and to learn from each other. The advanced technology of a Western recording studio can then be used to record some of these new mixes. How will music therapy adapt to this growing culture mix when we are realising with increasing clarity that music of all kinds is a key link with what it is to be human? The essence of our humanity is in our music, making it possible to integrate people of many backgrounds, experiences and ranges of ability in music.

This chapter begins with a review of an area where music can help people at all levels of cognitive ability, namely music therapy for adults with learning difficulties (formerly called mental handicap). For these clients music therapy can provide a needed support in the move out from the traditional hospital setting. Other areas of work not highlighted in previous chapters will then be summarised, alongside indicators for future work. We shall look briefly at the response of music therapists to current music technology. How do music therapists link with other disciplines? The creation of a community-based service and charity, MusicSpace, will be used as an example of one way in which music therapy is responding to the current situation. How does music therapy relate to trends in contemporary music and changes in the role of the musician in society? Can we adapt to many musical challenges without becoming a dabbler in too many approaches? How can a music therapist integrate such roles as performer, teacher, researcher and therapist?

MUSIC THERAPY AND THE ADULT WITH LEARNING DIFFICULTIES

Historically music therapy has developed expertise in meeting the needs of adults with some of the gravest cognitive and physical impairments. Departments of music therapy have been set up in many of the formerly large institutions where people with such severe problems lived, often for many years. In such settings a music therapy culture is able to develop and staff become used to referring Johnny and Sarah for music therapy not 'because they like music' but for other reasons over and above music's aesthetic, pleasurable and recreational aspects. Connections with the cognitive, emotional, physical and spiritual areas of a person's life become increasingly the area of therapeutic focus. We begin to see that whatever the degree of impairment a music therapist can contact the person behind the problem and make an emotional connection through the musical transaction. Therapeutic objectives can then be discussed to help develop physical mobility or some aspect of learning, social or emotional behaviour, even in the areas of so-called 'challenging behaviour'. The range of problems presented is vast, from the very withdrawn and passive to the hyperactive and self-stimulating. All of this range can be said to present a challenge to the music therapist. Isolation seems to link many of these difficulties, and the situation of an adult with a profound learning problem is often further complicated by overlapping problems such as visual or hearing impairments, physical disabilities or mental health problems such as acute depression.

The history of the profession indicates that music therapy can offer a great deal to an adult with such difficulties. A music therapist can make links with the essential personal qualities that lie beneath some of the presenting problems. In what way do the problems interfere with or frustrate the process of communication through music? As observed in Chapter 3, responses to sound and musical elements can be very basic, not necessarily relying on complex intellectual reasoning for comprehension. By bypassing some of the functions necessary for decoding speech, for example, music can make a deep impact on people for whom a verbally saturated environment can only add to confusion and further isolation. Stephanie Zallik reminds us that developmental or physical delay does not prevent a person from feeling with the full range of intensity of somebody whose mental and physical faculties are more developed.[1] As a music therapist she is wanting to understand and work through these outer layers so as to reach for the innermost layer where she feels the real needs of the person are met.

Sally, a 27-year-old with profound learning difficulties, would sit curled up in a foetal position in her chair. She appeared to be completely withdrawn into herself. She was referred to music therapy to see if any communication system could be established. I had very mixed feelings about inviting her for the first session. How could I intrude on a world she had created for herself, possibly as a means of protection from the aural invasions of ward noises, including both the television and the radio? I sat beside her and began to play some long and quiet sounds on a small pipe. I sang her name gently and slowly. Over the weeks she began to express some curiosity about these sounds. She began to uncurl herself and turn sideways towards the source of the sounds. A few weeks later she began to reach out and touch some of the instruments. This led to her facing me as I began to sit opposite her. All this took place within an extremely slow time framework; any sudden or loud intrusion would set her back into herself. She eventually began to vocalise and to make long sounds and sighs. We improvised such long sounds together. After a period of nine months of weekly sessions she would come into the small room off the main ward, sit in a chair facing me, sing and reach out for the instruments. Towards the final stages of our work together she would get out of her chair as soon as I entered the ward and lead me to the room, singing *en route*. The speech therapist observed and notated a wide range of sounds that she produced in her singing, sounds that could perhaps be the basis for some kind of communication system. She began to attend for speech therapy.

I do feel that sensitivity to Sally's own time framework helped the very gradual establishment of the simple interactions with her. This was not an easy process and there were times when we were not able to make any contact and we were definitely not part of the same time framework.

This description relates well to the discussion on duration in Chapter 3. We can be critical of this example from the viewpoint that any individual attention over a sustained period of time could result in changes, particularly if the adult is being supported in a consistently safe environment. Research is nevertheless indicating that music therapy can be effective with people who have the profoundest of difficulties and can make specific contributions above and beyond those expected from a period of such sustained attention. Amelia Oldfield, for example, investigated the efficacy of music therapy in accomplishing a set of individualised objectives when working with adults with profound learning difficulties. She compared the results with a similar period of play activities. Extensive video analysis of some of the behaviours of four adults indicated improvements as a result of music therapy by comparison with play activities. Oldfield points out that the objectives were often very simple but that music therapy can be an effective means of achieving such objectives:

- Resident A was more active, held on to objects more and participated more in music therapy than in the play activities.
- Resident B progressively relaxed his arm more in the music therapy sessions, contributing to the general aim of helping him to 'reduce time spent curled up in a foetal position with head down and arms over ears'.
- Resident C took part in and tolerated more activities in music therapy than in the play sessions. He also made fewer negative comments in music than in play.
- Resident D was the only adult who was more active in the play than in the music sessions.[2]

Oldfield's study also indicated the sporadic nature of the changes. There were few trends indicating cumulative changes over the weeks, the behaviour tending to vary from week to week. We have met this theme before alongside the need for a long period of sustained and regular intervention in order to observe changes.

Tony Wigram has recently reported an example of such a sustained period of work. He charted the development of a group of five highly disturbed and at times aggressive young adults. Weekly sessions over a period of two years helped this group to increase in tolerance of each other. The group became less resistant both to being involved in the music and to physical contact. The music therapists adapted the musical approaches as the behaviour of the group members developed, with noticeable changes in social behaviour. There was a deeper level of contact between all of the people involved in the music-making.[3]

Clearly stated objectives, observations and reporting can help the profession to gain more external validity and acceptance with other professionals. We can indicate that music therapy is a viable medium for working with this population, both inside and outside the hospital setting. This kind of descriptive work relates to an early stage in the history of the profession and it is understandable that researchers such as Oldfield have chosen to focus initially on observable behaviour, behaviour that can translate more readily into strong, time-based measures. In adopting this perspective we are all aware that we are choosing to overlook some very central issues. To date it has been difficult to set up research projects that examine, for example, those fleeting feelings and emotional responses that pass between therapist and client in any musical transaction. We need to develop finer research tools to explore some of these central issues. A period of solid outcome work, indicating changes related to objectives across many parameters, will hopefully lead into areas of research involving deeper levels of analysis.

A BRIEF SURVEY OF SOME OTHER AREAS OF WORK

The practical examples used in this book have, for the most part, been descriptions of work with children, adults with learning difficulties and adults with mental health problems. The most recent development described in detail was the work relating to cancer care. If we look at the new *Journal of British Music Therapy* we can observe how music therapy is extending into other areas of child and adult health.

Serious interest is developing in working with adults with neurological problems such as Parkinson's Disease and Huntington's Chorea. Jennie Selman has described a period of music therapy with a 64-year-old man diagnosed as having Parkinson's Disease. She described how the music therapy enabled him to channel some of his feelings of frustration, thereby reducing some of his stress and anxiety. The session brought some physical relief, which her client noted remained with him for about twenty-four hours after the session. She included singing specifically in the sessions to help relax movements of the mouth, tongue, jaw and face and to improve breathing and posture. She observed, as is often the case, that words were more clearly sung than spoken.[4] This case study indicates the relevance of music therapy in this area not only for providing a physical release but also as an aid for improved communication and emotional and spiritual integration.

Early in her music therapy career Sarah Hoskyns completed a piece of research on the short-term effects of music therapy with adults diagnosed as having Huntington's Chorea. The positive effects of the intervention and the implications for further work with both the physical and the speech and language problems involved were written up and published in medical journals, including *The Lancet*.[5]

Sarah Hoskyns has developed research into another pioneering area, that of the adult recidivist offender. Here she has taken Kelly's Personal Construct Theory as reference in preparing a music therapy grid for use in the evaluation. In this way the clients themselves have been very involved as partners in the research process.[6]

Sarah Hoskyns carried out this recent research while employed as Research Fellow in Music Therapy at the City University, London.[7] The work of the research fellow has been at the forefront of many of the new developments in music therapy in recent years. Colin Lee, another holder of the post, has been pioneering work with adults living with the HIV and AIDS virus. During his work at the London Lighthouse he has brought his musical gifts as both pianist and composer to this area of work. His research on 'significant moments' during an improvisation developed the partnership approach instigated by Hoskyns. Both client and therapist are able to comment on the music and discuss moments of significance.[8]

Penny Rogers is extending the work of the Fellowship into the area of sexual abuse. In a recent review of her work she highlighted some of the important factors in this work, including the symbolic use of instruments; the importance of boundaries; and what she calls 'the power of the secret'.[9] She also indicated how some of the issues apply to other areas of work, including eating disorders and substance abuse.

We are increasingly becoming aware of the interconnections of problems presented by clients. A learning difficulty may be influenced by a complex range of emotional problems. Margaret Heal has recently adopted the term 'psycho-analytically informed music therapy' to describe the links she makes between psychoanalytic theory and music therapy when working with people with learning difficulties.[10]

A further link is with the ever-expanding field of technology. Recent developments in computer technology, such as the MIDIGRID system, make it possible for a child or adult with even the slightest of available movements to access and be in control of a wide range of musical experiences. A client with a profound physical disability may be very frustrated by a more traditional use of instruments. Music therapists could link up with music educators and other researchers in discovering how such technology can improve the quality of life of these people. Such is the motivation for the Drake Research Project.[11] There are further implications for uses of such technology when working with people with visual or hearing impairments.

WORKING LINKS WITH OTHER DISCIPLINES

Many music therapists work as part of a para-medical or creative therapy team. There are many ways in which an approach in music therapy can complement work within other disciplines. Some of the links will be discussed here; in other chapters we have already described close working relationships with occupational therapists, physiotherapists, speech therapists and clinical psychologists.

Music therapy and physiotherapy

In Chapters 4 and 5 I described how the motivational and attentional aspects of sound and music can be used in joint interventions with physiotherapy. Bryce and Alvin have described such an approach when working with a child with cerebral palsy.[12] Wigram and Weekes have outlined a specific joint programme for working with adults with severe mental and physical disabilities.[13] They describe how the tempo, style and timbre of the music are carefully adapted for a wide range of planned movements. Movements do not take place in isolation but are given an added framework and support by the enveloping music. Wigram and Weekes describe how the rhythm and tempo help to motivate and stimulate any movement; the melodic and harmonic content sustains curiosity, awareness and any fluidity in a movement; style and timbre are linked to the support and encouragement of either relaxation or stimulation, depending on the context. They stress the care needed to find the appropriate speed for the music. Fast and stimulating music has its place when motivating people to move very spastic limbs, but care needs to be taken not to over-arouse or increase tension in often already tense bodies. Such music can also over-stimulate people with many involuntary movements, such as in athetosis, when calmer music is needed to help focus the movements. In this joint approach the two disciplines work to a common purpose, a carefully structured piece of work. Every individual's needs and resulting approach will be slightly different. Care is also needed to balance the level of physical response expected with the cognitive demands of the task: on some occasions a client may be able to comprehend at a higher level of functioning than demonstrated by the range of movements available. Careful observation will be needed to find the appropriate balance. Over the course of weeks both staff and clients begin to anticipate both the individual's specific movements and the phrasing and structure of the music. Music supplies a very appropriate grid for the placing of movements and can help instil many kinds of memory traces, both physically and mentally. There is much motivation derived from the music in wanting to move and place these movements. As Oldfield and Peirson note in describing their joint approach with people with physical disabilities, people may not be able to waltz but they can still feel the musical impulse and they are highly motivated by the music to move.[14]

Kevin, a 7-year-old with profound physical and learning disabilities, was very responsive to the sound of single tones sung to him or played on the chime bars. We developed a combined music therapy and physiotherapy approach. He made every effort to look up to the source of sound, to smile and to vocalise. We began to have short vocal interactions. These interactions covered a wide range of moods, from the quietly inward to the very outward and excited. The physiotherapist was aiming to help Kevin develop his motivation to stand. We found that singing or playing his favourite sounds from above was such a strong motivation for him that he would uncurl and make a great effort to move upwards, with the support of the physiotherapist, to reach those sounds. To see this profoundly disabled boy work so hard to stand with support in response to the musical invitations was a very moving experience for all concerned, other staff and parents often being part of the session.

Writing in general about a combined physiotherapy/music therapy approach, one colleague commented:

It was noticeable that in each session: a) a better understanding of the speed of the physical activities of the children was understood by the music therapist, helping the physiotherapist; b) working with a music therapist encourages the children to obtain more physical skills themselves, music therapy stressing the self-motivation of the children rather than a requirement of therapist skills as in physiotherapy; and c) communicating with a severely disabled child is helped by music therapy; sometimes movement is stressful and upsetting to such a child and combining music therapy with physiotherapy makes movement more enjoyable and the child is happier.

Music therapy and speech therapy

Working non-verbally with sound can often prepare the groundwork for the gradual introduction of speech therapy. It is becoming increasingly common for units assessing the needs of pre-school children with learning difficulties, for example, to have a music therapist on the staff or within easy reach as part of the local resources. I described in Chapter 5 how research has indicated that music can stimulate and sustain much vocalising among children. There are parallels with the stressing, phrasing and timing procedures involved in both musical processes and stages in language development. Oldfield and Parry have developed a system of combined speech therapy and music therapy that focuses on the areas of pre-linguistic skills: vocalisation, articulation and intonation.[15] They stress that music can help develop skills at a very basic level in the development of motivation and awareness of self and others. Music can help in listening and in focusing attention and concentration, all prerequisites of any communication system. A child can be motivated by the music to vocalise in a pause or at a moment of anticipation or heightened musical excitement. Music can help children produce sounds sequentially. A child may be able to understand the concept of joining two sounds to form a pattern in music before being able to utter two syllables or place two words together.

Annie, a 2-year-old with Down's syndrome, was well able to vocalise using single sounds. We were able to engage in vocal turn-taking when playing with single sounds. We developed a combined speech therapy and music therapy approach. She was particularly curious about musical sounds and could extend her playing for more than one sound. We wondered whether she could learn about placing two sounds in sequence in a musical context before practising such a development outside the music room. Such was our specific aim. We explored contrasts of pitch and timbre to see if Annie could understand the difference. We noted that both of our names were composed of two syllables and over the weeks began to explore a variety of sounds contrasting these two syllables. A high and low chime bar became her favourite sound quality and she began to explore one sound on the high bar and one on the lower. We made even more of a contrast by the visual stimulation of the high bar up in the air and vice versa. After three or four sessions she began to vocalise while playing these two different sounds. She then added the specific sounds of her name. We moved from free vocal interactions using one to two sounds. We had achieved the objective and Annie was then seen more regularly for intensive speech therapy.

It is always necessary to be aware of the limits of the brain's functional potential. If there is any organic brain damage, we will need to look for ways to help compensate for the damage, to optimise responses, all within the limits imposed by the disorder. An adult, for example, can help ease articulation or intonation difficulties through vocalising and singing. As with movement and sound, a rhythmic and melodic grid can help in acquiring clarity of articulation. There are many examples in music therapy literature of people who have had major strokes still being able to sing words. This relates to neurological research that has found that linguistic faculties are processed largely in the dominant hemisphere, for most people the left, whereas the overall processing of music tends to be a minor-hemisphere specialisation (for most people the right). The left hemisphere is concerned with logical and analytical features, the right dealing with holistic, spatial, non-verbal and intuitive features. The neurologist Hans Borchgrevink has labelled these two broadly contrasting features as 'pattern analysis over time' (left) and 'pattern analysis in an instant' (right).[16] Recent research is indicating that exposure to musical training can develop functions within the major hemis-phere, in particular rhythmic and temporal processing. There is much cross-over between the two hemispheres. It is also possible that very basic responses to the emotional and patterned aspects of music are stored at a deep level of con-sciousness. It appears that some melodic and rhythmic well-learned patterns may be stored at such a basic level for long periods and brought into focus to be performed as wholes. This is concurrent with the research of Marin, for example, who gives the example of a person with diffuse damage across both cortices being able to sing with good prosody, rhythm and intonation as well as being able to perform an automatic function such as counting aloud.[17] It is also possible that very young children whose speech and language function is impaired may be able to discriminate simple rhythmic patterns and develop alternative channels for communication. Detailed knowledge about the extent of any damage will caution against an over-optimistic approach.

Evidence for the plasticity of the central nervous system has provided impetus for the development of melodic intonation therapy, where a short linguistic statement is paired with a musical pattern, often the music of a well-known song.[18] Speech and music therapists working with this technique note its benefits but reject any possibility, particularly at an older age, of the minor hemisphere re-acquiring or taking over the language functions of the major hemisphere.[19] But it does give rise to more questions, and combined music-therapy and speech-therapy approaches could be the basis of much fruitful research in areas of neurologically-based problems.

Some criticisms of joint approaches, and some creative solutions in mental health

We could debate that the effectiveness of music therapy may be diluted in these joint approaches. By finding commonalities of approach we may lose track of what music therapy has to offer as a unique discipline. Are we firmly established enough as a discipline to begin to set up joint interventions? Music is a vast enough subject to be broken up into component parts, but perhaps music therapy's greatest strengths lie in its sense of integration and the specific differences from other approaches. The more elusive aspects of music may be the areas that we find eventually are the root causes of its appeal and effectiveness. Such attitudes could become elitist but need to be considered. How is it possible to be part of a team, work closely and effectively with other colleagues and yet retain the central purpose and ethos of music therapy?

We have noted the developing interest in music therapy in the field of mental health in the previous chapter. Given that words and confusion of meanings are often linked to emotional and social problems, music does appear to be offering something quite different and unique in this field. Perhaps one answer lies in keeping some of these essential qualities of music in mind when setting up joint interventions. Joint interventions in the field of mental health seem to confront some of these critical issues. Given that clients may gain personal insights during a musical improvisation, how and where are they going to process such material? Do music therapists also need further extensive training in counselling or psychotherapy in order to offer support and insight to any issue that may be translated from a musical to a verbal medium? Odell finds one answer by linking with a co-therapist.[20] She has evolved close working relationships with drama therapists, in particular when she uses various role-play procedures. Sometimes work is enacted individually; at other times other members of the group are involved, as directed by the individual member concerned. Odell emphasises the importance of looking at what is happening in the moment within and between members of the group. Her clients are then helped to gain more insights to help themselves adapt to life outside the hospital.

David Aldridge and the team of therapists at Herdecke University in Germany have explored the links between music and art therapy. In a joint paper they describe a series of individual art and music therapy for a 36-year-old lady suffering from nervous depression. Different perspectives can be highlighted by the two therapies. They conclude that the experience can be positive:

> The advantage of the creative arts is that they allow us to express our pathologies, they also allow for the expression of potential. In this tension we can then appreciate that both poles can be used creatively; opposites can be reconciled within form. This is the aesthetic act where the negative sign is transformed by the act of creation into the positive.[21]

Music therapy and music teaching

A number of music therapists have also previously been trained as teachers. Some trained therapists later train as music teachers so as to be able to gain full-time employment as therapists or teachers within the British education system. There is much debate on the relationship between teaching and therapy and the bordering areas between these two disciplines.

In the USA a study of both music education and therapy has until very recently been part of music therapy training programmes. In 1967 George Duerksen stressed the similarities in goals, techniques, and groups of children involved.

Helping children to reach their full potential was a goal held by both educationalist and therapists alike. Both disciplines make use of musical behaviour,
Duerksen adding:

> Music education attempts to develop artistic or aesthetic activity and attitudes
> in the particularly human activities we call music; music therapy uses such
> artistic activities and attitudes to help persons develop the most human be-
> haviour patterns of which they are capable.[22]

Ten years later Jayne Alley stressed more of the unique characteristics of music
therapy, noting that a therapist's role in an educational setting could be regarded
as that of a 'specialist to resolve individual problems which negate a student's
ability to fully participate or benefit from his or her educational opportunities'.[23]
In a survey of the differences between music therapy and music education
William Salaman feels the fundamental difference to be one of attitude. At a very
basic level pupils are occupied in studying a subject, whereas in therapy the
clients themselves are the subjects.[24]

In spite of these apparent differences of approach and attitude, developing
therapeutic work does often produce musical changes in the children in addition
to the central emphasis on developmental or therapeutic objectives. There are
also many music educationalists who work in a very child-centred and therapeutic way. Increasingly music therapists are being invited to contribute a basic
introduction to music therapy on teacher-training courses. John Strange has
recently argued that 'educational and therapeutic work are complementary and
not opposed'.[25] In his work as a music therapist at a school for children with
severe learning difficulties he has found that his wide involvement in the work of
the school – such as supervising classes in play periods; covering when staff are
ill; playing the piano for school assemblies; training a choir and helping with
school events – enhances his work as a therapist. It helps him see the children
responding in other contexts and complements his understanding of the children
in music therapy. He also understands more about the needs of the teachers. Other
therapists, including myself, would agree with the complementary nature of the
two disciplines and, when working in a school, would stress the role of therapist
so as not to confuse the children involved in therapy. In this way the work could
be viewed in a similar way by children and staff alike, as akin to that of the
visiting speech therapist, the physiotherapist and other members of the para-
medical team.

MUSIC THERAPY AND THE PSYCHOLOGY OF MUSIC

A further link is between music therapy and the growing specialism of psychology
of music. This link provides two-way opportunities for further understanding:
music therapists stand to benefit from working with musicians researching the
details of musical processes, and music psychologists would be able to ask
questions relating to the raw and spontaneous musical material from people of all

ages. The link is not straightforward, as was demonstrated in a series of joint seminars held in the early 1980s at the City University, London, and in a recent discussion between two music therapists and two music psychologists.[26] There is often confusion over jargon – technical over clinical – and differences in aims and context. One area where there seems to be some future potential is in understanding the musical processes in any period of music therapy. Colin Lee, for example, is researching into some of the surface and deep musical structures and processes of improvisation in music therapy.[27] Such work is at the frontier of trying to understand what is going on in the music in music therapy. It contributes towards a growing sense of 'internal validity' for members of the profession and other interested musicians.[28] We can be supported in such research by more musicians beginning to work as music psychologists. The influence of these musicians will be reflected in a corresponding growth in the awareness of significant events in the music itself rather than in more microscopic analysis of minute aspects of auditory processing. When we turn to any form of musical transaction or interaction we are faced with streams of musical phenomena. In music therapy interactions we face such wide-ranging streams of musical behaviour from the level where a child or adult finds it difficult to formulate a simple pulse, through music that is fragmentary or disconnected, to music that is highly organised, intricate and developed. We could look at some of these processes together with music psychologists. We could look at such processes in their totality as broad changes develop over the weeks of musical interaction, or home in on some small part of the musical behaviour to understand more about a detail in relation to the whole. Recent advances in formulating a cognitive base to music psychology may help us here. Cognitive psychologists are beginning to look into the musical processes that many music therapists consider really matter: that is, what goes on in people's heads when they are making or listening to music. By observing how people behave in music we can begin to understand more about what is going on inside.

SOME THOUGHTS ON THE FUTURE STATUS OF MUSIC THERAPY IN THE COMMUNITY

Members of a relatively new profession such as music therapy are understandably going to have conflicting ideas on how the profession might evolve. Some therapists are interested in developing more links with other creative arts therapies – art, drama and dance movement – by setting up local creative therapy resource centres. Projects could develop from this stimulating mix, with a continuation of joint work already carried out by some therapists in hospital settings – art and music, drama and music, and dance and music would be natural partners. Such integrations could reflect ancient healing traditions, where there appeared to be no need to split up into various specialisations. A tribal healer made full use of dance, music, drama and art.

Other therapists focus on working within para-medical teams and are strengthening existing links with physiotherapists, community nurses, speech therapists, clinical psychologists, psychotherapists and other such disciplines. Some music therapists are finding a base as part of community-based teams providing local resources for people with mental health problems or learning difficulties. It is difficult to maintain links with clients once they have been discharged back into the community. Sometimes the new homes are not in the vicinity of the therapist's base. Some of these clients may have been involved in music therapy for a long period and further music therapy may still be indicated, even if only as a temporary measure to help support and bridge the movement from living in the hospital to living outside. An obvious problem here is the time factor. It may be impractical to continue the individual sessions or set up groups with people living so far apart. In addition to trying to continue seeing those clients who could benefit from further work, a community-based therapist will also be challenged to develop a system for giving priority to the large number of people living outside the old hospitals for whom music therapy may be very appropriate. Such groups of potential clients may have previously not come under the direct care of the hospital.

At present there are very few established links with local general practitioners and health centres. With the changes in local management, budgeting and financial controls it may be possible to offer packages of work that can link in with some of the priorities of a local general practice. Blocks of sessions with a focus on specific client groups could be offered to general practices, even if starting off on a trial basis. Perhaps there will be a time, in the not too distant future, when there will be a music therapist living at a reasonable distance from a practice to whom a local doctor can refer people direct. As medical practice begins to examine the efficacy of more complementary approaches and include them in treatment plans we could also predict a time when access to a music therapist would become part of the many resources of your local surgery.

Several music therapists have set up as freelance, peripatetic therapists, running sessions at different locations or setting up a specific space for sessions. By working on a sessional basis a music therapist has the freedom of movement to make commitments to work within environments that feel comfortable and to meet individual philosophical standpoints. I used to work as a sessional therapist, and an example of part of a working week was: a session at a children's assessment centre; a session at a day hospital for adults with mental health problems; a teaching session; and a session for writing up notes and research. Another therapist may choose to be even more radical by becoming a resource to a local community centre, for example suggesting that a regular music group could become part of the evening young people's club. Mary Troup carried out some pioneering research along these lines by offering her skills as a musician (omitting the sometimes off-putting term 'therapist') to locally based self-help groups.[29] She has documented how such groups gradually included her as trust developed and how various music projects evolved. Her sensitivity and skills as an experienced therapist were very much put to the test in adapting to such situations.

THE SETTING-UP OF MUSICSPACE

A further answer to current needs is to set up local music centres in the midst of where people live. These could become community-based music centres with music therapy at the heart of the local service. Able-bodied and disabled people alike could come together through active participation in music. This is a core philosophy of the charity MusicSpace, the trust recognising that music has the potential to be a very powerful social equaliser. The charity was the practical outcome of a two-year project that explored how a community music therapy service might develop within the County of Avon.[30] The first MusicSpace centre was officially opened in Bristol in November 1991. The main objective of MusicSpace is to set up a network of centres nationwide to:

- provide individual and group music therapy service for people of all ages
- assist in the training of music therapy students
- run training days and workshops on the use of music for all working in the fields of child and adult health
- carry out research into the effects and processes of music therapy
- support the rehearsal and performance of as wide a range of music as possible.

After the first eighteen months of operations the music therapists at the Bristol Centre were seeing over 250 children and adults per week, either at the Centre or as part of a busy outreach programme. Three full-time, one part-time and two sessional therapists were being employed by the trust in January 1993.

In conjunction with Bristol University, MusicSpace set up the first British part-time postgraduate diploma course in Music Therapy, and the first group of students began their studies in January 1992. The course offers an alternative to the present full-time courses and could be viewed as a model for the development of other part-time courses, since the present economic climate makes part-time training a more practical option for mature musicians.

During the first year MusicSpace ran specific training and music workshop days for staff and parents working with adults with learning difficulties; adults with mental health problems; the elderly; pre-school children; and children with learning difficulties. There are plans to develop more workshops, including sessions for adults with hearing impairments.

MusicSpace was commissioned by the Wessex Regional Health Authority to carry out an investigation into the effects of music therapy with elderly mentally ill residents at one of the region's hospitals. The project was set up in collaboration with the hospital's senior clinical psychologist, and three blocks of fifteen sessions have been carefully monitored and evaluated.

MusicSpace is setting up a national development strategy with a firm intention to create other centres nationwide. Each new centre will reflect the need of the particular community. Therapists and colleagues from many cities and also from more rural settings have expressed serious interest in establishing such centres in their own communities.

MusicSpace has already promoted a wide range of musical performances which not only helps secure more funding for the various projects but also brings more people in touch with different kinds of music. Several of the charity's patrons have been involved in these performances.

MusicSpace is setting up a musician-in-residence scheme. There are also plans to create a small electronic studio at the Bristol Centre. This would double up as a space for exploring how current technology can help people with disabilities and a recording studio.

MusicSpace is managed by its council, which includes leading figures from the musical, academic, educational and business communities. Hard-working groups of volunteers support some of the administrative work and fund-raising activities. The growing list of well-known patrons adds support to the development of the trust.

FURTHER CHALLENGES TO THE CONTEMPORARY MUSIC THERAPIST

Music therapists are hard-working and dedicated musicians, some of whom have left rather more financially secure and regular positions within the music profession to develop their expertise as therapists. They face many challenges, and during one week these could include:

- seeing a number of individual adults or children for regular music therapy
- facilitating some music therapy groups
- writing up case notes
- discussing work in regular supervision
- presenting a rationale for increased funding to managers
- supervising the work of a student in training
- preparing material for a lecture
- planning a practical staff training day
- practising and rehearsal for future musical performance.

Such a programme extends both our musicianship and our personal skills. It is likely that we shall meet a wide range of musical behaviour from our clients, who demand empathic and genuine musical responses from us. We will spend time thinking and writing about the music therapy work. Talking to colleagues about the work taxes our ability to be clear about music therapy. In the present climate we need to be increasingly aware of how to market our work, dressing it up in packages that will appear acceptable to the potential funding agency. All in all, not a soft option but an all-embracing occupation that unites many aspects of ourselves. I like to compare such challenges to those that must have been faced by those early musical ambassadors and apprentices the troubadours, or by a busy court or church composer of the seventeenth or eighteenth century. Each day would bring new musical and personal challenges. On a very practical and down-to-earth level, responding effectively to such challenges was also crucial to any financial reward.

If we look at the music therapist from this perspective we see that music therapy can be part of a very contemporary view of music. Well-established groups of musicians, such as members of our leading orchestras, are realising that there is a great deal to be gained by extending work outside the concert hall and recording studio. Many orchestras are now setting up community-based pro-grammes, taking their music-making to new settings such as schools, day centres, hospitals and prisons. There are many fruitful links to be made between these musicians and music therapists, a two-way learning process. Such a two-way interaction is at the hub of the next and final chapter. A synthesis of the artistic and scientific aspects of music therapy is proposed as a response to some of the challenges both in contemporary music-making and in health care.

Chapter 8

Music therapy as a synthesis of art and science: Orpheus as emblem

INTRODUCTION

Benjamin Britten based his last opera on Thomas Mann's novella *Death in Venice*. Here we encounter a highly articulate artist, the writer Gustav von Aschenbach, being unable to use words to communicate directly some of his deepest feelings. The two protagonists of the story, Aschenbach and the boy Tadzio, never communicate verbally, a situation made even more ripe for operatic treatment through Britten's casting of the boy and his family as dancers. A crisis surfaces when Aschenbach tries to warn Tadzio's mother of the dangers of the developing cholera epidemic. She walks into the hall of the hotel; Aschenbach goes up, as if to speak to her, but turns away at the crucial moment. The medium of opera now comes into its own; music provides a vehicle for the articulation of these unspoken emotions. We hear two conflicting forces within Aschenbach personified by the Voice of Apollo (counter-tenor) and the Voice of Dionysus (baritone).

Aschenbach falls victim to the whims of the gods. 'Let the gods do what they will with me', he sings. What do the protagonists, these two polar opposites, Dionysus and Apollo, represent? Traditionally the Greek god Dionysus stands for unbridled energy, free instinct, all that is irrational, all body- and feeling-centred: 'He who denies the god, denies his nature', Dionysus sings. By contrast, Apollo is striving for clarity of mind, rational order and control from out of the potential Dionysiac frenzied chaos: 'Love reason, beauty, form', he sings.[1] His music is in fact part of an ancient Delphic hymn.[2] Apollo tries to discipline the overwhelming and orgiastic emotions that Dionysus is rousing. Dionysus will lead to anarchy if left unbridled. Apollo goes, Dionysus remains and we are led to the final catastrophe – Aschenbach's total collapse and eventual death.

The conflicting pulls of these two Greek gods are at the heart of this chapter. Such ancient themes have resonance today as we try and make sense of our work as music therapists. Apollo and Dionysus can be observed at work in the Cartesian mind and body split that still permeates debates within our profession and other health care disciplines. In Chapter 2, when discussing Freud's later views on the ego, we noted that the creative process provides an opportunity to detach ourselves from the centre of the emotional conflict. This does not mean that we use the art as an escape, but that the Dionysiac unbridled energy can be mastered into pleasurable Apollonian forms and structures. We noted in Chapter 3 how music can be thought of as originating from inner stirrings and movements in the body and articulated externally in musical patterns and forms. This is a very action-based and balanced process; we are not totally overwhelmed by the strength of the feelings. Balance and integration are themes of many contemporary commentators, with writers such as Capra merging strands from physics, medicine, psychology, politics and ecology into a new fusion.[3] Could such fusion and integration be part of music therapy? The main proposition of this final chapter is that both artistic and scientific processes can be synthesised in our research and practice as music therapists. We can begin to bring together some of these apparently conflicting opposites.

EXPRESSION AND ORDER IN MUSIC THERAPY

The musical process is rich in interplay between these two polar opposites. It is clear that making music can bring us and our clients into touch with all manner of irrational material. On the one hand this is very liberating and positive, even if painful at times, but an overemphasis on the irrational and self-expressive function of music can lead to further chaos and inward-looking trends. The Danish philosopher Hans Siggard Jensen presents a vibrant image of this danger in relation to some trends in how music is being used in society, pointing out how we:

> on the one hand have humans that tend to create their identity in relation to computers, and then, due to the one-sidedness of their communication situation, just express their frustrations, and cope with them, through the passive narcissistic enjoyment of a form of music only meant to be used for such fulfilment of needs.[4]

A romantic notion of art tends to stress these indulgent and self-realising aspects. Jensen considers that some pop music videos are the ultimate expression of indulgent narcissism, with their dominance of heavy rhythms and images. Do we as musicians and music therapists want to perpetuate this use of music by feeding into such an over-indulgence?

But music and art in general are also about structure, logic and order. We need Apollonian order and clarity to make sense out of what is happening:

> Art is not only an emotional expression, but also, and mainly, a way of understanding reality. Through artistic activity and the perception of art, we come to see and understand things we would not otherwise have understood.[5]

Nietzsche realized that we can understand the world, even with all its horrors, through our perception of art. He was aware of the interconnections of opposites and that even the painful and tragic in music can be life-affirming. In discussing Nietzsche's views about music Anthony Storr points out that, to him:

Music not only makes life possible, but also makes it exciting. He refers to music as a means by which the passions 'enjoy themselves'; not as escapist, or other-worldly; but as an art which, by exalting life as it is, transcends its original tragedy.[6]

There are as many realities and dimensions as there are artistic expressions. A stress on the cognitive aspects of music, the organisation of expression into forms and structures, will add further meaning to our search for truth. As McNiff states, 'Art allows for the expression of inner chaos and pain through a reassuring external order.'[7] This reassuring balance is needed. Self-expression within the living forms of an artistic medium can therefore at one and the same time be liberating and informative: 'One essential feature of creativity is that it can express both irrational phantasies and the needs of a rational, objective task in one single image or structure.'[8] Such activity is also rooted in communication: it is relational, interactive and transactional. A more cognitive, socially orientated, interactive and communicative position can therefore be a radical alternative to the towering edifices of the commercial music business. Our work as music therapists is helping people to understand that such balanced and focused artistic activity is no luxury, no mere diversion or idle pastime, but an indispensable part of our lives. Music can help us find our lives worth living; perhaps we have never needed it so much, a viewpoint elaborated by Stockhausen:

Music is the medium that touches human beings most deeply, capable of impelling the most delicate inner vibrations. Our Central European culture is more than ever in need of general sensitisation to music. The full significance of that will only be recognised in a few centuries when the crisis of the 'religion of science' will be dying away, and a time will come when humanity's musical aspects – the resonance of all human rhythms and their harmonisation through music – will exert an impact on the entire culture.[9]

We are working in the medium of music, which is able to integrate all aspects of a complex whole to the extent of expressing opposite emotions simultaneously. If we are able then to move from an understanding of these processes in music itself, then, if we identify with the label 'music therapy', are we not also accepting this fusion of artistic and scientific processes within the notion of developing relationships? Bruscia observes of music therapy:

As an art, it is concerned with subjectivity, individuality, creativity and beauty. As a science it is concerned with objectivity, collectivity, replicability and truth. As an interpersonal process it is concerned with empathy, intimacy, communication, reciprocal influence and role relationships.[10]

He goes on to spell out how in music therapy these aspects mutually interact, being both subjective and objective, individual and collective, for example. A sign of maturity and health could be seen as the fusion of objective knowledge with subjective feeling. We can point out even further interconnections of these apparent opposites than Bruscia. To take up only one apparent paradox: there are surely as many creative scientists who talk of striving for beauty as there are artists striving for objectivity and truth. But to echo Bruscia it is apparent that music therapists can embrace multiplicity and diversity while preserving their integrity.

RESEARCH AS SYNTHESIS OF ART AND SCIENCE – TOWARDS MULTIPLICITY OF FORMS

Building up a body of research is well timed in a profession's late adolescence and early adulthood. An apprentice needs to try out different ways of looking at a problem and to ask many multi-faceted questions. A rich descriptive background can be built up that can contribute to understanding and the growth of knowledge and any potential theoretical model-building. As discussed, such research arrives on the back of much practice. Interpretations and inferences can be made, arising out of periods of extensive and detailed description. Sarah Hoskyns noted that in music therapy: 'The art/science dichotomy seems to be our biggest hurdle in developing effective research. We fear that we lose the meaning of art by evolving strategies for research.'[11] An alternative proposal could state that the art/science synthesis is one of the biggest challenges facing the music-therapy researcher. We shall briefly explore the potential fusion of five pairs of what on one level could be regarded as potential opposites.

1   Outcome vs. process

Music therapy is coming of age but there is still a need to demonstrate efficacy. The new purchasers of the skills provided by music therapists continue to ask for evidence of potential effects. We can argue that it is their due, as it is that of clients, parents and all interested in the developing service. We need to discover what is accomplished by any intervention. Positive results are obviously welcome but we can also learn from negative results, which in turn can help set up future questions and further investigations. We may have been asking the wrong sort of questions, using too gross measures or methods. We are at a stage when the 'Does it work?' question seems rather meaningless given the complex interaction of the many variables involved in any piece of therapeutic work – a point noted by John Sloboda at a music therapy conference.[12] This question is different from devising specific outcome measures in order to indicate efficacy and change. In this way the complex stream of behaviours observable in music therapy sessions can be reduced to questions of a manageable size. Such was the background for the series of outcome studies discussed in Chapters 5–7.[13] We can be challenged to work within existing reliable measures: for example, using standardised 'before-and-after' tests, or using such tests in conjunction with specifically constructed outcomes such as target objectives or behaviours. Such work also includes the constraints of constructing reliable measures.

Outcome research occupies one side of a research continuum. It can be criticised by therapists interested in the musical processes as not asking questions at the centre of music therapy. It can tell us very little about how people move to the particular outcomes and the nature of the music used. Detailed research into the musical processes can teach us a great deal about the internal processes of the musical journeys and contribute a great deal to our understanding of musical techniques and structures. However, this side of the continuum can also be criticised for its narrowness and the potential exclusive and inward-looking traps of using music to describe music, as well as for the problems of devising effective systems of notation. Having established change in outcome measures, either positive or negative, would it not then be possible to look at the very processes by which these outcomes were reached? In this way outcome and process work can become more connected: we make our first synthesis. If this becomes a pattern in future work, we would not face the situation in this book with clinical case material and speculations being slightly separated from the more quantitative surveys of work.

2   External vs. internal validity

A clear piece of outcome research provides increasing external validation for the developing discipline of music therapy. Results can be published in language that is understood by members of other professions and by people outside music therapy. Such work contributes to improved professional credibility and academic recognition. The outcome studies referred to earlier indicated, using established research methods, that music therapy has an application and relevance for specific client groups, even if only a narrow band of questions was asked.

On the other side of the continuum, publication of detailed analyses of the musical processes involved may only reach a limited readership of music therapy colleagues, students and other musically-minded people. Such detailed discussions can contribute to an increase in the internal validity of the discipline. I have argued previously for a new synthesis in which both external and internal validity could co-exist within a publication, readers taking from the material what is of personal interest.[14]

Some recent British research appears to be attempting to form such a synthesis. In the abstract of her recent thesis on improvisation in music therapy Mercedes Pavlicevic writes: 'I propose that improvisation in music therapy provides a pivotal synthesis for demonstrating the duality of music and basic emotional responses, and support this with experimental work.'[15] Her first study evaluated how a severe mental health problem such as schizophrenia affects the reciprocal processes in musical improvisation. Her second study analysed the connections between changes in the musical processes and the clinical state of the clients.

3   Quantity vs. quality

This introduces the concepts of 'hard' (quantitative) and 'soft' (qualitative) research. Some of the projects described in Chapters 4 and 6 used statistics as a means of establishing any levels of significance (or not) for results and as a method of generating more questions. I could argue, with hindsight, that in some of my project work there has been an over-reliance on statistics, but not to the extent of accepting criticisms of losing touch with the art of music therapy or becoming a 'numbers man'. It may appear that the complexity of a rich artistic process such as music therapy can be reduced to almost naive proportions by attempts to quantify results. Nevertheless, as argued earlier, it is possible to organise research into rigorous strategies that will not lose touch with the empathy that we establish with our clients. Our sensitivity in the practice of music therapy will not suffer by asking rigorous questions about the how, why, what of our work. This could lead to a period of rigorous story telling. David Aldridge points out that ideas have been presented in story form for centuries. The case study provides an opportunity for such rigour when a behaviour or group of behaviours is observed at stages both during and outside the therapeutic intervention. 'Single case study designs are an attempt to formalise clinical stories with factors of rigorous experimental design being grafted on to the clinical process.'[16] Practising music therapists would not need to alter their current practice to any great degree to carry out such forms of observation and documentation. There is growing evidence that more therapists are turning to the single case study and writing about their work without recourse to jargon, anecdote or over-interpretation.[17] As Sarah Hoskyns reminds us, such work is also economical in resources, time and personnel.[18] Oliver Sacks is a prime contemporary example of a writer who is able to carry out such rigorous story telling. He blends medical neurological background with insightful and, at times quite fanciful, interpretative material. His 'stories' also provide opportunities to examine any underlying phenomena; wider issues are drawn out from the detailed examination of the stories.[19]

Once again different approaches can converge in increasing our understanding of the whole picture. 'Softer' methods, such as interviews, self-evaluations and questionnaires, can add richness to what may appear on the surface to be hard numerical information. But we still need to do our counting – surveys of where therapists work, training records, numbers of therapists, and so on. Such work adds to our growing external validity. Can we then move away from the notion of 'hard' or 'soft' research and begin to think more of evolving different and complementary research strategies?

4   Individual vs. group

There are both advantages and disadvantages to the individual case study and the group study. On the one hand individual studies contain rich detail, illuminate but lack a generalising effect; on the other hand group studies gain on the generalising but lose on the detailed richness. It would be interesting to make specific studies of individual progress within a group and thereby integrate the two approaches. We come face to face with the hot issue of control in order to carry out efficacious research. Clearly the tightly controlled strategies employed when testing a new drug within medical research are impractical in music therapy action-based research, yet we can learn lessons relating to rigour and consistency, still a pre-requisite in people-centred research. In the recent work on case study design we are discovering more how individuals can be used as their own controls.

5   Subjectivity vs. objectivity

We still face our Greek protagonists in this debate. Increasingly we are observing the direct synthesis of this polarity. It becomes joined in the term 'objectively subjective' in new paradigm research.[20] 'There is no single reality in the sense that there are different perspectives, subjectively held, of objective reality.'[21]

Some recent British research is attempting to blend subjective and objective approaches. Sarah Hoskyns, in her original work with offenders, is using clients' self-reports on both their expectations and their reactions to a course of music therapy intervention alongside the more established and reliable methods derived from Personal Construct Psychology.[22] Subjective reporting is increasingly becoming accepted as a means of imparting further meaning and richness to evidence. The clients themselves can make significant contributions to a research process, the new-paradigm researchers including the client in the planning, execution and interpretation of the research.

To this group of five apparent polarities we could add many more, including: right-brain/left-brain; active/passive music therapy techniques; verbal/non-verbal; directive/non-directive approaches; inner/outer forms; background/foreground; observer/observed. The meeting points between the opposites may be the source of the real inspiration. We need not fight from one position or the other but can begin to enjoy the paradoxes. Positive and negative features seem to be present in any chosen research method. Working on several dimensions at the same time, using several procedures, may be one means of integration.

THE PROBLEM OF LANGUAGE

Working in the field of music integrates many factors: practical and therapeutic aims, the setting, all the people involved, the complexities of the musical medium. We want to do justice to the whole, to the richness and multiplicity of the material. In Britten's opera, Aschenbach cannot find the words to articulate his emotions. Words are often highly intrusive after a deeply moving musical experience. We often at moments of ecstasy and intense moments of expressive communication, such as making love, only utter the most elemental of sounds.

The very fact that music therapists have decided to work in such a field may be linked in some way with the inadequacy of language in articulating some of our deepest and most personal feelings. We may be expecting too much of ourselves in writing about the art and science of music therapy. How can we begin to translate the untranslatable?

We have come round full circle. The early anecdotal descriptions demonstrating music's almost innate power to do good evolved into a period of increased rigour. There was a striving for objectivity and much borrowing from well-established research methods. The development of outcome studies has been, for the most part, very much under the control of the researcher, with the various designs and measures set up in response to the different contexts and based within the researcher's value system. This period has led in turn to a stage in which rigour is applied in both objective analysis and subjective self-reporting.

We could think more in images, metaphors and gestures rather than complex interpretations in describing the connections between people and music. James Hillman is convinced that standard psychological language is: 'impoverished, without imagination and incapable of giving good descriptions of phenomena. Clinical language had become too abstract, too professional, and is consequently less and less capable of describing sensuous experience'.[23] The call for an 'imaginative inquiry' is a tall order, being at the same time rigorous and clear, warm, sensitive and highly readable. Descriptive writing can be multi-dimensional; it can be non-linear; it can take on multiple forms. Hillman refers to Joyce's *Ulysses*, which clearly acknowledges multiplicity. Joyce gives us much detail about the lives of some people in one city on a particular day but the writing also embraces vast and universal themes. Hillman and Joyce return us again to Greece and to the deep connections between myth and culture.

We may be entering a stage in music therapy where forms of language will stress both the uniqueness of our work and the connections with other disciplines. Such forms of language could emerge in antithesis to the discursive nature of language used in psychotherapy, for example. If we consider music therapy as a form of psychotherapy, we may run the risk of preventing new forms of description from evolving. Problems of meaning, symbolism and the search for truth seem central to psychoanalysis, for example. Any new forms of reference for music therapy could arise from the work itself, from earlier musical and cultural traditions, and need not be over-dependent on existing models. Meaning seems to be more ambiguous in music; it is impossible to use such terms as 'true' or 'false'. We seem to be dealing more in metaphor and poetic forms. We may not yet have discovered the appropriate language but stand Janus-like on the edge, respecting the past and with tantalising glimpses of what might be.

A SPACE–TIME APPROACH TO HEALTH

There continue to be major changes in how physicists view the world. To the classical physicist nature is objective; time is linear; matter, energy and space are absolute. To the modern, post-Einstein physicist nature is not entirely objective; matter, energy, space and time are not absolute. At the sub-atomic level cause and effect are no longer fundamental. If we think about music therapy from the viewpoint of the determinism or causality of Freudian or behaviour therapy, then we keep alive the earlier fixed positions. Perhaps music therapy, alongside the other creative arts therapies, will begin to move into the uncharted waters of non-linear space–time. The ever-changing, open-ended, connected and inter-active nature of these artistic processes has much that is complementary to these new constructs. There is a multiplicity of connections in musical transactions, as there is in the higher levels of healing. Here there is no mind and body split but a dance-like interplay between mechanistic and non-mechanistic patterns. In his book *Space, Time and Medicine* Larry Dossey proposes that many of our prob-lems and illnesses are related to a misperception and misordering of times. His concept of the 'biodance', where humans are in constant interaction not only with each other but also with larger and even smaller universal patterning, is beauti-fully musical.[24] Dossey does not dispose of the major advances in medicine but places them in synthesis with other complementary non-mechanistic approaches.

A more open-ended, cyclical and spiral-like view of health presents a challenge to music therapists. It is symptomatic of some present directions in music therapy that a medical practitioner with such views as Larry Dossey gave the keynote address at the National Association of Music Therapy's annual conference in Atlanta in 1988. The concepts he was proposing seem to go beyond a holistic model of health to a new ordering of reality. Such an order seems to permeate non-Western cultures, where the numinous, mystical and inexplicable elements of life are accepted with a less questioning attitude. Such attitudes can be seen in the recent re-awakening of the more spiritual qualities of music. A piece such as John Taverner's *A Protecting Veil* becomes a best-selling re-cording, and the rather mystical compositions of Arvo Pärt, for example, are performed to large audiences. There is a growing interest in the ancient healing traditions that use music as a central core, and several texts have recently been published.[25] It seems that interest in such self-healing potential of sound and music is part of a deeper search for meaning and a sense of belonging. Alterna-tives to a fast, hectic life-style are being sought. We can send messages almost instantaneously across the globe but find continuing difficulties in communi-cating with family, friends and colleagues.

We make music in a space–time continuum, using a highly subjective art form that gains meaning through the translation of inner impulses into recognisable pattern, objective form and structure. We bring to our music-making much of the past, which is translated into the present moment. At the same time this moment is instantly predicting the next event. We are beginning to realise the healing potential of music for us all and not only for the traditional client populations referred to music therapy in the past. If we view music in this way, it can release potential as a cohesive force, a spiritual integrator that can bring people of all ages together for a common purpose.

ON THE ANCIENT AND THE NEW IN MUSIC THERAPY

The role of the musician as an active healing force in society is not new. Music therapists such as Joseph Moreno are teaching us that there is a historical connection of music and healing in ancient shamanic traditions.[26] Such traditions are still practised in non-technological and in tribal cultures. We also learn about these ancient traditions from the ethnomusicologists, who, by focusing on the common musical processes, could become instrumental in helping to connect aspects of present-day music therapy with these very ancient roots. Moreno observes that the sustaining, stimulating and organising aspects of rhythm are at the roots of relationships set up by both shaman and music therapist. Rhythmic drumming of a hypnotic and repetitive nature helps the shaman to enter a trance state or altered state of consciousness. This state is considered to be necessary if the shaman is to enter a different sense of reality to gain insights to help the person. It is customary for the shaman to work with a musical assistant, who provides the rhythmic accompaniment. This triadic arrangement has a parallel in some music therapy approaches, where one therapist supports the client and another works with the musical material. I have a vivid memory of one of Jo Moreno's workshops at a music therapy conference, where rhythmic drumming was used to induce such an altered state.

The aim of the workshop was explained at the outset, namely an invitation to explore connections with different levels of awareness. We divided into pairs, with one person as the guide for the other person's internal journey. Jo Moreno played a regular and hypnotic rhythm on a large tambour, inviting us to use the rhythm to visit an imaginary but favourite special natural place, be it a deep pool, a field or whatever. Once there we were invited to look for an animal and to follow it. Where does the animal take us? What is it like? How often do we see it? The guide was asked to clear all extraneous thoughts so as to be open to support the inner journey of the partner. I had a vivid and repeated image of a bird flying from one mountain top to the next and sweeping low over the valleys. On surfacing from this inner journey I found, to my sceptical amazement, that my partner had a very similar image. In the group discussion there were many more such connections between guide and guided. We emerged from the workshop a less cynical group of music therapists, with more questions than answers. There was more of a sense of respect for not knowing than at the start of the workshop.

The use of music as a trigger to guided imagery is a central part of a specific approach known as Guided Imagery in Music (GIM for short). Deep relaxation is paired with concentration on the music to guide the client through various inner journeys. The therapist keeps a written record of the images recounted by the client during the exposure to the music. The images are then discussed. On such journeys areas of personal problems or difficulties may arise which can also be the focus for discussion and future work. This approach is very much based on the work and writings of Helen Bonny, who has carried out extensive research on the kinds of music used in the work.[27]

There are very positive moves in current music therapy, exploring how music therapy can be used preventatively to promote good health, almost as a self-help tool. At the 1988 Atlanta conference one symposium included these titles:

1 Health communication: the relationship of the immune system to imagery, relaxation and music effect.
2 Music, mind and immunity.
3 The influence of preferred relaxing music on measures of state anxiety, perceived relaxation and autonomic responses.[28]

Here is the return of some of the factors – affective responses, autonomic reactions, relaxation – that gave rise to the early interest in music therapy with music's close relationships to basic physiological functioning. The very problems that present-day life-styles create can, paradoxically, be studied by the sophisticated technology that may be adding to our degrees of stress and problems. There is still much controversy over how music, particularly music-listening, can be used in stress reduction. As Susanne Hanser points out, there are many personal issues of preference to consider in selecting the most relaxing music.[29] There are also problems connected with mood changes, and what may be relaxing on one day may irritate the next. It is difficult to generalise about the effects of music over and above commonly held views: for example, that long, slow and soft melodies can contribute to a more relaxed or soporific state.

The use of music as a distractor has also moved into the delivery room and the dental surgery, and it appears that, for the most part, people respond to music in a positive way in these stressful situations.[30] The field is wide open to future carefully monitored research where individual reactions and preferences are respected. Individual profiles need to pre-dominate above any barren attempt at prescriptions for general use.

ORPHEUS – THE RATIONAL SHAMAN

> Orpheus with his lute made trees,
> And the mountain-tops that freeze,
>   Bow themselves, when he did sing:
> To his music plants and flowers
> Ever sprung; as sun and showers
>   There had made a lasting spring.
>
> Everything that heard him play,
> Even the billows of the sea,
>   Hung their heads, and then lay by.
> In sweet music is such art,
> Killing care and grief of heart,
> Fall asleep, or, hearing, die.[31]

Our Greek protagonists at the start of this chapter were Dionysus and Apollo. In conclusion, the myth of Orpheus brings together in a beautiful synthesis many of the apparently opposing paradoxes highlighted in this chapter and throughout the book. Here is a mythical son of Apollo who may also have been historically a Dionysian priest. Here we can observe free expressive energy within formal constraint, a synthesis of the elements of both deities. There is a mix of both the sacred and the profane, the rational and the irrational. In his book *The Masks of Orpheus* Wilfrid Mellers echoes the Shakespeare song and reminds us that Orpheus, as shaman and healer, uses his singing and art to arouse and calm beasts, to chase away shadows (including those internal ones).[32] He counteracts gravity, telescopes time and even confronts the gods by defying death itself. He strives for this balance between the objective demands of rational Apollo and the subjective all-embracing passions of Dionysus. After the death of his beloved Eurydice he makes the descent to Hades (we must note the psychological implications of an implied descent into the unconscious). He is human after all and fails his prescribed task by looking back to check if Eurydice is still following on their journey out of Hades. She is summoned by Pluto back to the underworld. He was not able to die for love and cannot gain full redemption, as is common in full redemption legends such as Tristan and Isolde and in the mystical part of the Christian story. He loses Eurydice for a second time (a double fall?) and, if we look at the myth in Jungian terms, there is no full integration of *anima* and *animus*. He is not complete. If he was able to find a complete balance between rational Apollo and the passions of Dionysus, then he would be, as Mellers says, 'whole and holy, not far from a god himself'.[33] Some endings of the myth have female followers of the god Dionysus dismembering him and scattering his remains on the river Hebrus, yet his head (spirit) carries on singing. A few years ago I worked on Striggio's text, used by Monteverdi in his opera *Orfeo*. Here the ending is more joyous, with the *deus ex machina* figure of Father Apollo reclaiming his son. He becomes united with his father, climbing heavenwards with him. Mellers talks of Orpheus reclaiming the spiritual realm through his art. The music becomes increasingly animated as they soar heavenwards, Orpheus at one point taking over the higher part. There is a spiritual integration, but this is not the final story. The myth presents us with a quest: the constant struggle to unite Dionysus and Apollo, to discover the whole, to discover an earthly paradise. Consequently the opera ends, as Mellers reminds us, with a repetition of this eternal pattern. The shepherds sing and dance with the same energy and freedom as at the start of the opera.

In Orpheus the music therapist has an emblem. Like Orpheus, the contemporary music therapist can synthesise science and art in both practice and research. Like Orpheus, we are searching not necessarily for the only truth, but for aspects of the truth. We cannot answer all the questions at once, and each set of questions inter-connects beautifully with the next. What we can do is gradually to build up our understanding of part of the whole.

Music and music-making can be a focus of real beauty and transformation, helping us to define our humanity and all that is vibrant in living to our creative potential. Music can contribute to making life possible and liveable. According to the great Sufi master Hazrat Inayat Kahn, 'The whole of life in all its aspects is one single music; and the real spiritual attainment is to tune oneself to the harmony of this perfect music.'[34] There may well be the dance at the still point of the revolving world, to paraphrase Eliot.[35] At the source of the dance, we may yet find the resonating and rhythmic vibration.

Appendix

For general information about music therapy in the UK, including the training courses, write to:

The Administrator
British Society for Music Therapy
25 Rosslyn Road
East Barnet
Hertfordshire EN4 8DH

For specific information about the local provision of music therapy and other professional issues, write to:

The Administrator
The Association of Professional Music Therapists
Chestnut Cottage
38 Pierce Lane
Fulbourn
Cambridge CB1 5DL[1]

For information about MusicSpace, write to:

The MusicSpace Trust
The Southville Centre
Beauley Road
Bristol BS3 1QG

When writing within this country for further information to these addresses, please include a stamped addressed envelope.

Notes

INTRODUCTION

1 A. Sher, *Year of the King*, London: Methuen, 1985, p. 215.

1 THE GROWTH OF MUSIC THERAPY

1 W.B. Davis, 'Music Therapy in Victorian England', *Journal of British Music Therapy*, 1988, vol. 2, no. 1, pp. 10–17. Groups of female singers and instrumentalists of either sex (violins and harp) were employed to play in adjoining rooms to the patients' wards. The musicians were encouraged not to see or talk to the patients. This interesting early development is also briefly discussed in J. Alvin, *Music Therapy*, London: Hutchinson, 1975.
2 D. Blair, 'Arts in Society: Music Therapy', *New Society*, 30 January 1964, p. 26.
3 E. Feder and B. Feder, *The 'Expressive' Arts Therapies: Art, Music and Dance as Psychotherapy*, New Jersey: Prentice-Hall, 1981.
4 S. Licht, *Music in Medicine*, Boston, Massachusetts: New England Conservatory of Music, 1946; E. Podolsky, *Music Therapy*, New York: Philosophical Library, 1954; D.M. Schullian and D. Schoen, *Music and Medicine*, New York: Henry Schuman, 1948; W. Van de Wall, *Music in Institutions*, New York: Russell Sage Foundation, 1936.
5 Podolsky, op.cit., p. 18
6 G.W. Ainlay, *The Place of Music in Military Hospitals*, in Schullian and Schoen, op.cit., pp. 322–51.
7 For further details of the development of the profession in the USA, see: B. Fleshman and J.L. Fryrear, *The Arts in Therapy*, Chicago: Nelson-Hall, 1981; E.T. Gaston, *Music in Therapy*, New York: Macmillan, 1968; and D.E. Michel, *Music Therapy – an Introduction to Therapy and Special Education through Music*, Springfield, Illinois: Charles C. Thomas, 1976.
8 Like its American counterparts, the BSMT organises conferences and workshops, helps finance the publication of a journal and generally disseminates information about music therapy. Membership is open to all.
9 The Guildhall course was set up originally in cooperation with the BSMT and is currently validated by York University.
10 This course is currently based within the Nordoff–Robbins Music Therapy Centre in North London and since 1984 has been validated by the City University, London.
11 The APMT represents the professional interests of qualified therapists.
12 This course is currently validated by the Roehampton Institute.
13 *Hansard: 29 April 1980.*
14 *DHSS Memorandum: PM (82) 6.*

15 Michel, op. cit., p. vii.
16 Alvin, op. cit., p. 4.
17 Quoted in K.E. Bruscia, *Defining Music Therapy*, Spring City, Pennsylvania: Spring House Books, 1989, p. 172.
18 NAMT career leaflet, 1980, p. 1.
19 Fleshman and Fryrear, op. cit., p. 59.
20 P. Nordoff and C. Robbins, *Therapy in Music for Handicapped Children*, London: Gollancz, 1971; P. Nordoff and C. Robbins, *Music Therapy in Special Education*, London: Macdonald & Evans, 1975; P. Nordoff and C. Robbins, *Creative Music Therapy*, New York: John Day, 1977.
21 Alvin, op.cit., p. 82.
22 E.H. Schneider, R.F. Unkefer and E.T. Gaston, Introduction to Gaston, op.cit.
23 K.E. Bruscia, *Improvisational Models of Music Therapy*, Springfield, Illinois: Charles C. Thomas, 1987, p. 9.
24 R.O. Benenzon, *Music Therapy Manual*, Springfield, Illinois: Charles C. Thomas, 1981, p. 50.
25 P. Steele, 'Foreword', *Journal of British Music Therapy*, 1988, vol. 2, no. 2, p. 3.
26 C. Kenny, *The Mythic Artery: The Magic of Music Therapy*, Atuscadero, California: Ridgeview Publishing Co., 1982, p. 6.
27 *NAMT Standards of Clinical Practice*, 1983.
28 Bruscia, op. cit. (1989), p. 47.
29 Leaflet published by Association of Professional Music Therapists, 1990.
30 D. Soibelman, *Therapeutic and Industrial Uses of Music: a Review of the Literature*, New York: Columbia University Press, 1948. Also see Alvin, op. cit. and Licht, op. cit.
31 Benenzon, op. cit., p. 143.
32 Alvin, op. cit., p. 38.
33 K.D. Goodman, 'Music Therapy', in S. Arieti and H.K.H. Brodie (eds), *American Handbook of Psychiatry: Volume 7 – Advances and New Directions*, New York: Basic Books, 2nd edition, 1981, pp. 564–83.
34 H.E. Sigerist, 'Tarantism', in Schullian and Schoen, op. cit., pp. 96–116, and see Alvin, op. cit.
35 Alvin, op. cit., p. 48.
36 Licht, op. cit., p. 18.
37 Feder and Feder, op. cit., p. 43.
38 C. Rogers, *On Becoming a Person*, London: Constable, 1976.
39 E. Ruud, *Music Therapy and its Relationship to Current Treatment Theories*, St Louis, Missouri: Magnamusic-Baton, 1980, p. 1.
40 J.A. Jellison, 'The Frequency and General Mode of Inquiry of Research in Music Therapy, 1952–72', *Council for Research in Music Education Bulletin*, 1973, vol. 35, no. 3, pp. 114–29.
41 J.P. Gilbert, 'Published Research in Music Therapy, 1973–1978: Content, Focus and Implications for Future Research', *Journal of Music Therapy*, 1981, vol. 16, no. 3, pp. 102–10.
42 L. Bunt, 'Research in Music Therapy in Great Britain: Outcome Research with Handicapped Children', *British Journal of Music Therapy*, 1984, vol. 15, no. 3, p. 3.
43 Jellison, op. cit., p. 7.
44 C. Kenny, Conference presentation, NAMT, Atlanta, 1988.

2 THE RELATIONSHIPS BETWEEN MUSIC THERAPY AND OTHER FORMS OF THERAPEUTIC INTERVENTION

1 J. Alvin, *Music Therapy*, London: Hutchinson, 1975, p. 3.

2 G. Ansdell, 'Limitations and Potential: A Report on a Music Therapy Group for Clients Referred from a Counselling Service', *Journal of British Music Therapy*, 1990, vol. 4, no. 1, p. 22.

3 I.D. Yalom, *The Theory and Practice of Group Psychotherapy*, London: Basic Books, 3rd edition, 1985, pp. 3–4.

4 N. Spender, 'Music Therapy', in S. Sadie (ed.), *New Grove Dictionary of Music and Musicians*, London: Macmillan, 1980.

5 M. Critchley and R. Henson, *Music and the Brain*, London: Heinemann, 1977. This text provides extensive documentation of this rare condition in chapters 19 and 20.

6 G.E. Arrington, 'Music in Medicine', in E. Podolsky (ed.), *Music Therapy*, New York: Philosophical Library, 1954, pp. 264–73.

7 E. Ruud, *Music Therapy and its Relationship to Current Treatment Theories*, St Louis, Missouri: Magnamusic-Baton, 1980, pp. 18–19.

8 D.S. Ellis and G. Brighouse, 'Effects of Music on Respiration and Heart-Rate', in Podolsky, op.cit., pp. 158–69.

9 E.W. Weidenfeller and G.H. Zimny, 'Effects of Music upon GSR of Children', *Child Development*, 1962, vol. 33, pp. 891–6, and 'Effects of Music upon GSR of Depressives and Schizophrenics', *Journal of Abnormal Psychology*, 1962, vol. 64, pp. 307–12.

10 M. Rieber, 'The Effect of Music on the Activity Level of Children', *Psychonomic Science*, 1965, vol. 3, no. 8, pp. 325–6.

11 From time to time the NAMT publishes short summaries of research. Many physiologically based studies are summarised, for example, in M.L. Sears and W.W. Sears, 'Abstracts of Research in Music Therapy', *Journal of Music Therapy*, 1964, vol. 1, no. 2, pp. 33–60.

12 N. Spender, 'Psychology of Music,' in S. Sadie (ed.) *New Grove Dictionary of Music and Musicians*, London: Macmillan, 1980.

13 See: C.E. Furman, 'The Effect of Musical Stimuli on the Brainwave Production of Children', *Journal of Music Therapy*, 1978, vol. 15, no. 3, pp. 108–17; J.M. McElwain, 'The Effect of Spontaneous and Analytical Listening on the Evoked Cortical Activity in the Left and Right Hemispheres of Musicians and Non-Musicians', *Journal of Music Therapy*, 1979, vol. 16, no. 4, pp. 180–90; M.J. Wagner, 'Brain Waves and Biofeedback: a Brief History – Implications for Music Research', *Journal of Music Therapy*, 1975, vol. 12, no. 2, pp. 46–58; M.J. Wagner and A. Menzel, 'Effect of Music Listening and Attentiveness Training on the EEG's of Musicians and Non-Musicians', *Journal of Music Therapy*, 1977, vol. 14, no. 4, pp. 151–65.

14 I.M. Altshuler, 'The Past, Present, and Future of Music Therapy', in Podolsky, op.cit., p. 31.

15 R.O. Benenzon, *Music Therapy Manual*, Springfield, Illinois: Charles C. Thomas, 1981, pp. 33–7.

16 M.S. Rider, 'Treating Chronic Disease and Pain with Music-Mediated Imagery', *The Arts in Psychotherapy*, 1987, vol. 14, no. 2, pp. 113–20.

17 Ruud, op. cit.

18 A comprehensive survey of this literature is provided by P. Noy, 'The Psychodynamic Meaning of Music', *Journal of Music Therapy*, 1966, vol. 3, no. 4, pp. 126–35; vol. 4, no. 1, pp. 7–18; vol. 4, no. 2, pp. 45–52, vol.4, no. 3, pp. 81–95; vol. 4, no. 4, pp. 117–26. A summary can be found in Ruud, op. cit.

19 J. Strachey (ed.), *The Standard Edition of the Complete Psychological Works of Sigmund Freud*, London: Hogarth Press, 1953–64, vol. 13, pp. 11–12.

20 R. May, 'The Nature of Creativity', in H. Anderson (ed.), *Creativity and its Cultivation*, New York: Harper & Row, 1959, p. 57.

21 A. Storr, 'Psychoanalysis and Creativity', in A. Storr, *Churchill's Black Dog, and Other Phenomena of the Human Mind*, Glasgow: Collins–Fontana, 1989.
22 C.G. Jung, 'On the Relation of Analytical Psychology to Poetry' (1922), in *The Collected Works of C.G. Jung*, London: Routledge, vol. 15, para. 115.
23 Jung, op. cit., vol. 6, para. 197.
24 May, op. cit., p. 57.
25 D.H. Hitchcock, 'The Influence of Jung's Psychology on the Therapeutic Use of Music', *Journal of British Music Therapy*, 1987, vol. 1, no. 2, pp. 17–21.
26 F. Jensen, *C.G. Jung, Emma Jung and Toni Wolff*, San Francisco, California: The Analytical Club, 1982, pp. 125–8; and see M. Tilly, 'Music Therapy', in *Notes for Californian Music Libraries*, vol. 1, no. 9, pp. 1–9.
27 Jensen, op. cit., p. 126.
28 E. Fromm, 'The Creative Attitude', in Anderson, op. cit., p. 44.
29 R. May, *The Courage to Create*, New York: W.R. Norton, 1975.
30 Fromm, op. cit., p. 48.
31 Noy, op. cit.
32 H. Racker, 'Psychoanalytic Considerations on Music and the Musician', *Psychoanalytic Review*, 1965, vol. 52, pp. 75–94.
33 P. Ostwald, 'Music in the Organisation of Childhood Experience and Emotion', in F.R. Wilson and F.L. Roehmann, (eds), *Music and Child Development*, St Louis, Missouri: Magnamusic-Baton, 1990, p. 18.
34 Ruud, op. cit., p. 40.
35 C.K. Madsen, V.M. Cotter and C.H. Madsen, 'A Behavioural Approach to Music Therapy', *Journal of Music Therapy*, 1968, vol. 5, no. 3, pp. 69–71 (p. 70).
36 The NAMT's official publication the *Journal of Music Therapy* contains many examples of work within this framework, for example: K. Roskam, 'Music Therapy as an Aid for Increasing Auditory Awareness and Improving Reading Skill', *Journal of Music Therapy*, 1979, vol. 16, no. 1, pp. 31–42; D.M. Miller, L.G. Dorow and R.D. Greer, 'The Contingent Use of Art for Improving Arithmetic Scores', *Journal of Music Therapy*, 1974, vol. 11, no. 2, pp. 57–64; K. K. Underhill and L.M. Harris, 'The Effect of Contingent Music on Establishing Imitation in Behaviourally Disturbed Retarded Children', *Journal of Music Therapy*, 1974, vol. 11, no. 3, pp. 156–66.
37 See: A.L. Steele, 'Programmed Use of Music to Alter Uncooperative Problem Behaviour', *Journal of Music Therapy*, 1968, vol. 5, no. 4, pp. 131–9; H. Jorgenson, 'The Use of Contingent Music Activity to Modify Behaviours which Interfere with Learning', *Journal of Music Therapy*, 1974, vol. 11, no. 1, pp. 41–6; T.J. Scott, 'The Use of Music to Reduce Hyperactivity in Children', *American Journal of Orthopsychiatry*, 1970, vol. 40, no. 4, pp. 677–80; W. Lathom, 'Music Therapy as a Means of Changing the Adaptive Behaviour Level of Retarded Children', *Journal of Music Therapy*, 1964, vol. 1, no. 4, pp. 132–4.
38 See: C.L. Dileo, 'The Use of a Token Economy Program with Mentally Retarded Persons in a Music Therapy Setting', *Journal of Music Therapy*, 1975, vol. 12, no. 3, pp. 155–60; L.P. Hauck and P.L. Martin, 'Music as a Reinforcer in Patient Controlled Duration of Time Out', *Journal of Music Therapy*, 1970, vol. 7, no. 2, pp. 43–53.
39 C.V. Wilson, 'The Use of Rock Music as a Reward in Behaviour Therapy with Children', *Journal of Music Therapy*, 1976, vol. 13, no. 1, pp. 39–48.
40 L.H. Ponath and C.H. Bitcon, 'A Behavioural Analysis of Orff–Schulwerk', *Journal of Music Therapy*, 1972, vol. 9, no. 2, pp. 56–63.
41 A.L. Steele, 'Application of Behavioural Research Techniques to Community Music Therapy', *Journal of Music Therapy*, 1977, vol. 14, no. 3, pp. 102–15 (p. 103).
42 D.F. Carroccio and B.B. Carroccio, 'Towards a Technology of Music Therapy', *Journal of Music Therapy*, 1972, vol. 9, no. 2, pp. 51–6 (p. 51).

43 J.K. McGinty, 'Survey of Current Functions of a Music Therapist', *Journal of Music Therapy*, 1980, vol. 17, no. 2, pp. 148–66.
44 Ruud, op. cit.
45 D.E. Blackman, 'Images of Man in Contemporary Behaviourism', in A.J. Chapman and D.M. Jones (eds) *Models of Man*, Leicester: British Psychological Society, 1980, pp. 99–112.
46 Blackman, op. cit.
47 Ruud, op. cit., pp. 63–86.
48 ibid., pp. 75–7.
49 W.W. Sears, 'Processes in Music Therapy', in E.T. Gaston (ed.) *Music in Therapy*, New York: Macmillan, 1968, p. 33.
50 L.G.K. Bunt and S.L. Hoskyns, 'A Perspective on Music Therapy Research in Great Britain', *Journal of British Music Therapy*, 1987, vol. 1, no. 1, p. 4.
51 For a recent review of applications of cognitive therapy, see: J. Scott, J.M.G. Williams and A.T. Beck (eds), *Cognitive Therapy in Clinical Practice*, London: Routledge, 1989.
52 Ruud, op. cit., p. 1.

3 SOUND, MUSIC AND MUSIC THERAPY

1   J. Alvin, *Music Therapy*, London: Hutchinson, 1975, p. 61.
2   H. Gardner, *Frames of Mind*, London: Heinemann, 1984, pp. 99–127.
3   J. Blacking, *A Common-Sense View of All Music*, Cambridge: Cambridge University Press, 1987, p. 30.
4   Alvin, op. cit., p. 61.
5   G. Ansdell, 'Limitations and Potential – A Report on a Music Therapy Group for Clients referred from a Counselling Service', *Journal of British Music Therapy*, 1990, vol. 4, no. 1, p. 25.
6   A. Copland, *Music and Imagination*, Cambridge, Massachusetts: Harvard University Press, 1952, p. 24.
7   ibid., p. 14.
8   See D. Ward, *Hearts and Hands and Voices*, London: Oxford University Press, 1976 and *Sing a Rainbow*, London: Oxford University Press, 1979.
9   Alvin, op. cit., pp. 16–17
10 T. McLaughlin, *Music and Communication*, London: Faber, 1970, p. 21; D. Cooke, *The Language of Music*, London: Oxford University Press, 1959, p. 105.
11 R. McClellan, *The Healing Forces of Music*, Shaftesbury: Element Books, 1991; and see P.M. Hemel, *Through Music to the Self*, Shaftesbury: Element Books, 1978, particularly chapter 5.
12 See review of pitch and pitch discrimination in N. Spender, 'Psychology of Music', in S. Sadie (ed.), *New Grove Dictionary of Music and Musicians*', London: Macmillan, 1980.
13 I remain grateful to Juliette Alvin for providing this striking example during one of her classes at the Guildhall School of Music and Drama, 1976.
14 O. Skille, T. Wigram and L. Weekes, 'Vibroacoustic Therapy: The Therapeutic Effect of Low Frequency Sound on Specific Physical Disorder and Disabilities', *Journal of British Music Therapy*, 1989, vol. 3, no. 2, p. 7.
15 Skille *et. al*, op. cit., p. 7.
16 P. Nordoff and C. Robbins, *Therapy in Music for Handicapped Children*, London: Gollancz, 1971, p. 7.
17 L. Dossey, *Space, Time and Medicine*, Boston, Massachusetts: Shambhala Publications, 1982, pp. 26–7.

18 See Gay Gaer Luce's extensive study of durations in both animal and human physiology: *Body-time – The Natural Rhythms of the Body*, St Albans: Granada, 1973.
19 McLaughlin, op. cit., pp. 31–40.
20 P. Fraisse, 'Rhythm and Tempo', in D. Deutsch (ed.), *The Psychology of Music*, London: Academic Press, 1982, pp. 151–4.
21 O. Sacks, *Awakenings*, revised edition, London: Pan, 1991, p. 60.
22 R. Ornstein, *On the Experience of Time*, Harmondsworth: Penguin Books, 1969.
23 S. Langer, *Feeling and Form*, London: Routledge & Kegan Paul, 1953, p. 108.
24 ibid.
25 N. Spender, 'Music Therapy', in *New Grove Dictionary of Music and Musicians*, op. cit.
26 E.T. Gaston, *Music in Therapy*, New York: Macmillan, 1968, p. 17.
27 Fraisse, op. cit., p. 150.
28 A. McGlashan, *Gravity and Levity*, London, Chatto and Windus, 1976, p. 137.
29 Gardner, op. cit., pp. 104–5.
30 F. Capra, *The Turning Point*, London: Fontana, 1983, p. 355.
31 Spender, 'Psychology of Music: Rhythm', in Sadie, op. cit., p. 403.
32 Gaston, op. cit., pp. 17–19.
33 See Spender, 'Psychology of Music: Rhythm', in Sadie, op. cit., pp. 405–6.
34 ibid., p. 409.
35 Fraisse, op. cit., pp. 154–5.
36 Nordoff and Robbins, op. cit., p. 52.
37 ibid., p. 63.
38 ibid.
39 Plato, in Jowett's translation, *The Republic, Book Three*, section 399, London: Sphere, 1970.
40 A. Storr, *Music and the Mind*, London: HarperCollins, 1992, pp. 46–8.
41 W.J. Dowling, 'Melodic Information Processing and its Development, in Deutsch, op. cit., p. 415.
42 Zenatti, 1969, discussed in Dowling, op. cit., pp. 418–19.
43 J. Sloboda, 'Empirical Studies of Emotional Response to Music', in M. Riess-Jones (ed.), *Cognitive Bases of Musical Communication*, Washington DC: American Psychological Association, 1991, pp. 33–46 (p. 36).
44 J. Sloboda, *The Musical Mind*, Oxford: Oxford University Press, 1985, pp. 253–7.
45 Cf. J. Blacking, *How Musical is Man?*, Seattle: University of Washington Press, 1973.
46 See McClellan, op. cit., pp. 9–20 for a straightforward account of the physical world of sound, including the natural harmonic series.
47 L. Bernstein, *The Unanswered Question*, Cambridge, Massachusetts: Harvard University Press, 1976.
48 Storr, op. cit., pp. 59–62.
49 P. Nordoff and C. Robbins, *Creative Music Therapy*, New York: John Day, 1977, p. 102, and see Part Five for a series of comprehensive practical exercises on exploring intervals and different scale-systems.
50 Plato, op. cit., p. 166
51 Cooke, op. cit., pp. 146–51.
52 Sloboda, op. cit., (1991) p. 41.
53 L.B. Meyer, *Emotion and Meaning in Music*, Chicago: University of Chicago Press, 1956.
54 See Chapter 4, 'Music in early childhood'.
55 Spender, 'Psychology of Music', p. 410.
56 Blacking, op. cit. (1987), p. 26.
57 Sloboda op. cit. (1991), pp. 33–46.
58 Meyer, op. cit., pp. 22–32.

59 Sloboda op. cit. (1985), p. 265.
60 A. Storr, 'Music in Relation to Self', *Journal of British Music Therapy*, 1991, vol. 5, no. 1, pp. 5–14.
61 Blacking, op. cit. (1973), p.111.
62 ibid., pp. 32–53.
63 R. Sessions, *The Musical Experience of Composer, Performer, Listener*, Princeton, New Jersey: Princeton University Press, 1971, p. 4.
64 Blacking, op. cit. (1973), p. 54.
65 ibid., pp. 8–10.
66 Sloboda, op. cit. (1985), p. 268.
67 B. Chatwin, *The Songlines*, London: Pan, 1987, p. 120.
68 Storr, op. cit. (1991), p.8.
69 Sessions, op. cit., p. 24.
70 S.K. Langer, 'On Significance in Music', in *Philosophy in a New Key*, Cambridge, Massachusetts: Harvard University Press, 1942, p. 243.
71 Langer op. cit. (1942, 1953).
72 Sloboda op. cit. (1985), pp. 11–66; see Chapter 2.

4 MUSIC THERAPY AND CHILD HEALTH

1 John Sloboda provides a thorough summary of both musical enculteration and learning in his book *The Musical Mind*, Oxford: Oxford University Press, 1985. For other surveys of the influence of musical training, see R. Shuter-Dyson and C. Gabriel, *The Development of Musical Ability*, 2nd edition, London: Methuen, 1981, and D. Hargreaves, *The Developmental Psychology of Music*, Cambridge: Cambridge University Press, 1986.
2 See Hargreaves, op. cit.; Shuter-Dyson and Gabriel, op. cit.; and J. Funk and J. Whiteside, 'Developmental Theory and the Psychology of Music', *Psychology of Music*, 1981, vol. 9, no. 2, pp. 44–54.
3 J-E. Berendt, *The Third Ear*, Shaftesbury: Element Books, 1988, p. 37.
4 ibid., p. 38.
5 L. Salk, 'The Effects of the Maternal Heartbeat Sound on the Behaviour of the Newborn Infant: Implications for Mental Health', *World Mental Health*, 1960, vol. 12, pp. 168–75.
6 See recent review by P.F. Ostwald, 'Music and Emotional Development in Children', in F.R. Wilson and F.L. Roehmann (eds), *Music and Child Development*, St Louis, Missouri: Magnamusic-Baton, 1990, pp. 11–27.
7 Hargreaves, op. cit., p. 61.
8 See: E. Ockelford, 'Response to Rhythmical Sound in Pre-Term Infants and Term Neonates', *Journal of Reproductive and Infant Psychology*, 1984, vol. 2, pp. 92–6; and E.M. Ockelford, M.A. Vince, C. Layton and M.R. Reader, 'Response of Neonates to Parents' and Others' Voices', *Early Human Development*, 1988, vol. 18, pp. 27–36.
9 D.J. Shetler, 'The Inquiry into Prenatal Musical Experience', in Wilson and Roehmann, op. cit., p. 54.
10 Ostwald, op. cit., p. 13.
11 I am grateful to John Chesney for this personal communication.
12 Sloboda, op. cit., pp. 198–202.
13 H. Moog, *The Musical Experience of the Pre-School Child*, London: Schott, 1976.
14 D.N. Stern, *The Interpersonal World of the Infant*, New York: Basic Books, 1985, p. 10.
15 Stern, op. cit., pp. 138–62.
16 See H.R. Schaffer, *Studies in Mother–Infant Interaction*, London: Academic Press, 1977; and T.G.R Bower, *A Primer of Infant Development*, San Francisco, California: W.H. Freeman, 1977.

17 Bower, op. cit.
18 C. Trevarthen, 'Descriptive Analysis of Infant Communicative Behaviour', in Schaffer, op. cit.
19 M. Lewis and L.A. Rosenblum, *The Effect of the Infant on its Caregiver*, New York: Wiley, 1974.
20 J.S. Bruner, 'Early Social Interaction', in Schaffer, op. cit., p. 287.
21 W.S. Condon, 'A Primary Phase in the Organisation of Infant Responding Behaviour', in Schaffer, op. cit., pp. 153–76.
22 Stern, op. cit., p. 85.
23 K. Kaye, *The Mental and Social Life of Babies*, London: Methuen, 1984, pp. 64–79.
24 S.J. Pawlby, 'Imitative Interaction', in Schaffer, op. cit., pp. 203–24.
25 D. Stern, *The First Relationship: Infant and Mother*, London: Fontana, 1977, pp. 81–105.
26 M. Bullowa, *Before Speech*, Cambridge: Cambridge University Press, 1979, p. 71.
27 Stern, op. cit. (1985), p. 139.
28 ibid., p. 142.
29 K.S. Robson, 'The Role of Eye-to-Eye Contact in Maternal–Infant Attachment', *Journal of Child Psychology and Psychiatry*, 1967, vol. 8, pp. 13–25.
30 G.M. Collis and H. R. Schaffer, 'Synchronisation of Visual Attention in Mother–Infant Pairs', *Journal of Child Psychology and Psychiatry*, 1975, vol. 16, pp. 315–20.
31 M. Scaife and J.S. Bruner, 'The Capacity for Joint Visual Attention in the Infant', *Nature*, 1975, vol. 253, pp. 265–6.
32 S.B. Miranda and R.L. Fantz, 'Visual Preferences of Down's Syndrome and Normal Infants', *Child Development*, 1973, vol. 44, pp. 555–61.
33 C. Hutt and C. Ounsted. 'The Biological Significance of Gaze Aversion with Particular Reference to the Syndrome of Infantile Autism', *Behavioural Science*, 1966, vol. 11, pp. 346–56.
34 S. Fraiberg, 'Intervention in Infancy: A Programme for Blind Babies', *Journal of the American Academy of Child Psychiatry*, 1971, vol. 10, pp. 381–405.
35 L. Bernstein, *The Unanswered Question*, Cambridge, Massachusetts: Harvard University Press, 1976, p 129.
36 M.R. James, 'Sensory Integration: A Theory for Therapy and Research', *Journal of Music Therapy*, 1984, vol. 16, no. 2, pp. 79–88.
37 D.W. Winnicott, *Playing and Reality*, London: Tavistock, 1971, pp. 1–30.
38 J. Alvin, 'The Musical Instrument as an Intermediary Object', *British Journal of Music Therapy*, 1977, vol. 8, no. 2, pp. 7–13.
39 K.D. Goodman, 'Music Therapy', in S. Arieti and H.K.H. Brodie (eds), *American Handbook of Psychiatry: Volume 7 – Advances and New Directions*, 2nd edition, New York: Basic Books, 1981, pp. 564–83.
40 M.R. Pflederer, 'The Responses of Children to Musical Tasks embodying Piaget's Principle of Conservation', *Journal of Research in Music Education*, 1964, vol. 12, pp. 251–68.
41 M.S. Rider, 'The Relationship between Auditory and Visual Perception on Tasks employing Piaget's Concept of Conservation', *Journal of Music Therapy*, 1977, vol. 14, no. 3, pp. 126–38; M.S. Rider, 'The Assessment of Cognitive Functioning Level through Musical Perception', *Journal of Music Therapy*, 1981, vol. 18, no. 3, pp. 110–19.
42 Funk and Whiteside, op. cit., pp. 46–9.
43 Hargreaves, op. cit., pp. 31–50.
44 Cited by Funk and Whiteside, op. cit., pp. 45–6.
45 Shuter-Dyson and Gabriel, op. cit., p. 101.
46 K. Swanwick, *Music, Mind and Education*, London: Routledge, 1988; and K.

Swanwick and J. Tillman, 'The Sequence of Musical Development: A Study of Children's Composition', *British Journal of Music Education*, 1986, vol. 3, no. 3, pp. 305–39.

47 Swanwick and Tillman, op. cit., p. 309.

5 MUSIC THERAPY AND CHILD HEALTH

1 See the classic texts published in the 1960s and 1970s: J. Alvin, *Music for the Handicapped Child*, London: Oxford University Press, 1965, and *Music Therapy for the Autistic Child*, London: Oxford University Press, 1978; P. Nordoff and C. Robbins, *Therapy in Music for Handicapped Children*, London: Gollancz, 1971; P. Nordoff and C. Robbins, *Music Therapy in Special Education*, London: Macdonald & Evans, 1975, and *Creative Music Therapy*, New York: John Day, 1977.

2 L. Bunt, 'Research in Music Therapy in Great Britain: Outcome Research with Handicapped Children', *British Journal of Music Therapy*, 1984, vol. 15, no. 3, pp. 2–8.

3 For example, see: J. Brown, 'The Psychological and Physical Responses to Music Therapy of Very Young Retarded Children', *British Journal of Music Therapy*, 1974, vol. 5, no. 3, pp. 2–8; A. Lee, 'Music Therapy and the Handicapped', *British Journal of Music Therapy*, 1981, vol. 12, no. 1, pp. 6–12; F. Morgenstern, 'Music Therapy for the Mentally Handicapped: Some Theoretical Considerations', *British Journal of Music Therapy*, 1974, vol. 5, no.1, pp. 9-16.

4 A. Warwick, 'The Role of Music in the Treatment and Education of the Autistic Child', *British Journal of Music Therapy*, 1984, vol. 15, no. 1, pp. 2–8; J.W. Austin, 'The Use of Music in the Education of the Deaf', *British Journal of Music Therapy*, 1970, vol. 2, no. 1, pp. 2–10; T. Sheppard, 'Relationship Therapy through Music with Maladjusted Boys', *British Journal of Music Therapy*, 1977, vol. 8, no. 3, pp. 6–10; F.M. Wolf, 'Music Therapy with the Blind, *British Journal of Music Therapy*, 1978, vol. 9, no. 3, pp. 6–9; B. Reaks, 'The Physically Handicapped Child', *British Journal of Music Therapy*, 1971, vol. 2, no. 2, pp. 31–5.

5 E. Streeter, 'The Role of Music Therapy in the Assessment and Treatment of a Pre-School Language Delayed Child', *British Journal of Music Therapy*, 1978, vol. 9, no. 1, pp. 2–6.

6 J.C. McQueen, 'Two Controlled Experiments in Music Therapy', *British Journal of Music Therapy*, 1975, vol. 6, no. 3, pp. 2–8.

7 J. Chesney, 'Keeping in Tune with the Patient: Choosing Music for Therapy', *British Journal of Music Therapy*, 1980, vol. 11, no. 2, pp. 8–15.

8 L. Bunt and D. Alberman, 'The Role of Music Therapy with Handicapped Children in a London District – a Pilot Study', *British Journal of Music Therapy*, 1981, vol. 12, no. 2, pp. 2–10.

9 W. Lathom, 'Role of Music Therapy in the Education of Handicapped Children and Youth', Report to National Association for Music Therapy, 1980.

10 J. Carr and M. Collias, 'A Controlled Study of the Effects of Music Therapy with Severely Subnormal Children using Blind Assessments' unpublished paper.

11 Nordoff and Robbins, op. cit. (1977), pp. 177–208.

12 R.A. Hinde, 'On Describing Relationships', *Journal of Child Psychology and Psychiatry*, 1976, vol. 17, pp. 1–19; J. Richer, 'Human Ethology and Mental Handicap', in S.A. Corson (ed.), *Ethology and Nonverbal Communication in Mental Health*, Oxford: Pergamon Press, 1979.

13 See Hinde, op. cit.

14 The project, funded by the National Medical Research Fund, was based within the Department of Paediatrics, Charing Cross Hospital Medical School, London.

15 Quoted in L. Bunt, 'From Individual to Group Music Therapy with Very Young Children in a Nursery Unit', in *Music Therapy for the Young and the Aged*, London: British Society for Music Therapy, 1979, p. 24.
16 For details of the results and statistics from all three of the projects discussed in this chapter, see L. Bunt, 'Music Therapy and the Child with a Handicap: Evaluation of the Effects of Intervention', unpublished Ph.D. thesis, The City University, London, 1985.
17 From the speech therapist at the school for the deaf.
18 This project was based within the Department of Music, The City University, London, and was funded by the Music Therapy Charity. All the practical work took place in pre-school nurseries and special units within the Haringey and Islington Districts of North London (see Bunt, op. cit. (1985) for further background to the project).
19 For more details of the tests used, see Bunt, op. cit. (1985).
20 The project was based within a school in Hackney and The City University, funding being continued with the research grant from the Music Therapy Charity.
21 Bunt op. cit. (1985), pp. 226–72.
22 A. Warwick, 'Questions and Reflections on Research', *Journal of British Music Therapy*, 1988, vol. 2, no. 2, p. 7.

6 MUSIC THERAPY AND ADULT HEALTH

1 W.J. Dowling, 'Melodic Information Processing and its Development', in D. Deutsch (ed.), *The Psychology of Music*, London: Academic Press, 1982, p. 421.
2 L. Bunt (ed.), *Music Therapy in Psychiatry* (conference proceedings), Bristol: The Bristol Music Therapy Centre, 1986. Copies available from The MusicSpace Trust, The Southville Centre, Beauley Road, Bristol BS3 1QG.
3 K.E. Bruscia, *Improvisational Models of Music Therapy*, Springfield, Illinois: Charles C. Thomas, 1987, p. 5.
4 ibid. pp. 7–8.
5 Dr Bruscia's text provides a comprehensive description of the many different models of improvisational music therapy. It is a must for all interested in learning more about the development of music therapy worldwide. The first units of the book focus on some major models of improvisational music therapy, including: Paul Nordoff and Clive Robbins ('Creative Music Therapy'); Juliette Alvin ('Free Improvisation Therapy') and Mary Priestley ('Exploratory Music Therapy'). Also see K.E. Bruscia, 'A Survey of Treatment Procedures in Improvisational Music Therapy', *Psychology of Music*, 1988, vol. 16, no. 1, pp. 10–24.
6 H. Odell, 'A Music Therapy Approach in Mental Health', *Psychology of Music*, 1988, vol. 16, no. 1, pp. 52–61.
7 M. Priestley, *Music Therapy in Action*, London: Constable, 1975, passim.
8 Odell, op. cit., p. 57.
9 ibid., p. 58.
10 The project was funded by the Emperor Fine Arts Trust, London.
11 A. Levinge, in *Music Therapy in Psychiatry*, p. 22.
12 ibid., p. 21.
13 ibid.
14 For a detailed account of this project, see L. Bunt, D. Pike and V. Wren, 'Music Therapy in a General Hospital's Psychiatric Unit – An Evaluation of a Pilot Eight Week Programme', *Journal of British Music Therapy*, 1987, vol. 1, no. 2., pp. 3–6.
15 Funding was donated by the Hospital's League of Friends.
16 This and all other statements from the clients are published in: Bunt, Pike and Wren, op. cit.

17 For background, see G.A. Kelly, *The Psychology of Personal Constructs*, vols 1 and 2, New York: Norton, 1950.
18 S. Siegel, *Non-Parametric Statistics for the Behavioural Sciences*, New York: McGraw-Hill, 1956. My thanks to the unit's senior clinical psychologist at the time, David Pike, for help in analysing the data and discussing the results.
19 H. Odell, 'An Investigation into the Effects of Music Therapy with Elderly Mentally Ill People', unpublished M.Phil. thesis, The City University, London, 1988, p. 112.
20 My thanks to the assessor, Joanna Marston-Wyld, who also helped in the preparation of this material.
21 E.H. Erikson, *Childhood and Society* (1st edition 1950), Harmondsworth: Penguin, 1965, and *Identity and the Life Cycle: A Reissue*, New York: W.W. Norton, 1980.
22 U. Brondfrenbrenner, *The Ecology of Human Development*, Cambridge, Massachusetts: Harvard University Press, 1979, pp. 21–7.
23 Leonie Sugarman has reviewed some of the key concepts in *Life-Span Development*, London: Routledge, 1986.
24 A.H. Maslow, *Motivation and Personality*, 2nd edition (1st edition 1954), New York: Harper & Row, 1970.
25 J.B. Davies, *The Psychology of Music*, London: Hutchinson, 1978, quoted in J. Sloboda, *The Musical Mind*, Oxford: Oxford University Press, 1985, p. 2.
26 A. McGlashan, *Gravity and Levity*, London: Chatto & Windus, 1976, pp. 102–3.

7 MUSIC THERAPY AS A RESOURCE FOR THE COMMUNITY

1 S. Zallik, 'In Search of the Face – An Approach to Mental Handicap', *Journal of British Music Therapy*, 1987 vol. 1, no. 1, pp. 13–16.
2 A. Oldfield, 'The Effects of Music Therapy on a Group of Profoundly Mentally Handicapped Adults', unpublished M.Phil. thesis, The City University, London, 1986, p. 64.
3 T. Wigram, 'Music Therapy, Developments in Mental Handicap', *Psychology of Music*, 1988, vol. 16, no. 1, pp. 42–51.
4 J. Selman, 'Music Therapy with Parkinson's Disease', *Journal of British Music Therapy*, 1988, vol. 2, no. 1, pp. 5–9.
5 S. Hoskyns, 'Huntington's Chorea: Striking the Right Chord', *Nursing Mirror*, 1982, vol. 154, no. 22, pp. 14–17, and a research note describing the project in The *Lancet*, London, 29 May 1982, vol. 1, no. 82/3, p. 1259.
6 S. Hoskyns, 'Studying Group Music Therapy with Adult Offenders: Research in Progress', *Psychology of Music*, 1988, vol. 16, no. 1, pp. 25 – 41.
7 This is currently the only full-time appointment within a music department of a British university. The funding of the post has been possible since 1980 owing to the continued support of the Music Therapy Charity.
8 C.A. Lee, 'Structural Analysis of Therapeutic Improvisatory Music', *Journal of British Music Therapy*, 1989, vol. 3, no. 2, pp. 11–20; C.A. Lee, 'Structural Analysis of Post-Tonal Therapeutic Improvisatory Music', *Journal of British Music Therapy*, 1990, vol. 4, no. 1, pp. 6–21.
9 P. Rogers, 'Issues in Working with Sexually Abused Clients in Music Therapy', *Journal of British Music Therapy*, 1992, vol. 6, no. 2, p. 5.
10 M. Heal, 'Mutual Respect: Therapeutic Approaches to Working with People who have Learning Difficulties', in D. Brandon (ed.), *Tune with the Mind*, Surbiton: Good Impressions, 1989, pp. 45–56.
11 See A. Fitzwilliam, 'An Assessment of the Benefits of Micro Technology in Music Therapy', *Journal of British Music Therapy*, 1988, vol. 2, no. 1, pp. 24–31.
12 J. Alvin and J. Bryce, 'Physiotherapy and Music Therapy for Physical Handicap', in

Music Therapy for Mental and Physical Handicap, London: British Society for Music Therapy, 1978, pp. 14–22.

13 A.L. Wigram and L. Weekes, 'Music and Movement', *British Journal of Music Therapy*, 1985, vol. 16, no. 1, pp. 2–12.

14 A. Oldfield and J. Pierson, 'Using Music in Mental Handicap – 2. Facilitating Movement', *Mental Handicap*, 1985, vol. 13, pp. 156–8.

15 A. Oldfield and C. Parry, 'Using Music in Mental Handicap – 1. Overcoming Communication Difficulties', *Mental Handicap*, 1985, vol. 13, pp. 117–19.

16 For a summary of these functions that links with key issues for music therapists, see H.M. Borchgrevink, 'The Brain Behind the Therapeutic Potential of Music', in E. Ruud (ed.), *Music and Health*, London: Chester, 1986, pp. 63–97.

17 O.S.M. Marin, 'Neurological Aspects of Music Perception and Performance', in D. Deutsch (ed.), *The Psychology of Music*, London: Academic Press, 1982, p. 458.

18 T. Krauss and H. Galloway, 'Melodic Intonation Therapy with Language-Delayed Apraxic Children', *Journal of Music Therapy*, 1982, vol. 19, no. 2, pp. 102–13; D. Allen, 'An Exploration into Musical Speech Therapy', *British Journal of Music Therapy*, 1981, vol. 12, no. 1, pp. 2–6.

19 R.D. Price and C. DeFosse, 'Music and Language Processing in the Central Nervous System: State of the Art', in *Second International Symposium of Music Education for the Handicapped*, Bloomington, Indiana: Frangipani Press, 1983.

20 H. Odell, 'A Music Therapy Approach in Mental Health', *Psychology of Music*, 1988, vol. 16, no. 1, pp. 52–62.

21 G. Brandt, D. Wohler and D. Aldridge, 'Working Together: A Comparative Study of Music Therapy and Art Therapy', *Journal of British Music Therapy*, 1991, vol. 5, no. 1, p. 17.

22 G.L. Duerksen, 'Some Similarities between Music Education and Music Therapy', *Journal of Music Therapy*, 1967, vol. 4, no. 3, pp. 95–9 (p. 95).

23 J.M. Alley, 'Education for the Severely Handicapped: the Role of Music Therapy', *Journal of Music Therapy*, 1977, vol. 14, no. 2, p. 54.

24 W. Salaman, 'The Elusive Jewel of Music Therapy: Psychological and Other Factors', *Journal of the Education Section of the British Psychological Society*, 1982, vol. 6, no. 1, pp. 38–43.

25 J. Strange, 'The Role of the Music Therapist in Special Education', *Journal of British Music Therapy*, 1987, vol. 1, no. 2, p. 31.

26 L. Bunt, E. Clarke, I. Cross and S. Hoskyns, 'A Discussion on the Relationship between Music Therapy and the Psychology of Music', *Psychology of Music*, 1988, vol. 16, no. 1, pp. 62–71.

27 Lee, op. cit.

28 See L.G.K. Bunt and S.L. Hoskyns, 'A Perspective on Music Therapy Research in Great Britain', *Journal of British Music Therapy*, 1987, vol. 1, no. 1, pp. 3–6.

29 M. Troup, 'Music – A Resource for Mental Health in the Community', unpublished M.Phil. thesis, The University of Glasgow, 1986.

30 This project was based within the Institute of Child Health, University of Bristol and funded by the Barnwood House Trust and the Emperor Fine Arts.

8 MUSIC THERAPY AS A SYNTHESIS OF ART AND SCIENCE

1 Quotations from Myfanwy Piper's libretto by kind permission of Faber Music Ltd.

2 See Donald Mitchell's introduction to the Decca recording of the opera. The Delphic Hymn is no. 7a in Davison's and Apel's *Historical Anthology of Music*, London: Oxford University Press, 1946.

3 F. Capra, *The Turning Point*, New York: Simon & Schuster, 1982.

4 H.S. Jensen, 'Music and Health in Postmodern Society', in E. Ruud (ed.), *Music and Health*, London: Chester, 1986, p. 185.
5 ibid., p. 178
6 A. Storr, *Music and the Mind*, London: HarperCollins, 1992, p. 166.
7 S. McNiff, *The Arts and Psychotherapy*, Springfield, Illinois: Charles C. Thomas, 1981, p. vii.
8 T. Dally (ed.), *Images of Art Therapy*, London Routledge Tavistock, 1987, p. 10.
9 K. Stockhausen, *Towards a Cosmic Music*, translated by T. Nevill, Shaftesbury: Element Books, 1989, p. 34.
10 K. Bruscia, *Defining Music Therapy*, Spring City, Pennsylvania: Spring House Books, 1989, p. 8.
11 S. Hoskyns, 'Music Therapy', in *Arts Therapies Research: Proceedings of the First Arts Therapies Research Conference*, London: The City University, 1989, p. 14.
12 J. Sloboda, 'A Discussion of Case Study Research in Psychology of Music: Implications for Music Therapy', in *The Case Study as Research: Proceedings of the Fourth Music Therapy Day Conference*, London: The City University, 1988, p. 27.
13 The outcome studies of A. Oldfield, H. Odell and L. Bunt in particular.
14 L. Bunt and S. Hoskyns, 'A Perspective on Music Therapy Research in Great Britain', *Journal of British Music Therapy*, 1987, vol. 1, no. 1, pp. 3–6.
15 M. Pavlicevic, 'Music in Communication: Improvisation in Music Therapy,' unpublished Ph.D. thesis, University of Edinburgh, 1991.
16 D. Aldridge, 'The Single Case in Clinical Research, in *The Case Study as Research*, p. 3.
17 Recent volumes of the *Journal of British Music Therapy* contain several articles in case-study format, for example: F. Ritchie, 'Behind Closed Doors, A Case Study', 1991, vol. 5, no. 2, pp. 4–10; A. Davies and A.R.K. Mitchell, 'Music Therapy and Elective Mutism: a Case Discussion', 1990, vol. 4, no. 2, pp. 10–15; A. Agrotou, 'A Case Study: Lara', 1988, vol. 2, no. 1, pp. 17–24.
18 S. Hoskyns, in Introduction to *The Case Study as Research*.
19 O. Sacks, *The Man who Mistook his Wife for a Hat*, London: Pan, 1985.
20 See P. Reason and J. Heron, *Human Inquiry*, London: John Wiley, 1981.
21 J. Chesney, 'Is Psychotherapy Research Possible?', *Starting Research in Music Therapy: Proceedings of the Third Music Therapy Day Conference*, London: The City University, 1987, p. 21.
22 S. Hoskyns, 'Studying Group Music Therapy with Adult Offenders: Research in Progress', *Psychology of Music*, 1988, vol. 16, no. 1, pp. 25–41.
23 Quoted in S. McNiff, 'Research and Scholarship in the Creative Arts Therapies', *The Arts in Psychotherapy*, 1987, vol. 14, p. 290.
24 L. Dossey, *Space, Time and Medicine*, Boston, Massachusetts: New Science Library, 1985, pp. 72–81.
25 For a recent summary, see R. McClellan, *The Healing Forces of Music*, Shaftesbury: Element Books, 1991.
26 J. Moreno, 'The Music Therapist: Creative Arts Therapist and Contemporary Shaman', *The Arts in Psychotherapy*, 1988, vol. 15, pp. 271–80.
27 H.L. Bonny and L.M. Savary, *Music and your Mind*, New York: Harper & Row, 1973.
28 NAMT 1988 National Conference, Atlanta, Georgia.
29 S. Hanser, 'Controversy in Music Listening/Stress Reduction Research', *The Arts in Psychotherapy*, 1988, vol. 15, pp. 211–17.
30 A recent survey of the use of music therapy in these contexts is J.M. Standley, 'Music Research in Medical/Dental Treatment: Meta-Analysis and Clinical Applications', in C.E. Furman (ed.), *Effectiveness of Music Therapy Procedures: Documentation of*

Research and Clinical Practice, Bristol: National Association for Music Therapy, 1988, pp. 9–61.
31 W. Shakespeare, *King Henry VIII*, Act III, sc. i., line 3.
32 W. Mellers, *The Masks of Orpheus*, Manchester: Manchester University Press, 1987, p. 4.
33 Mellers, op. cit., p. 4.
34 H.I. Khan, *The Music of Life*, New York: Omega Press, 1988, p. 129.
35 T.S. Eliot, 'Burnt Norton', in *Four Quartets*, Faber & Faber, 1944.

APPENDIX

1 The British Society for Music Therapy and the Association of Professional Music Therapists recently combined resources to organise a European Music Therapy Conference at Cambridge University. See: M. Heal and T. Wigram (eds), *Music Therapy in Health and Education*, London, Jessica Kingsley Publications, 1993.

Name index

Ainlay, G.W. 4
Aldridge, D. 169, 181
Alex (case study) 77–80
Alley, J. 170
Altshuler, I.M. 33
Alvin, J. 4, 6, 43, 45, 47, 49, 50, 54, 97, 165
Ansdell, G. 47
Apollo 176–7, 186–7
Arrington, G.E. 31

Beethoven, L.V. 61, 158
Benenzon, R.O. 7, 10, 33
Berendt, J.-E. 75–6
Bernstein, L. 66, 96
Blacking, J. 70–2
Blackman, D.E. 41
Bonny, H. 185
Borchgrevink, H. 168
Bower, T.G.R. 90
Brighouse, G. 31
Britten, B. 68, 132, 176, 182
Bruner, J.S. 95, 99
Bruscia, K.E. 7, 8, 135–6, 178–9
Bryce, J. 165
Bullowa, M. 93

Capra, F. 61, 177
Chatwin, B. 72
Chesney, J. 109
Chomet, Dr 11
Chomsky, N. 73
Condon, W.S. 91
Cooke, D. 54, 68
Copland, A. 47

Davies, J.B. 159
Dionysus 176–7, 186–7
Dossey, L. 56, 184

Dowling, W.J. 65
Duerksen, G. 169–70

Eagle, C. 61
Einstein, A. 61, 184
Ellis, D.S. 31
Erikson, E.H. 157

Fantz, R.L. 95
Fraisse, P. 60
Freud, S. 11, 34–8, 176
Fromm, E. 37
Funk, J. 99

Gabriel, C. 99
Gabriel, P. 160
Gardner, H. 46, 61, 99
Gaston, E.T. 61
Gilbert, J.P. 14
Glennie, E. 61
Goodman, K.D. 10

Hanser, S. 186
Harford, Canon 3
Hargreaves, D.J. 76, 99
Heal, M. 165
Hillman, J. 183
Hitchcock, D.H. 36–7
Hitler, A. 64
Hoskyns, S. 43, 164–79, 181–2
Hutt, C. 95

Jellison, J.A. 13
Jensen, H.S. 37, 177
John (case study) 17–22, 31–3, 36, 39, 41–2
Joyce, J. 183
Julia (case study) 101–4, 114
Julian (case study) 104–8

Subject index

residential homes for 9; *see also* music therapy: efficacy; pre-composed music: old time songs

elements: of music 45–6, 60, 158; *see also* harmony, melody, rhythm; of sound 45–7, 56, 59–60; *see also* duration, loudness, pitch, tone quality; use of by clients 47, 69

embryo 75–7; auditory world of 76

emotional: disturbances 6, 9, 109, 118; release 28, 154–5

emotional health 8, 36, 61

empathy 90, 178

engagement 150

epilepsy 29; musicogenic 30

ethologists 110, 120

existentialism 42

exploration: of experience 50; explorative play 19, 35, 37, 83, 93; of habits 27; of melodies 65, 67, 81, 143; of modes 67–8; of problems 85; of range of musical stimuli 39, 53, 84, 107; of sounds 50, 57, 77, 79, 93, 123; *see also* feelings, instruments

feelings: communication of 9, 20, 22, 52, 84, 134, 176; of depression 153, 155; destructive 97, 135; experience of 42, 81, 91, 115, 134–5, 152, 176; exploration of 22, 53, 97–8, 115, 133; expression of 9, 20–2, 23–4, 27–8, 43, 68, 71–2, 105, 107, 147; fear 105, 107, 133, 135, 145; frustration 83, 102, 105, 115–16, 151, 153, 156, 177; happiness 147–8; reflection of by therapist 18–19, 21, 143; relaxation 147–8, 185; of self-worth 147–8; therapist's 18, 21–2, 24, 84; therapist's support of 20, 22; understanding of 71–3, 93–4, 116; *see also* language

focus 21–2, 25, 27, 51–2, 132, 137, 155, 167; focal point 78; *see also* duration of sounds

funding agency 174

general practitioners 172

Gestalt therapy 42

gesture 95, 111, 183; musical 93, 97, 99, 104, 135, 143, 158

Goldie Leigh Hospital 110

Greek medicine 10; music 10, 67, 72

ground rules in improvisation 134

group 'iso' 33

groups 8–9, 22–9, 35, 51, 108, 111, 115, 119, 133, 136–7; activity 70; celebration 71; cohesion 28, 33, 68, 146, 157; commitment to 26, 144, 148; curative factors 26–8, 148–9; emotional support from 71, 83; group session 22–6, 137–8; identity 16; leadership of 134, 139–40, 147; open 22–6; and pentatonic scale 67; self-help 172; sense of caring for members 27, 52; size 138, 145, 151; support between members 27, 144, 156; *see also* behaviours, exploration of melodies, modes, ritual

group therapy 146

Guided Imagery in Music 185

Guild of St Cecilia 3

Hackney project 124–8

Hammersmith intervention study 109, 111–20, 124, 129

harmony 45, 55, 69–70, 165; dissonance/consonance 65, 68–70, 143; drone 66, 69; and melody 69; repeating chord patterns 69; *see also* duration, pitch, tension, tone-colour

harmonic: context 46; passage 30; patterns 70; series 66–7

health 74, 178, 184, 186; health care 175

hearing impairments: adults 51, 61, 161, 165, 173; children 83, 109, 116, 118–19; pitch discrimination 53; problems with loud sounds 50–1

home environment 79

homeopathy 43

hope 26

hospice 9

hostels 42, 160

House of Commons 5

humanistic psychology 11, 42–4, 110; goals 12, 42, 157; growth 42; joint negotiation 42

Huntington's chorea 63, 164

imitation 19, 27, 52, 84, 91–4, 96, 99, 101–5, 111, 123, 139; and language 92; skills 40, 81–2, 89, 101, 128; *see also* music (uses of): contact

improvised music 23, 28, 31, 35–6, 49, 71, 73, 93, 107; analysis of 16, 171; descriptions of sessions 18–20, 24–5,

puzzlement 37

quality: of life 71, 151, 165; of sound 81

reality, escape from 34–5
recorded music: listening 32, 40–1, 43,
   49–50, 72; use of tape recorder in
   sessions 84, 137
regression *see* psychoanalysis
relationships: client–therapist 6–8, 15,
   20–1, 28, 88, 90, 107, 123; developing
   through music 8, 15, 28, 85, 90, 93,
   123, 136–7; with others 22, 114–15,
   120, 136, 144; with parent 22, 90–2,
   130; role 178; therapeutic, core factors
   12; therapeutic, evolution of 47, 90, 93;
   therapist–group 28, 136–7; within
   group 25, 27–9, 37, 106–8, 136–7, 144,
   146, 152
repetition 38, 96–7, 102; melodic patterns
   82; minimalist school of composers 64;
   rhythm 64, 82
research 12–15, 43, 179; assessment
   procedures 4, 15, 110–11; case study
   13, 109, 129, 181; clients' self-reports
   147, 181–3; design of studies 33, 43,
   119–20, 139, 147, 181; experimental
   work 11, 13–15, 31, 46, 58, 120–8,
   181; group study 13, 129, 181–2;
   inter-observer reliability 110, 122, 124,
   140, 142–3; into long-term effects 124;
   measuring equipment 33, 90; musical
   processes 171, 173; need for 108–9;
   objective analysis 40, 43, 110, 115–16,
   145, 151–4, 182–3; outcome studies
   11, 15, 56, 109, 129, 163–4, 179–80,
   183; physiological 30–2; projects 32,
   110–30, 136–49, 163–4; psychological
   46; quantitative 31, 110, 115–16,
   148–9, 181; questionnaires 111,
   113–16, 145–8, 181; resources 30, 124,
   144, 147; time-based measure 120–5,
   163; use of video 110, 120–8, 163
resistance *see* psychoanalysis
resonance 21, 47, 51, 54–5, 61, 70–1,
   176; resonant frequency 47
responses to music 15–16, 20–1, 46, 79;
   association with nature 70; emotional
   32–3, 46, 67–9, 72–3, 107, 129, 132,
   137, 153–6, 158–9, 163, 178, 180;
   learned 51; to particular pattern of
   intervals 68; to particular tempo,

changes of tempo 57, 62; to particular
   timbre 49; physical reactions 68, 70,
   79, 166; relation to problems 47, 137,
   153, 156, 186; spontaneous 82
Rett's syndrome 62
rhythm 60–4, 93, 96, 99, 119, 134, 137,
   140, 165, 168, 185; definitions 60, 63;
   dependency 102–4; emotional
   responses to 64; entrainment 62;
   expectations 61; as focus of energy 60;
   intention 80; internal 57, 92, 153–5,
   178; matching client's 33, 86; melodic
   105–6; patterns 18, 22, 24, 32, 34, 41,
   45–6, 52, 62, 64, 101–2, 129, 139, 168;
   patterns in nature 61, 63, 76; pulse 24,
   56, 59, 62, 101–2; reflexive rhythmic
   activity 80; rhythmic forms 60, 177;
   skills 101–2, 104, 106; structure 57, 63,
   65, 87, 139; synchrony with self as
   measure of health 61; variation of 102;
   of words 80; *see also* tension
risk-taking 27, 49, 52, 103–4, 157, 159
rituals 49, 66, 70–1, 131; group 71; tribal
   70; ritualistic behaviour 101

safety 22–3, 26–8, 79, 85, 103, 134, 145,
   157, 162
scale: diatonic system 65–7; Indian
   system 53; modal 66–8; modes,
   emotional effects 67–8; pentatonic
   66–7; twelve-tone 53
self-esteem 9, 42, 59, 105, 115–16, 147,
   157
sensory integration 97
sexual abuse *see* abuse
silence 51, 85, 93, 134, 137, 147
singing 9, 21, 49–50, 68, 74, 80–1, 86,
   105–6, 133, 141; action songs 80, 106;
   with backing track 131; *bel canto* 54;
   in construction of society 72; effect on
   unborn baby 76; learned songs 82;
   nursery rhymes 81; singing games 82;
   songs as repositories of knowledge 72;
   use of to aid relaxation 164, 187; *see
   also* pre-composed music, spontaneous
   singing
sleep 56
social activity 71; interaction 9, 20, 41,
   77, 83, 118–19, 121, 143; responses
   96; skills 9, 20, 89–90, 108, 111, 113,
   115; tasks of group 27
social worker *see* para-medical team